T0381159

THE POWER OF SPEAKING ATOMIC, NUCLEAR, EXPLOSIVE DECREES & DECLARATIONS INTO EXISTENCE

THIS INFORMATION & INSTRUCTIONS WITH RESULTS WILL CHANGE YOUR LIFE FOREVER.

PRAYERS DECREES & DECLARATIONS, WARFARE TRAINING, DELIVERANCE & HEALING & TEACHING SERIES #1

BY CARL A BURDEN
GOD' SCRIBE WRITER

WESTBOW
PRESS®
A DIVISION OF THOMAS NELSON
& ZONDERVAN

WestBow Press books may be ordered through booksellers or by contacting:

WestBow Press
A Division of Thomas Nelson & Zondervan
1663 Liberty Drive
Bloomington, IN 47403
www.westbowpress.com
844-714-3454

Scripture taken from the King James Version of the Bible.

ISBN: 979-8-3850-1193-3 (sc)
ISBN: 979-8-3850-1192-6 (e)

Library of Congress Control Number: 2023921701

Print information available on the last page.

WestBow Press rev. date: 12/12/2024

CONTENTS

ACKNOWLEDGEMENTS

GRACE MERCY & PEACE ALWAYS GIVING THANKS TO MY HEAVENLY FATHER, GOD, THAT IS GREAT and AWESOME EMPEROR. WHICH IS MY GOD, SUPPLIER, PROTECTOR, RESTORER, REBUILDER OF THE BREACH. Those areas in my life that have been lacking and missing coming behind. He has blessed them and cause them to flourish as the green and beautiful fresh amazon forest after the fresh Rain. WHO IS MY EVERYTHING THAT I EVER DID NEED IN JESUS NAME AND IT IS SO.

I WANT TO SAY THANK YOU SO VERY MUCH TO MY LORD & SAVIOR, YESHUA, THE CHRIST. MY REDEEMER, MY SUPPLIER, MY DELIVERER, AND SO MUCH MORE, MY SACRIFICIAL LAMB THAT WAS SLAIN AND CRUCIFIED JUST FOR ME AND THE SINS OF MY WHOLE WORLD.

THE HOLY SPIRIT, MY FRIEND, MY TEACHER, BRINGING ALL THINGS TO MY REMEMBRANCE, WHATEVER I NEEDED TO REMEMBER AND GET DONE. I JUST WANT TO SAY THANK YOU, FOR DOWNLOADING INSIDE OF ME ALL THE INFORMATION THAT IS IN THIS BOOK.

FOREWORD

To ; My Husband; Prophet, Carl. A. Burden.

It gives me great joy to talk about this man, my husband, Prophet Carl A. Burden. This journey of his life has been rewarding and enlightening and more. I can't count the days, weeks, months, and years that he has been working, praying, and studying for this purpose. There are many hours of quietness and loneliness, even on secluded days. Days I had to endure and pray for peace and GOD to keep me. Times of shutting in and not coming out till hours later, my! What a journey! The blessing of all of that is the level of maturity that came. Then, the level of increase of wisdom came. The seed time and harvest are forever. The wine was poured out, and it overflowed into the house and more. The greater prayer life was extended from day to day. Seeking GOD for greater revelation, wisdom, knowledge, and understanding takes patience, endurance, and long suffering. It takes a level of commitment, sacrifice, and dedication. The more he cried out to GOD, the more GOD poured into him, and he poured into me.

Now I see the victory in the labor. The tears and the healing that took place because of his faithfulness. To see how prayers, and warfare prayers can change people's lives, their hearts, and health my GOD.! I thank GOD for what he has put in Prophet Carl Burden, my husband. The one who prays for me and covers me as an Apostle of GOD. The Dunamis, power, and the anointing of this man of GOD are powerful. It's an honor to know an Elite Atomic Warrior who will tear satan's kingdom down with the Word of GOD. I pray just as this book has been a blessing to us (Carl & Cheryl Burden) that it will be a blessing to help heal and deliver you as well, in Jesus name.

Apostle Cheryl L. Burden

To My Wife, Cheryl Burden, who is an Apostle, with the Ministry of House of Prayer Impact Ministries along with myself, joined in together as well, The LOVE OF MY LIFE, for Praying and Prophesying to me what the Lord is showing and telling her to say and give to me. For being a blessing to me, for many years throughout our lives.

Cheryl has been very encouraging, standing by my side, through this writing, and helping me in many ways, such as, giving me some feedback on some of my writings and chapters, various viewpoints, advise, information that's, helpful, for my book with suggestions. She is my life companion, friend, and many other great attributes in the Lord as GOD instructs her. For that I just want to say THANK YOU and I love you so very Much.

By Prophet Carl. A. Burden Author & writer.

Apostle John. A. Duncan. Jr, Ministry The Ruah Kingdom Creations Global Arts, which is the Breath of GOD, for his Love for GOD and all that he does in the Kingdom, for all his wonderful fiery Prayers, for his encouragement, correcting some things in my life that were off course slightly as the Lord has spoken to him. That's anointed and powerful, with instructions, information, his wisdom that he shares and cares for others from the Lord. Many things that he has imparted into my life, and I will never be the same ever again. Also, He was a great mentor, even as a spiritual father, and he guided and supported me in many ways. He is a blessing in Yeshua's name, helping to cultivate the gifts that GOD, has He has imparted many things into my life, and I will never be the same graciously given to me.

Apostle: James Fairbanks, The Ministry of the Apostle's Brigade, has really been a great friend to me. Through the years of knowing him he has allowed GOD to use him to prophesy into my life concerning many things that GOD is doing, in my life, even right now so, for that, I want to say thank you for being my best friend in many areas of my life as a support.

Apostle: Rodney Wade, with the Ministry, called Constant Flow, Prophet Gwen Lackey, The Ministry, that speaks into others for guidance. Prophet Devontae Gaines, The Ministry that represents the last days for the young people. and many others have prophesied over My life. Things concerning upcoming future events that are taking place. I just want to mention them for their support and obedience to the Lord concerning my life.

Apostle: Frank & Stacie Johnson, The Ministry, called The Ironmen International Ministry, and Adonai International Kingdom Ministry, Along with Pastor Delisa McIntosh, have allow GOD, to use her in the whole set up. The Johnsons have prayed over us, for us, and with us, and have given us platforms, as the Lord has led them to do so. The use and exercise our gifts and treat us with great gratitude. They have been a wonderful blessing to me and my wife. When we were at a low place and going through many trials and tests, they stepped in and began to help us out.

Apostle: Solomon & Carolyn Stewart, The Ministry of the Prophetic, & Revelational knowledge of GOD, also has been a complete blessing to me as well. Allowing the Lord to prophesy to me concerning this book that it will be a blessing to all of those who are reading it. Those who want a change in their lives and that it will be an awesome teaching tool, for anyone who wants to pursue it, in the Mighty name of Yeshua, Jesus the Christ.

Evangelist: Michelle Yates, having the love, desires, and care to pray for me and my wife and has given many wonderful gifts that are treasured right today.

Evangelist; Monica Osei not only did she love us and prayed for us both, but she gave us some wonderful Gifts to kick off our Ministries,

And if any others who have helped with their prayers, I just want, to say thank you so very much and speak many blessings upon each one of you for your love and care. For showing the LOVE OF CHRIST AND GOD IN YESHUA NAME, it is so, and so it is.

I want to give a warm thanks to Roderick. S. Smith. whom I had the privilege of raising at the age of 13 months as a Son, I want to say thank you as well for all your help.

I want to add my gratitude with GRAMMARLY which has really been great for those who need help with improving their writing skills and other writing adventures.

FOR THOSE THAT HAVE BEEN A BIG HELP I WANT TO SAY A GREAT BIG GOD BLESS AND PROSPER YOUR LIVES RICHLY IN JESUS NAME IT IS SO & SO IT IS.

INTRODUCTION FOR THE BOOK

From the Desk & Words, thoughts, and feelings of the Author, Welcome, to All & Thank you, for purchasing, and also for your support, of the book, and all that it has to offer, this great Book full of wealth, to all that again I say THANK YOU SO VERY MUCH. To My LORD GOD ALMIGHTY, MY HEAVENLY FATHER, A PERSONAL THANKS, for choosing me to write & author this book of training and information. TO ALL THAT WILL EMBARK UPON or take such A GREAT ADVENTURE TO GET THIS INFORMATION YOU ARE OFF TO A GREAT START. PLEASE TAKE SOME TIME TO READ THIS INTRODUCTION. IT WILL HELP YOU TREMENDOUSLY. IT WILL GIVE YOU SOME INSTRUCTIONS.

THESE INSTRUCTIONS WILL BE VERY IMPORTANT FOR YOUR PROGRESS THROUGHOUT THE REST OF YOUR TIME WITH THIS TRAINING AND LIFE-CHANGING INSTRUCTION AND INFORMATION. DO NOT OVERLOOK THIS PART OF YOUR TRAINING. IT FULFILLS A GREAT GAP IN YOUR LIFE THAT WAS MISSING, AND NOW IT WILL BE FILLED AND RUNNING OVER.

THANK YOU SINCERELY BECAUSE I
REALLY GENUINELY CARE:

SIGNED: Carl A Burden, Author.

Ephesians 6:10-12 says to us;

[10] <u>Finally, my brethren, be strong in the
Lord, and in the power of his might.</u>

¹¹ <u>Put on the whole armour of GOD, that ye may be able to stand against the wiles of the devil.</u>

¹² <u>For we wrestle not against flesh and blood, but against principalities, against powers, against the rulers of the darkness of this world, against spiritual wickedness in high *places*.</u>

This is a book for Spiritual Warriors and Soldiers in the Army of the Lord. This book will teach you how to fight the battles you face from moment to moment and from day to day. This book is also for Intercessors, who have been called, to pray, chosen, to a prayer ministry, and faithful in this type of prayer work: Standing in the GAPS, being a mediator for the WORLD, better known as the globe, and getting a fervent prayer through to reach GOD on behalf of others.

Those who want to become! Better equipped in this spiritual work for Our Lord, GOD, and Savior, of the Whole world and the ministry of the Holy Spirit & more. To my book Entitled, The Power of Speaking, ATOMIC & NUCLEAR, EXPLOSIVE, DECREES & DECLARATIONS INTO EXISTENCE.

It is a book that is long overdue to help, train, and instruct, in many ways, the lives and settled in the hands, hearts, and the emotions of those that need some more intense instructions. This book also has many levels to reach, such as those that are just starting out with the basic foundation. To graduating to other deeper levels that will propel you and them, being those that you may be teaching soon, into more realms & dimensions. These set of instructions will give you some ammunition and information on how to fight the good fight of faith. In 1 Timothy 6:12 says, Fight the good fight of faith, lay hold on Eternal life, whereunto thou art called, and hast professed a good profession before many witnesses.

Lives and various walks of life and Ministries of all people that are interested, worldwide. This book will fill in some blanks give some understanding as to why things happen the way that they do. This book will give you some of the answers as to how to fix some things in your life and how to maintain your spiritual life with some growth, maturity training, and discipline. The training that will take place to advance, yourselves to other levels, dimensions, and realms, in the mighty name of Yeshua. THIS, BOOK IS POWER PACK INFORMATION, TRAINING EXTENSIVELY, GOING INTO SOME DETAILS. In each and every chapter of the book go deep within the recesses of your life, mind, will, and emotions. Your spirit and body as well. These are training exercises to follow as you will gain information on why and how attacks come and how to see them. This training material will give you the ability to stop them before they reach their full potential.

This book is for extensive learning and training that will be needed during your life, for enhancing your thoughts a long with the thoughts of GOD ON PAPER. That is what the words of GOD are. This book has the ability to help all Saints, Sons of GOD, who are Ambassadors while here on earth. Saints and Sons ON every level that they may be treading on.

It will encourage the building of lives and other areas of impact. If you are hungry for a lot more results, to be introduced, give access to, Educate, your spiritual life, then this is the book to give you a great start. This information will open up and expand, your knowledge base, to OPEN UP some blinded minds, blinded eyes that may be IGNORANT TO THE FACTS AROUND YOU. You have the right book and information, in your hands at this moment. To get you on your way, this book will help, you on your way. This book will help you to fall in love with our lovely FATHER AND SAVIOR, YESHUA, THE CHRIST. This information will give you some revelations and insights and will add some more blessings to your life and the lives of others; then, I suggest you get ready for life-changing results. All who are interested.

in living a better life that will be fulfilled to the fullest. People from all walks of life can and will be helped.

If, in fact, they follow all the procedures, which is a series of steps. These steps, that must be taken are just reminders that there are no shortcuts taken to get to the top. To reach the goals and standards of your life in GOD that you desire.

To get and expect the results that is mentioned in this book. Going forward, they apply all the content in this.

book. This book is packed with experiences for more than (forty & five)forty-five plus years. What is written in this material, that has been going on through, tried, and tested with proven tactics, skills, success, victories, and triumphs, that causes me to spoil the works of the enemies' mess and strategies. All requires some TIME and patience with yourself and others. All types of reading, studying, and using what GOD IS GIVING YOU ACCESS IN will be needed. It requires some extensive studying from the Words of GOD. IN THE KING JAMES VERSION because of the current words in this volume that stand out with many.

Meanings; are ancient with hidden mysteries and the truth behind it.

That is, this book is from ancient writings that cannot be disputed nor debated; this is why the KJV is chosen, mostly because I was raised in a fellowship with this.

version. There is so much to gain from this version. there are other versions that I recommend, and those are the amplified versions and the new King James versions of the words of GOD. MANY versions have been, and have been watered down, dumbed down, and diluted with lies or part truth, but not all that you may need. Some of the meanings that are in the KJV are not written in other versions. I am not here to criticize other versions and will not mention them by name, but YOU WILL SEE FOR YOURSELF. the many words that stand out for meaning

and purpose. I must say that I love it and thoroughly enjoy all the content. The information that is available to me and others over the years of using this powerful word of truth through Our

Lord & Savior Jesus Christ & Our HEAVENLY FATHER GOD ALMIGHTY, NOT TO FORGET THE HOLY SPIRIT which is the SPIRIT OF TRUTH in Jesus name. The information in this book is first Powerful and one of its kind. This book is very powerful.

explosive in the use of it with Authoritative actions taking Dominion over certain areas of your LIFE with great teachings from the APOSTOLIC FOUNDATIONAL TEACHINGS JESUS LEFT US BEFORE HE ASCENDED INTO THE HEAVENS Ephesians 4:1-thirty-two. St Luke 24:6-7,

It commands & demands your attention. The nature of its contents, ingredients, compounds, equations, and words spoken that will no doubt bring.

manifestations, real results in the mighty name of Jesus. Hopefully, you know what you are getting, yourself into with this book. I am very sure you are ready to tackle and swallow up all its CONTENTS. As do a hungry & thirsty, from spiritual food and drink in the spirit, a person who is ready to sit down to eat and nourish themselves from starving, malnutrition of some kind; you get the point. It has been.

carefully arranged, put together over some periods of time guessing over two in one half years of more, forming this info for all. not rushed over, or just thrown together like a beginner or a novice for a fast meal spiritually. There has been much fasting and praying over the content. In this book is GODS WORDS which is SPIRIT AND LIFE. It will produce results when spoken with faith, in faith, by faith, and through faith in Jesus name. Belief and total trust in the Lord. It will give and add some life to your years and add years to your life.

To my Book Entitled, The Power of Speaking Explosive, Atomic Nuclear Decrees & Declarations into Existence.

ENJOY!!!

THE MINISTRY THAT BRINGS UNDERSTANDING
& INNER STANDING, with COMPREHENSION

FROM THE INSIDE OUT!!!

Grace Mercy & Peace, Welcome to the Ministries that brings understanding to the people of GOD.

THE VISION & MISSION OF THIS MINISTRY IS THAT; Everyone in the body of Christ wants to know with knowledge, wisdom, and understanding that will give them peace of mind with a calm mindset. The word of GOD requires for us to understand, what the word is saying to us. The ability to bring the body of Christ to a level of understanding of what GOD is saying to us as his people. OUR Goal are to reach, and train, equipped, and cause them to be always battle ready, and many prayer intercessors as we can while here on the earth, for my assignment. To bring the word with clarity, that's in every area of our lives. For example, prayer studying the word of GOD. What is the purpose of fasting??? Why do I need to pray if GOD is all-knowing? And HE IS ALL KNOWING. What does the blood of Jesus do for me and how to apply it to my life? What are demons and can, a child of GOD, open themselves up to an evil spirit?. The answer is most certainly, yes. They, being those that need deliverance; may have many as, one two or maybe three,, or more, inside of them. There will be more info as other books are being written for more training and teaching, in the near future. As of this moment you can go to the book of Matthews and read of the many accounts of Jesus dealing with all types of demons, from all sizes and countries and how he dealt with them. These are questions that will come to your mind as you read. This ministry is designed to answer these types of questions and more. THE MINISTRY THAT DIVES DEEP INTO STUDIES. Finding out what is going on and why it is.? How to apply these principles to your lives. MORE INFORMATION will be taught on this subject as the Lord GOD ALMIGHTY LEADS AND GUIDES us.

For more information about, anyone wanting to schedule for a conference, Platforms to host a meeting, speaking engagements, to come, interviews about the book, meetings on live TV, or group talks Please feel free to contact me by email at atomicwarrior100@gmail.com

Prophet Carl Burden by email, and you will be responded back with in a few hours of your request.

THANK YOU. LOOKING FORWARD TO HELPING GOD'S KINGDOM CITIZENS MUCH AS POSSIBLE.

CHAPTER 1

EXPLOSIVE OUTCOMES, INTENSIFIED WITH IMPACT PART 1

Explosive outcomes trigger actions of some kind;
The thing is what kind will it set off?

What do we think about? What comes to our minds, or your thoughts, and thinking patterns? when we speak of atoms or Organic molecule structures.? Such as, protons, electrons, and neutrons? When put together into action, what kind of thoughts, feelings, words, or actions with ideas will you get.? When we hear about, Hydrogen, nucleus, electronics, cloud bursts, chemical compounds, and scientific discoveries.

All are attached to and mixed in with ATOMIC, NUCLEAR Energy. So, these men one day, just imagine with me just for a few moments in time. Writing something in their journals as they keep good notes.

The pictures or images are being captured here; think about this. Think about these men and women, somewhere sat down or standing up working on a very important or very special project; had some light bulbs! go off in their minds.

These are ways, and thoughts inside of these thinkers, that happen with much thinking behind them. What was going through the minds of these brilliant geniuses? just to name some of them, for highlight or bring to your memory. Some of these you have never heard of are Albert Einstein, Sir Isaac Newton, Marie Currie, Charles Darwin, Nikola Tesla, Galileo Galilei, Louis Pasteur, Michael Faraday, Rosalind franklin and others just to name of few.

These are people who have made an impact in our world. That may not have been mentioned: when they discovered the various things in their lives through studies. One comes to mind which is Albert Einstein. With the help of our Great Heavenly Father came up with these components and equations of. $E=MC^2$ which is a square that is broken down as Energy= Mass x 186, 000 miles per second to the 2nd power. Energy has massiveness with power to back it or possess the mass which is matter.

This is NUCLEAR POWER. The C = Speed of light X's energy itself is larger, keep in mind; matter it is converted or changed over into energy, which in turn, becomes powerful, light energy on a massive scale. They may have a hand in it, but was not mentioned, some of these working behind the scenes.

But Albert Einstein had discovered a very small portion of its content and ingredients enough to become well known in the secular world. That was his calling, mission, and purpose in life if you please; so much for that, let's get back to this great subject; this is what this type of power is all about, and I am referring to.

I do not know how much you know about the science world and the studies that takes place from time to time.

There is much to know about it BUT they have gotten all their information from the thoughts & Words of GOD. Our GOD, MY Glorious FATHER IS A CONSUMING ETERNAL FIRE THAT NEVER GOES OUT. NEVER CAN ANYONE PUT OUT OR EXHAUST GOD'S ETERNAL ALMIGHTY ABILITIES. HIS Omni's WHICH IS OMNIPRESENCE, UNLIMITED IN SPACE, AND NO PLACE ANYWHERE IS OFF LIMITS TO HIM.

OMNISCIENCE, WHICH IS HIS UNLIMITED KNOWLEDGE, KNOWS ALL THINGS ALL AT THE SAME TIME AND THERE IS NOT ANYTHING THAT HE DOES NOT KNOW AT ANY AND ALL TIMES NOW AND FOREVER ETERNALLY. HE ALSO HAS ALL THE POWER WHICH MAKES HIM OMNIPOTENT; UNLIMITED IN POWER OF ALL KINDS EVEN THE POWERS THAT WE DON'T YET KNOW ABOUT. A BURNING BUSH THAT DOES NOT BURN OUT OR DOWN TO NOTHING.

Also think about the Stars, Galaxies, reaches out to be hundreds of billions upon billions of times trillions of Milky Way. All the gases that make up these extraordinary pieces of beautiful work of art. They are burning continuously out there in the eight spheres which comprise balls of mass space,

And more.

PLEASE BE VERY PATIENT WHEN READING THIS INFORMATION, IT'S TAKING YOU SOMEWHERE.

I am sure, it is all composed of Atmospheres, hemispheres,' Troposphere's Stratospheres, Mesosphere's, Thermosphere, Ionospheres, and the last one is Exospheres. All those other spheres that are out there CONSIDER THAT. And yet all the gases and spheres out there cannot compare to the power we have when we are in full bloom, caught up in an anointed blanket of atomic prayer powers that flows out of our mouths with the SPIRIT OF GOD AT THE CENTER OF IT FUELING IT BY HIS AWESOME POWER AND AUTHORITY. Getting back to this great info.

This atomic energy Which is vigor, power, and the liveliness of the Explosions, powers moving with intensity, forces, fuel, water, air, fire, wind, and Oxygen.

Are all Various types of gases, and various liquids, and compounds MIXED TOGETHER INTO ONE COMPONENT. These components are then blended to form something awesome explosive spiritually and then naturally.

In this case the scientist has discovered this type of compounds, components, and equations of studies. All these interactions, and information, GOD has made for all belongs to him. He is before all things and by him all things consist of. Colossians 1:16-17, Never forget there are all types of man-made, artificial, synthetics and manufactured chemicals, compounds, liquids, and minerals along with HEAT, LIGHT & BLASTING Powers.' These compounds are created, carefully arrange. The people that use this type of information must be trained properly to mix and carefully handle these dangerous chemicals. that are intensified, that can cover a huge & large mass area of land air, and sea.

So again, this all came through knowledge of those who have studied researched applied this info. Here again but it all came from the Lord GOD. ALL belongs to him, and he created it, they just discovered what he has created, spoken into existence from billions of years ago.

No one really knows all the time in which all of this came about but one thing we do know is that GOD SPOKE IT ALL INTO EXISTENCE and here it is. These component's constitutes modules & sections of effects. That will bring such an outcome of what or whatsoever has been carefully planned studied and put together for some.

Explosive powers. Igniting to go off and either destroy or stop some things from taking place. The biggest part of this is what will it do? And what will be left after it is all over. The effect it will have after its finishes doing charting its course, landing, or taking its course of actions with the blast and velocity. That is the speed, rate, and rapid power of the flow moving at such a pace with sound, temperature is which that is burning, ever so hotly is fervent heats.

Sets off such a reaction that has been done will take place all at ONCE, which is simultaneously all AT THE SAME TIME FLOWING AND INTERMIXING BONDING TOGETHER, will flow together. This to me is what combustion is all about, that happens when it's in a full motion nonstop.

Atomic & Nuclear power is energy from the atom, the smallest part with protons, neutrons, and electrons. When put into place being split causes nuclear powers to be released into the atmospheres, the Cosmos, Hemispheres, air, and the skies.

Biological energy breaking down cells from the metabolic processes requires energy from raw energy and materials. When we begin to pray, full-blown not holding back, without limits. Put our Prayers into full-blown action along with fasting and abstaining from food for a period to increase. To move faster, to accelerate the destiny in our lives. Dedication brings with it disciplining our flesh, commitment, the ability to stay and focus with something until it is finished and complete, which will bring it to a level of maturity. Not to ever forget into submission coupled, together with the Sword of the Spirit, which you all are his creative word speaking from (He Himself) GOD. This is his word spoken out of our mouths, that his spirit is within us, as his anointing upon our lives speaking steadfastly in faith.

It is a deadly, destroying death weapon AGAINST our enemies. Which is far more powerful than anything in this entire world put together. No one cannot and will not be able to touch or even come close to reproduce and match what OUR GOD HAS GIVEN US ACCESS TO HAVE AND USE IN THE MIGHTY NAME OF JESUS. We need to start tapping into some of this great power and it is widely available to all that will take up the dare, opportunity. We need to take up some of these challenges adventures in prayer. I call it getting my degree, in knee- ology. We can start with our born-again degree. This born-again degree starts with us giving our lives, wills, which is our choices to the Lord GOD ALMIGHTY.

Remember that we were born into sin and shaped in wrongdoing, seeds of darkness, and wrongfulness, planted deep and sown inside of us. He then takes us and begin to form, shape, and make, renew all over again. We become believers from our born-again degree.

We will shift over to a degree of becoming an ambassador of Christ Yeshua or Jesus Warriors, and Saints that serve. To become part of the plan of GOD.

This all happens simultaneously, WE'RE JUST ONE PART of this great plan, not the whole complete finished work. He gave us the part, that fitted us. He designed, written, about us that we can handle according to his divine plans and callings. It is called his predestinated plan, before the foundations of the world. This plan for you and me, how EXCITING! Laborer in the vineyard degree, this takes a lot of prayer releasing, confessing, decreeing, and declaring the word of the lord. What happens when we decree speaking the words of GOD INTO the atmospheres, and the other spheres that we spoke about earlier in this book, in this chapter earlier.

The sound begins to go out like a powerful invisible force of GOD's SPIRIT. The Word of GOD is all in the mix and, midst of us and it is what gives us such power.

The word of GOD gives us strength to fight. The word of GOD gives us Authority and dominion over EVERY Jurisdiction in ALL THE WORLD. LET ME MAKE THIS STATEMENT CLEAR AND PRECISE RIGHT NOW. WE AS SAINTS OF THE MOST HIGH, GOD'S CHILDREN HAVE THE HIGHEST CALLING IN ALL THE WORLD AND WORLDS TO COME. WHY? BECAUSE WE ARE MADE IN THE LIKENESS AND HIS OWN POWERFUL IMAGE These jurisdictions are lands, areas, and waters in depth with no limitations or restrictions. Below and high up in the air as far as the second heaven or even higher. NO AREA IN THIS LIFE IS OFF-LIMITS TO US AS LONG AS WE FOLLOW HIS DIVINE PLANS.

Reason I am saying this is that, are prayers reaches all the way up into Heaven and He (GOD) begins to answer our prayers of faith. Belief victory and triumphing to receive the manifestations of what we are and have prayed while in our earth suit or this flesh. We are both KINGS and PRIEST; in Revelations 1:6. We are a Royal priesthood a holy nation, 1 Peter 2:9. WE SHOULD BE PORTRAYING WHAT WE WERE CALLED TO DO ON THIS EARTH.

In other words, there is not anywhere on the earth, under the earth that is off limits to us when where in full armor and obedience all at the same time. get your degrees in prayer, speaking in other tongues and the Spirit of GOD gives us the utterance. These weapons are very powerful within themselves.

When we put it into practice daily without ceasing or stopping. Let us be praying all through the day. When we begin to pray all through the day & moment by moment in constant prayers, praying boldly before the throne of grace. Which has been given to us, all of this will come about through, you, me, and the body of Christ coming together spending some time in prayer. So, then we have fighting equipment, made available for us because for protection, to be skillful, armed for war, armor. Our armour are reinforced protection on us in the spirit and on the inside with the armor tools, weapons that have been given to us metaphorically to use as we see fit within the confines of GODS jurisdictions. That he has freely given to us that is; set by his laws, rules, and commandments in the Mighty name of Jesus.

It will be a mighty awesome RELEASE OF GODS POWER THAT WILL PENETRATE. But only BY READING AND STUDYING HIS MIGHTY ALL-POWERFUL WORD and APPLYING IT TO OUR LIVES. One of the greatest ways to get the scriptures into us is through meditation, pondering, what we have read over and over into our memories, thinking about it, looking at it, and speaking it out loud to hear yourselves say it. Throughout their lifetime, individuals experience a multitude of events, actions, and changes that can impact their lives. These changes will grow us, them, and you and anybody that are willing to put GOD'S words and plans into, full actional operations. Spiritual giants' slayers will be born out of some of these experiences as you continue to engage in this great fight of faith. As you continue to pray,

WILL SEND OFF an ATOMIC, BIOLOGICAL, NUCLEAR BLAST, spoken in faith, power, belief, confidence, and secure of what is being said is going out into the many spheres' doing what its designed to do. That is to break up and consume, demolish our enemies, uproot till up the evil seeds that have been planted unawares known as tares, false harvest, imitations, look a likes, fakes, and a bunch of it. Even some metaphoric g.m.o.'s which is genetically modified organisms that have been designed to be a look-alike or a real thing, but it's not the real thing so do not be fooled by the fakes and look a likes. This is why we must pay attention and be alert and on guard for those that are what to be; s but they are phonies and imitators, they come to infiltrate, what we have and they become imposters. More on this subject for another time.

What is it designed to do? Tear up, break up, uproot crush, and demolish the hosts of hell. Yes, I said it this is what the word of GOD, PRAYER, FASTING CONFESSIONS DECREES, and DECLARATIONS are supposed to do to our evil and wicked fallen enemies in the mighty name of Jesus. THAT WILL ASCEND INTO THE HEAVENS FOR HIGHER AND GREATER in Power demonstration, signs wonders and even miracles with MARVELS. It will cause Exploits, Anointings, Imperial, Kingly anointings, mantels, and all that are attached to them of all kinds and much the more THAN THAT OF Any HUMAN BLAST OF INTENSE ENERGY. When MIXED with power air heat and all the component's that make up all materials, that will cause an explosion; bangs upsurges set off.

The things ALL MIGHTY GOD HAS GIVEN US, its ours because we are his children and the rights to all his inherited benefits. This is more than what the natural can and has produced. It SUPERSEDES ALL OF THIS MANY TIMES OVER In fact, the earthly things do not compare to the things that we have in our ARSENAL OF WEAPONS. We're going to do a series on the WEAPONS OF THE SAINTS AND SONS OF GOD, ON ANOTHER TIME.

Spiritual things of CHRIST LAUNCHED into the atmosphere will cause such explosions and the damage it will do, to the kingdom of darkness. Called the devils mess, or his place of abode, and all that he has set up and try to come against.

The ambassadors of Christ, the light of the Spirit of GOD IN US. It will do damage, severely, critically, chaotic, will have a crippling affect and may I add damming to the kingdom of the devil. Our adversary and all his agents. Those that work for him, demon spirits or evil spirits, fallen from a Celestial place and position.

Their main job and responsibility are to carry out, all their evil assignments, plots, schemes snares and traps across the spectrum of life. The devil makes it a priority, sure and certain with many attempts to stop us the Saints, from going forward to reach our destinies. Liberties that have been, assigned and given to us by our Heavenly Father & our Savior Yeshua. Jesus our Christ

The awesome use of the Holy Spirit is certainly not ever forgotten. These demons, sirens, monitoring, spying, snaring, and trapping unclean spirits that try to invade our lives. If they can, to get us to fall, give up, get tired, with a mind to quit, loose heart, cave in means, just plain old get burnt out, from doing the Lords will. With the many efforts, to keep moving with progress. If we are not careful will have loose heart do the lack of praying, feel like giving up. Sometimes these thoughts do hit our thinking. I have thought about at some times in my life and I want to be transparent in all that I do. That is to be true to the lord and to myself as well as others in the body of Christ.

This is where prayer constantly comes in and help us to be strong and very courageous.

Gaining ground in the mighty name of Jesus. Because of what we have will hit those demons, evil unclean spirits, leviathans, serpents, scorpions, vipers, restrictor pythons, cobras, and even dragons of all type's sizes and kinds.

Fallen angels can be transformed into all types of animals. These demonic spirits are in the forms of dogs, jackals, owls, foxes' dirty birds of all kinds even monster looking AND lurking demons just to name some. This gives us an ideal of what we're up against in the name of Jesus.

These are evil looking spirits nothing good or beautiful about them. They smell horrible, and their looks is nothing pretty. If you have ever seen them BUT we have the victory already,

In JESUS NAME, AND IT IS SO ANY HOW!

What has been already given to us is Tremendously awesome with the force behind what we represent, that is the power in the name of JESUS. What has been given to us, it will cause demonic entities damage to the kingdom of darkness.

These evil demons out there stirring up Havoc, they don't really know what to do, they really don't have a fighting chance, against us when we're in full gear, armed, and dangerous. They won't be able to escape from the velocity blast, that will take them out and damage and destroy them with the fires of GOD. His indignation fierce wrath and power, IT WILL LITERALLY CREMATE THEM INTO ASHES THEY WILL MELT WITH FERVENT HEAT. Despite what others may have heard or had said in the past.

Demons can be destroyed, cremated taken out, get rid of, and ceased to exist, do away with. We are the Children of GOD. We must know how to use what is handed down to us. We must learn how to use what was given to us. The weapons that are entrusted to us, inherited that we have through Jesus Christ our Lord. More will be explained in other chapters on weapons, and how to use them against our enemies. We must learn how to use what we have. Do we Really understand what has been given to us? Or do we neglect or not considering the price that has been paid for what we are enjoying right now in our lifetime. What I'm saying is that we need to enjoy and take full advantage of what we have.

Do not neglect or take for granted that it will always be here. It might not always be there. If we don't use it to our full advantage. If we don't live a clean and holy pure sinless life before our GOD & FATHER. We have it! but if we are living a lazy, slothful life then they will not work to the fullest, that's what I am talking about. LET ME SAY THIS IF WE ARE LIVING IN SIN, YOU HAVE NO POWER TO FIGHT AND WRESTLE AGAINST THE devils and HIS COHORTS. LIVING IN SIN, PRACTICING SIN AND BEING A SINNER SINNING ALL THE TIME THESE TYPE OF PEOPLE HAVE NO POWER DUE TO SIN ZAPS THEIR ANOINTING. YES, I SAID IT. LIVING LIKE TO WORLD NOT PRAYING, FASTING HAVING COMMUNION WITH OUR HEAVENLY FATHER WILL SURELY GIVE YOU A TICKET TO CHAOS, TURMOIL AND MISERIES, SO COME OUT OF SIN AND STOP IT IF THAT'S IS YOU. IF NOT CONTINUE AND PROCEED FORWARD.

There is a lot of things that can happen to cause us to lose out. We need to remember in the Kingdom of GOD. Things can always change unless the Lord tell us otherwise. Things that have been promised can be taken away, stolen, or not given at all. Just know this; it can diminish or be reduced to a little of nothing and be discontinued. For example, if King Saul's position can be taken away from him do not think that ours as well can be done to. Anointings can be withdrawn, other gifts can be taken away.

When lucifer fell, some of the gifts, and anointings that he had, were stripped from him, enough said. Make no mistake, we have got to take all that we have gotten, sacrificed for very seriously. What GOD has deposited to us, in us, and through us before the foundations of the world we are responsible to carry out without any excuses. What we have that is, if we stop practicing putting into action what we know and have been taught and displayed through the grace of GOD for us his people.

OUR lives are going to be as well, spiritually emotionally and physically healthy, prosperous, rich, successful, powerful progressively always moving forward as we put precious time in. What do you mean by saying time in. Time in with the Lord in Prayer, spending time in the Word of GOD. SPENDING time fasting. Spending time in GOD'S presence, soaking just sitting in his presence just enjoying him as your HEAVENLY FATHER. SPENDING time worshipping in, telling him how much you love him. Effort energy, support, discipline and passionate desires with a Great Hunger and thirst in the SPIRIT into all that our LOVING HEAVENLY FATHER & SAVIOR, (rescuers, Redeemer and Liberator has given to us. Our Heart must be a heart of putting out at a rate of 100%. The Spirit desires & passion into all that we do.

It will take Total commitment and dedication. We must stay focused on our efforts, steadfastness Disciplining ourselves, in the basics all the time throughout our entire life. This is how we grow spiritually. Sacrificially all for the cause of Christ Jesus. To bring all this to pass and about, to be able to meet our Divine Destiny. The lord Jesus has set for us on every level in the mighty name of Jesus Christ and it is so, and so it is Let it be done.

We will reap or get what we have sown into, experience our lives, whatever time energy, effort knowledge instructions, applications we follow and take to heart. What we have or (will) produce an AWESOME result. These results should make us feel better about ourselves. When it comes to making progress, our efforts should be from our spirit, that he has given us. ALL THAT HE HAS GIVEN US WE SHOULD HAVE BY NOW GIVEN ALL BACK TO HIM FOR THE USE AS HE SEES FIT..

It will be shocking even to ourselves good, bad, ugly, or whatever choices. Whatever thoughts, Ideals, or thinking patterns we chosen to follow. We are talking about a HARVEST HERE. Our activations will produce another reaction so we must make good sound decisions. All according to GODs plans instructions, gifts, and talents along with the fruits of the spirit. GOD has a wonderful Spirit, he has given us and the destiny that predestinated, that is Preplanned for us all.

LIFE IS WHAT WE MAKE IT, Be It; however, its according to what we are saying. LET ME PAUSE JUST FOR A MOMENT AND SPEAK and ask you a question. WHAT ARE, WE SAYING ABOUT OUR situations? Are we speaking positively or negatively to our situations? St Mark 11:22-24 You shall have whatsoever you say. We really need to define what are we saying. Is what we're saying moving us forward in the things of GOD? Or are they causing us to lose ground that we have gained. Remember the blood, sweat, and tears. We don't want to find ourselves in Our situations by the things we are saying and speaking. If it's not lined us with the words of GOD. ²² And Jesus answering saith unto them, Have faith in God. GOD WANTS US TO HAVE THE GOD KIND OF FAITH, ZOE, that speaks things into existence now.!

²³ For verily I say unto you, that whosoever shall say unto this mountain, be thou removed, and be thou cast into the sea; and shall not doubt in his heart but shall believe that those things which he saith shall come to pass; he shall have whatsoever he saith.

²⁴ Therefore I say unto you, what things soever ye desire when ye pray, believe that ye receive them, and ye shall have them.

When we're speaking the word of GOD under his anointing, or just simply believing what he has spoken and written his word for promises we need to just believe it and receive. This is what we have and has been given to us with intensity, impact, force, desire, passion, reason, purpose, and the strength of GOD.

IT WILL CAUSE A CATASTROPHIC OUTBURST OF EXPLOSION INTO THE ATMOSPHERE SENDING SHOCK WAVES OF ENERGY ENOUGH TO DESTROY THE WORKS OF THE ENEMY AND GET HIS ATTENTION. The things we have asked the Lord for will start to appear and show up. For this is what manifestations are all about. Asking what we desire, believe it, and watch the prayers, blessings begin to show up. Power with an abundant, blast, explosive igniting, in Jesus' name begin to form and materialize in front of us through us speaking words of life. The things we may speak and say with our mouths with sound and voice. Getting exactly what we ask for from our Heavenly and Glorious FATHER.

We must remember that our prayers are very powerful. We
are speaking, Spirit, and life into the atmospheres. The
words of GOD declare that verse (b) Effectual fervent prayer
of the righteous man availeth much. James 5:16

The choices we have made brought us these reactions. Our thinking,
thoughts on our minds flow with ideals, words, pictures, images, and the
like. We have just made which is called choices or our will into action,
without proper consideration from the MASTER OF THE UNIVERSE.
All other things that are in the world & worlds out there; decide the things
we say with our tongues. Speaking out our own mouths, Past, present,
and future. NOT counting the cost or rehearsing in GODS word. It is
making our actions as said before. Choices that we choose right now when
we speak things out of our mouths in the very present, will happen when
mixed with belief soon, will show up in whatever form we have spoken it.

Our words will begin to take shape and form whatever we are saying.
Experiences have a part, our words spoken, things in the matter but
do not put all our experiences in one thought. We need to learn to give
these things a chance to soak in our minds, not just speaking things
out of our mouths and the results are hurting, and painful to us as
well to speaking things to others. Seeking GODLY counsel, think
things through with prayer. Reading and asking a lot of questions
to others that can be trusted with a solid proven track record.

We are where we are; because we have made choices, mixed with
applications which is our actions on display putting our spoken plans
to work and they manifested, or they were and are seen. Sometimes
were not going to like what showed up. The things that have been
applied through knowledge, not considering what has or will be sown
or outlandish outcomes, that caused so much aftermath. Afterwards
which is our harvest or REAPING WHAT is put in the ground.
I am making this so plain that no one reading this book cannot
miss or get this info misconstrued and say I do not know what
happened. After you have read this my book from the Lord Jesus.

Our Heavenly All Mighty Father from this day, there will be some
great amount of accountability. Accountability will be required from
you to perform and help save and help others come out of their messes,

yes because some of them or most of them have more than one type of mess, so I said messes (Smiles). The things they have hastily made for themselves, though unwise choices, and the others that are connected.

That is our feelings thoughts and actions Experiences along with our applying applications to what we believe to be RIGHT. We cannot forget about how others may have influenced our lives as well. SOMETIMES ITS NOT RIGHT to be sown that will grow so don't be mad at anyone else. For whatever YOU OR I HAVE MADE OR ALLOWED TO BE SOWN. IN A WAY OF A SEED into OUR OWN THOUGHTS in our minds to come. The HARVEST THAT PRODUCES, WHEN IT SHOWS UP. But if we have followed what our LORD HAS TOLD us WE SHALL PRODUCE A 100%- AND 100-FOLD BLESSING IN JESUS NAME, and it is so. Don't forget about the 1000 X 's more, also make sure you take your time to go to chapter 15 on a 1000 X's more declarations.

Training and the will to learn and want to do better is the key, along with desires, passions determination steadfastness. Being unmoved by anybody else's actions, words, or their set of circumstances. What they may be saying at the time. It is all about CHANGE AND CHANGING. Doing something differently that we may have never done or considered before. That makes and will bring positive progress. Forwardness to see your results that will bring improvement. LISTEN, WE CAN'T HELP OR STOP WHAT OTHERS DO OR SAY TO us. BUT WE HAVE POWER TO NOT LET IT AFFECT us. IT'S NOT WHAT THEY DO or even say to us, ITS HOW WE TAKE IT.

SO, TAKE IT WITH A GRAIN OF sand or salt. IF ITS NOT GOING TO HELP YOU to grow, encourage, build, support or even enhance your life; Get rid of it. THROW IT OUT AND KEEP MOVING FORWARD; OK. This is what change is all about seeing something different than before. When we see something in our lives that need some attention or needs to be changed. Do not wait for others to tell you what or what not to correct in your lives. Make the change on your own; without anyone suggesting or advising.

The fact that you see and do something about it is a sign of having a desire, and wanting to do better for us, is a good sign we are catching on and learning, it will come out a lot better in the long run. Change should be a constant thing in our lives. Thoughts to ponder; Let us not be as others, or person, people have done in the past. Doing the very same thing, each and every day, week, month. And the year in and year out expecting different RESULTS, THAT'S THE DEFINITION OF INSANITY, OK. Saints people and the rest of the businessmen and women across the globe as well as all the leaders.

GOD has dropped and downloaded these thoughts into my spirit; that he is so concerned about people that he has created. That it's like he has divided all the people of his creation amongst his chosen ones, so that we can reach out to everyone, and no one is left out of this equation. In different parts of the world and be a witness to these and every individual.

Somehow help bring them advice, persuade, and admonish them, to be able to see for themselves, that they need to come to Christ. They are the ones that are not saved and into other religious settings, that's not real and true, they get no real results, because they are not serving the one TRUE GOD ALMIGHTY. GOD presence can be tangibly felt, he has a voice that can be heard, and we can see him moving across our lives, from time to time.

OUR THINKING: either will be blessed and empowered for success, or prosperity joy abundant achievements with progress. It will launch us, or it will take us down a path that will bring us a lot of upsets, worries, and distress, and make us feel like we are in a desert. The desert represents a place of dryness, stuck out in the middle of nowhere. Like we are on a long journey with no moving or movement, no water, moisture, hot and unquenched, and parched places is not where we should be whatsoever.

Plenty of confusions that is parched and cracked enough to share with others and then some; that's not what we want, not also what GOD ALMIGHTY wants for us as his children. Well let me assure you as well that is not what our Heavenly Father has desired for us; or designed to take place. These are choices we have carried out throughout our own lives.

What He wants for us is to live the ABUNDANCE OF OVERFLOW, CONSTANTLY GIVEN HIM ALL THE GLORY IN JESUS NAME, and it is so. We should be always working to do better and obtain more of our character, integrity, greatness, and wonderful habits that will enhance our personality. I just wanted to add this greatness only will come for us when we begin to master the fruits of the spirit. The fruits of the spirit as noted and quoted in Galatians 5:22-23 build character that will sustain us all the way through our lives.

The choices and seeds planted into our lives will in some cased have a lasting affect when done properly. All will come from the choices that we make today; the books we read, instructions we follow, information that will be read, giving out by others as well as ourselves will be very helpful while on our journey. Taken the time to hear instructions, listening to what others must impart into us, is some of the rich nuggets that we need to get, while on this journey.

The great and awesome times we have fasted and prayed intensely. The blessings of fasting and praying has its benefits; fasting and prayer speeds up the movement inside of us and heighten our spirit into a great dimension if we choose to stay here. If we choose to stay here due to our commitment in fasting and prayer it launches us to be exactly were GOD wants and sometimes can be many times exceed it by leaps and hurdles in Jesus name. Sacrificing ourselves, i.e... that is for the killing out of the deeds of this old flesh, living a renewed life in Christ Jesus for the furthering of the work of Jesus, the Christ.

Spending time in his (GOD) awesome presence, what do spending time in the presence of GOD do for us as his children, ambassadors, Sons of God. Spending time alone in the presence of GOD alone gives us rapid Acceleration, this is called fast movement. Things are and will be moving at such a fast rapid pace in our lives we have to put on our gym shoes to either keep up or catch up to the movement.

Spending time alone with HIM reading and studying his GREAT WORD; that brings EXPLOSIVE RESULTS THAT WILL change us. After all that's what this BOOK IS ALL ABOUT. Change If I'd said it once, I have said it many times, I've said it a thousand times; to drive this the meaning home, many times repeating a phrase, slogan, a word of truth, will certainly help strengthen us as we continue to speak and confess what the words of GOD is saying to us. Because if we get these points hiding them in our hearts and continue to meditate day and night upon the words of the spirit of GOD. if we get this understanding, its life-enhancing, propelling, projecting you and I to the next dimension.

Not only blow you away but will propel you to the next level. Sincerity and apply to our lives daily that will strengthen all your gifts & talents. This Project will also make you some money to share with others glorify GOD with many other blessings that comes alone with this supernatural change in our lives. When you discover who you are; and what it is that you are called to do, while being in this life. You get a chance to use your gifts, the things that come easy, when it comes to certain academics.

For example, when your good at math, adding numbers, in your head, just simply knowing how to calculate numbers, in a very easy manner, this is a gift for you. Things you did not trained for or wasn't taught by others, but these gifts are a GOD given, and talent, like for example: Getting on a piano and just messing with the keys. Finding out you are good at it, and you thoroughly enjoy playing it, and the sounds that comes from it. This is what we call talent to play instruments, this is just one example of what gifts and talents are and the ability will do for you; you must come to a point to discover your natural abilities and start using them to the fullest.

Now these abilities of gifts and talents, it has the potential to bring us before mighty prominent people. The Lord GOD will Open, Doors causing them to ask us questions; of how did you or I get to where we are. Asking questions, and how long did it take you, or I to get their? will begin to make room, to share their platforms; with us and reap awesome benefits and host our endeavors for Christ Jesus.

This type of teaching in details explaining how things get to be the way they are through careful calculations with respect to the words of GOD, proper planning, disciplining ourselves, before the Lord. Consecrating: ourselves behind the scenes, while others were doing whatever they do in public, or in private situations. But we did not let anyone stop or slow us down from reaching our spiritual goals, to please the lord:

The Lord bringing us before many others as an example for the world and the flocks of GOD. This is where preparation came in and done for us, this will put us fully and launched into an assault by the authority that has been given to us that is a part of our blessings. We want to always put out the very best quality of any goods and services; Not just given the Lord any leftovers, OR WHAT WE WANT TO GIVE HIM. No polluted offerings, sacrifices, or covenants, or gifts especially if we are representing our LORD & SAVIOR that's wonderful JESUS CHRIST, OUR HEAVENLY FATHER, and the PRECIOUS HOLY SPIRIT.

No doubt our desires passions gifts and talents will give us a great start in life. As we move forward up the great divine latter that has been allotted to us. As we are supposed to do and start, we are on an awesome destiny. This awesome destiny that will end up doing, fixing, and taking care of responsibilities. That means being accountable for our actions; exactly what we were put here to carry out in this life.

While we are here, but for now, where talking atomic and nuclear powers. This power that can obliviate a large area of land air and sea in a matter of minutes. Seconds, and in a quick blink of an eye, that's how fast it's moving, spiritually speaking, and is a metaphoric thoughts, actions, reactions, consequences, and rewards put into revolutionary momentum, steadily.

Philippians 4:8 - Finally, brethren, whatsoever things are true, whatsoever things are honest, whatsoever things are just, whatsoever things are pure, whatsoever things are lovely, whatsoever things are of good report; if there be any virtue, and if there be any praise, think on these things. Virtue here is referring to a type of strength, and it has to come from within from the Lord, remember that! What are we saying here, that if were using the power that our Heavenly Father has given us and begin to engage in it and take it to other powerful extreme anointed levels. The fields of the enemy that they are occupying, they will be destroyed and removed by the power of our prayers along with the word and the warrior angels of GOD.

CHAPTER 2

EXPLOSIVE OUTCOMES, INTENSIFIED WITH IMPACT PART 02

THE OUTCOME WITH OUR THOUGHTS, DECREES AND DECLARATIONS.

Accompanying GODS WORD; is also what we set for ourselves and guidelines for others as well. Those that have been set in place will be very helpful, useful, and POWERFUL, PLEASE take advantage of all this material written.

I decree & declare.

I say the truth in Christ and lie not.

I decree and declare that I am not a liar, and neither will I be engaged in a lying situation or let it be found in my life lying about something that is not truth.

I decree and declare that I will not cause myself to be used or put into a place of lying. Telling something that is not true, or real. But that which is original, authentic, pure, clean, and unadulterated in the mighty name of Jesus.

This information is used to quote, say Out loud, combat the works, and attacks of the enemy using the mighty name of Jesus, his Blood loosed against our enemies. But this same wonderful and powerful blood will indeed cover all our sins and protect us.

Listen by us speaking the word of GOD out loud the angels come to get and fulfill what they are hearing because it is the word of GOD.

Now when we speak these decrees and declarations out loud; we are encouraging ourselves building ourselves up, and strengthening what is already in place, that is GOD's work taking place on the inside and becoming a complete and solid steadfast unmovable work.

Romans 9:1

9 I say the truth in Christ, I lie not, my conscience also bearing me witness in the Holy Spirit,

I will be true with my feelings, but I will not be led by my feelings. I will not let my feelings dictate or control, or overtake me, but live by the word of GOD. My situation what I should and should not do but won't let it get the best of me. I will continue to be a true person in all that I do, say, think, act, apply, and perform for the Lord in the mighty name of Jesus.

I will not let these things overtake me, that is being caught in a deceptive ungodly situation. Some examples that we can get us caught up in a lie is doing these pagan holidays we are so engaged in the holidays that we are celebrating just as the other people in the world. Like eating the food that others may bring doing a halloween get-together. We are living a lie because we have just have been partakers of their dainty foods and not realized it.

When we eat something that is from a holiday my beliefs are that we are with the inn crowds celebrating just as they are. These pagan holidays really are for those demons and all of their fallen agents, and the devils people that love to celebrate right along with him that is ungodly, not for the ambassadors of Christ. Not to condescend, to bring me down to their levels, or reduce me in any way, shape, form, or fashion. When we begin to do other than what GOD tells us to do, then we are working for the enemy, that is called a spirit of disobedience, and it can carry a heavy penalty or a stiff correction if we're not going to catch it and repent, so we must be careful to follow his plan.

You and I know that we do not desire this in our lives. Do not let this be your case or allow us to be caught in devious lies.

I will not allow myself to come down to lower myself, or my standard in any other ways that are false. I will not allow others and their ways;

those men and women and their ungodly systems, that are worldly, and all their man-made standards, that are unlawful, & ungodly.

I do not want, anyone to set me up for a trap, or a devilish work of the enemy. I will Obey GODS word and instructions in the mighty name of Jesus.

I will be striving to reach up to his level, all that he requires, and he is asking of me. I will be responsible for, giving heed to, whatever instructions, that I am to follow in the name of Jesus.

I am very Honest in my thoughts, not only to myself but to others as well in the mighty name of Jesus.

Listen; to this statement, a lot can happen if we are with the wrong crowd or a brother or sister still needs some deliverance in certain areas of their lives. That do not give us the rights to do as we please. Just because we see a leader do something that seems to be ungodly does not give us a right to practice that deed, words or actions that may have been displayed, the things you may have seen them do or hear them say something, that does not sound like it should be flowing out of their mouth. We have better be asking a lot of questions and know who is laboring amongst us or over us.

I will take the right actions towards others whether they are in agreement with me or not.

I will remain to be honest in all that I do.

I will say, and speak, and perform, in truth, always while endeavoring, striving attempting to undertake in the mighty name of Jesus.

I will not side with the guilty, or unrighteous.

I will be honest, with my money, personal items, food, and drinks. I will be a leader with loyalty. When others that put me in charge of.

I will not let the enemy overtake, undermine, scheme take advantage or deceive me.

I will not manipulate, others and will not allow them to put me into one of his/her traps or snares.

I will not allow anyone to delay, deny, or hinder my
progress in the mighty name of Jesus.

I will walk and talk in truth and honesty with my Loving FATHER
& Savior. He (Jesus) is watching me right now as I read this, he is
RECORDING down all my deeds, actions, words, feelings, and thoughts.
So, what manner of person ought I to be when the LORD IS WATCHING?

I will never allow.

Always stay focused on the destiny that the Lord has set for me.

I will never allow myself to get, ahead of the Lord.

I will never allow myself to get in a boasting manner.

I will never allow myself to walk in pride, and
arrogance, being lifted within myself.

This is what gotten the devil thrust, driven out of Heaven, so if we
want to be driven out just be lifted in pride. When I think about it what
do we have to be lifted about? When it was Jesus precious blood that
delivered us from the darkness and the punishments of a burning hell!

I will not allow myself to go beyond the things that I know is wrong
but I will do that which is right in the sight of GOD and man.

I will not or never allow myself to be involved in illegal
scandals, crimes of any type, or dirty deeds that will take
away from others that I did not purchase or bought.

All that has been written about me that I will complete.

That I have been entrusted with,

Anything that will be put into my hands, my care, my
presents, and all the likes; with large sums of money,
people with stuff & things will be handled properly.

I decree and declare that ALL my thoughts, actions, spirit, mind,
deeds, and my intentions, will be pure, without any altered motives,
sincere, true, to the Core of my spirit, right before the Lord as
well as others all the time in the mighty name of Jesus.

I am a Just person, righteous, justified, Meaning I am in
right standing with the Lord and with his work.

My spirit is in right standing,

My soul is in right standing with myself and with the
others in my family and the rest of the world.

I walk in the right standing of the Lord and
make sure it is what he requires of me.

I walk in the right standing of GOD, because it is just right to do
and whatsoever is right, I will receive a reward from the Lord.

I will continue to search my heart and ask the Lord to
search my life, soul, to see if there are any ways that
are not right, and to always keep it together.

My home is in right standings.

The ministries he has given, or entrusted to me is in right standings.

With all the Saint, Ambassador, which is the
HIGHEST calling while on this earth.

I will always strive to be right. Which is, being fair to
myself treating others as I want to be treated, need to be
treated to be, treated in the mighty name of Jesus.

As well as being right, open-minded with others,
In Jesus name it is so; so, it is.

I will not allow myself to be willfully being out here, in life and society
to be in sin, making a mockery or displeasing or crucifying My Lord
and Savior all over again in the matchless name of Jesus. Hebrew 6:6

I will & continue to be a true person in all that I do, for
the cause of Christ, and set examples as a leader and an
AMBASSADOR FOR CHRIST in Jesus name, so it is.

I will give also that which is right to those things that
are lovely, kind, just, or whatever I may owe or need to
take care of at that time in my life, in Jesus' name.

I will not hold on to that which belongs to another if I do it will be given and delivered to them in Love in Jesus name, so it is.

I decree and declare that I strive to have a good report amongst all my brother's sister's family members church peers, business partners associates, companions, wife, children, and all that is & will be around me at any given time with others especially MY LORD GOD & SAVIOR JESUS CHRIST.

Proverbs 17:22 - A merry heart doeth good like a medicine: but a broken spirit drieth the bones.

I decree and declare that I have a MERRY HEART that is happy and full of joy and satisfaction, I do not suffer from A broken spirit, and if I did once before now in the mighty name of Jesus, I AM HEALED SET FREE AND DELIVERED IN THE MIGHTY NAME OF JESUS.

I AM HEALED BECAUSE I SAY THAT I AM.

I HAVE WHATSOEVER I SAY, SO I SPEAK TO THIS MOUNTAIN, AND DECREE THIS RIGHT NOW that I have and possess a healthy spirit in Christ Jesus name.

I take authority with this decree & declarations; they enable me to win all types of VICTORIES and TRIUMPH over each situation that I may face from time to time.

That I will not allow myself to suffer from a broken heart, to give in to any of its symptoms, these symptoms may include but not limited to, having a pity party, feeling sorry for myself, and shame & guilt, embarrassment of various sorts, for myself by myself.

The enemy may be on the other side making fun. So, it's not allowed, we will not accept or tolerate it.

Let's not render that to him, and his wicked demons, can make all types of fun over our situations and circumstances.

It's not given Glory to GOD.

This is what the people in the world and sometimes others in the body of Christ carry out.

Making fun, at us laughing at us, making sarcastic remarks, and having all types of jesters about us and think it is funny.

This type of attitude and character is from the devil. So, when you hear others making, such things like this come out of their mouths, just know they are being used by the devil and may not even know it, that's ignorant of the devil's devices.

Components are a part of some other parts & thoughts, that will add to what's already there.

Getting some help with these NEGATIVE THOUGHTS.

I WILL NOT ENTERTAIN ANY NEGATIVE THOUGHTS.

Negative thoughts: what are negative thoughts? Thoughts that the devil has interjected into our thought patterns and cycles of thinking. He is playing in the fields of our thoughts and we do not even know it. We think it's us but where do these thoughts come from? They are evil spirits in the air throwing out these thoughts and we picked them up because at the moment we are at a point of weakness. It's possible that this is an attack as well so lets not rule out what the enemy is trying to do. NEGATIVE THOUGHTS IS AN ATTACK ON THE THOUGHT PATTERNS OF OUR MINDS. WILL AND OUR EMOTIONS, WHICH IS AGAIN OUR SOUL.

These thoughts about myself or thoughts about others that GOD, did not think about us. Thoughts that are not true. Negative thoughts will weaken my appreciation, stains, blemishes, and wrinkles in my relationship, with GOD. Not to forget spots that can be heard and stamped into my feelings and thoughts, and will bring some shame to myself, my family members, and those in ministry with us, and will bring emotional, scars, bad and sometimes lasting thought of some type, to my friendship with my colleagues, associates, and comrades.

They do not build me up, instead, they degrade me, they tear me down, so low that I don't want to get up and ever make attempts again. This can be referred to self- condemnation, along with shame and being humiliated by one's own self, just because of a negative thought spoken out of the mouth of ourselves into the atmospheres amongst our associates and all who are listening, this is the works of the devils and evil spirits at work in the minds of those that are vulnerable, open to depressions oppressions, has become a victim of the enemy without warning or notice.

Negativity, this is the work of the devil, to steal your life, your image, your joy, and other healthy relationships, that has been built over the years. It takes a lifetime to build a great relationship, but only a moment to tear it down, destroy it or bring shame to us or others with our tongues, our mouths speaking doubt, that is not healthy to ourselves.

Negative words that hurt and cut deep like a knife.

Negative words, negative thoughts, ideals, brings harm to our soul, mind that causes other effects that can be lasting.

Negativity eats, at the great structures, chipped down those humongous mountains that were so carefully drawled out, skyscrapers, awesome buildings, that were erected by our Heavenly father in Heaven what has been planted to be good, and it will eventually tear down and destroy anything that was good, anything that was right, anything, that was planted as deep and righteous, morals that was handed down to us by our ancestors or great teachers or great teachings that we have acquired over the years. Any other things that he can find to steal. To kill out your desires, passions; to stop you and I from going forward, if he can. All things that are bad that's what he wants for our lives.

We have some news for the devil. We don't care what he wants, we will not let him overtake us in the things of GOD. These are those things that has been set before the foundations of the world. Let's not allow him to destroy us with his evil ways, using our own ways, against us that at times, in some way, become weak. No good trick the enemy set out against us no good. These thoughts could be about myself and how I feel about myself, how I look, how I see myself, and how I view myself. But for the record it does not matter what is going on with us, I declare that; this is not us, not you, or them, so we need to stop accepting things, the devil throws out at us. When I look in the mirror or thinking about what it is or is not, I am still, fearfully, and wonderfully made beautiful in the eyes of the LORD GOD ALMIGHTY this is all according to the word of GOD.

Ideas, or mind perceptions about this condition.

I do not let dictate to me what I can or cannot do, say, or go.

I always have victory in every area of my life
that come in the name of Jesus.

I decree & declare that I am not easily OFFENDED
by everything, Others may say.

I will not allow myself to be overtaken, by words from others
that attempt to hurt me intentionally, Emotionally, or maybe
even psychologically. It does not matter what others say about
me, but I will pray for them in the Mighty name of Jesus.

I decree and declare that my bones are not dry, I will not let dryness
set in my bones, causing me to have arthritis, a drying of the bones
due to extreme anger, hate, rage, bitterness, and contentions.

Neither will I let these thoughts in my heart. Because I
will guard my heart with all diligence, for out of it are the
issues of life the word of GOD declares. Proverbs 4:23

My life is guarded.

My family is guarded from the enemy.

My children are guarded from the snares of the enemy, as long as
they continue to walk in the laws, statues, and word of GOD.

I decree and declare that I do not suffer from any type of
sickness or diseases that comes from dry bones,

I decree and declare that I do not suffer from diseases that can cause
these, types of sicknesses to come. Nor do I suffer from unforgiveness,

I forgive everyone, anyone that has ever caused any type of pain, hurts,
or discomforts, wounds, or offences of any kind, I forgive them.

I decree and declare again with further expressions, that I do not
suffer from a person with an angry, anger, rage, hateful, mean
looking, type of person. Let me say this for explanatorial purposes,
just because a person looks very serious in the face, does not mean

they are mean, or have a nasty, ugly character, this does not mean that at all, so we need to be very careful not to put others, under this type of scrutiny, In the same category as others.

They may look like they are, does not mean that they are, so do not stand in judgement on others through speculations, or suspicions, hostility murdering, a person image or character assassination is still sin and considered to be a murderer, and no murderer can enter the kingdom of GOD, unless they truly repent and ask forgiveness, and make things right.

I decree and declare that I do not suffer from any of these types of spirits from the enemy in Jesus' name.

Revenge, retaliate, jealousies, envies, deceitfulness, stubbornness, rebellion, malice, which is wanting someone to hurt as they did once or even now, this is wrong and if you are, and or still going through, or you have suffered from this. We need to ask the Lord to forgive us, forgive yourself, others, and I forgive everyone and the persons that hurt me, all those that were involved, laughed, and made fun, whispered about me behind my back, I release all of them and let them go.

I release them and let them go free.

I decree and declare that I will not let the devil play with my thoughts or think someone is talking about me. If they are talking about me, I forgive them and ask The Lord to forgive them for their foolish, and childish ways.

I also want to make sure I do not give them anything in my life to talk about along with that, because if we give the devil an inch, he will take a yard and keep on growing so we do not owe him that, so we must keep ourselves in a neat and clean orderly fashion.

I release myself of any condemnation in the mighty name of Jesus.

I bind and rebuke the devil of any bad and wrong thoughts, evil ungodly, no good, unrighteous negative thoughts, that will make attempts to come into my thought life or me, you, or others. Those devils are REBUKED IN THE MIGHTY NAME OF JESUS AND I COMMAND YOU TO GO RIGHT NOW IN JESUS NAME.

I receive the medicine of GOD to heal any dryness, in fact there's no more dryness, or negative thoughts lingering in my life as of this moment, any more in Jesus name. No more Cracked, crushed, and damaged defects, neglected, deprived, forsaken, abandoned, unoccupied ways about me.

I renounced areas in my life, alone with no fragmented areas in my soulish man or my spirit in Jesus' name. Fragmented areas that have been broken separated and divided. All have been healed, set free, denounced, and released delivered and made whole and complete now. I decree and declare that all these areas that are mentioned are made totally whole and complete.

I will not go backward to indulge in these areas every again. That is all types of doubts, negative thoughts, attitudes, or any other ways that will cause setbacks.

NOR WILL I EVER OPEN the DOOR TO these spirits ever again in Jesus name. But I'm moving forward in the mighty name of Jesus Christ.

I even speak to my body and command it to heal thyself in the mighty name of Jesus.

My mind is healed, my thoughts, the things that I might think from time to time are healed.

I will not ponder, meditate on the negative of any one thing for long periods of time.

My Ideals are healed, the ideas that the Lord may drop in my thought patterns, pictures, images, or other ways. Thoughts comes to me they are all healed and decree and declare that my mind produce great thoughts and Ideas that will come to pass when I continue to be successful and have proper planning to fulfill my dreams. I am a person that will continue to thank the Lord for his great thoughts that is being downloaded in my mind in the mighty name of Jesus.

I am not a person that suffer from thoughts or needs to be a person of high maintenance. Which is upkeep, preservation, and allowances, always needing something, things are never right, never satisfied, always wanting something from someone or bothering someone about something, pertaining to something they are dealing with at the time.

Philippians 4:6 - Be careful about nothing; but in
everything by prayer and supplication with thanksgiving
let your requests be made known unto GOD.

I decree and declare; that I make my request to be known
to the Lord Jesus every day in Jesus name.

I decree and declare that I am not careful about nothing, but I have
purpose for everything I do for reasons and meaning in Jesus' name.

I decree and declare that my prayers are heart felt. My
cries, my feelings are true, real honest and very sincere
not putting on a show to get attention for myself while in
the presence of others to be seen or even heard.

I decree & declare that I am not insecure do not suffer from
low self-esteem. But knowing who I am excepting it comfortable
with all that has been dealt to me by the Lord King and GREAT
EMPEROR SOLID SOVEREIGN RULER OF MY LIFE.

When in supplications of prayers I will humble my soul before the
Lord, with thanksgiving, earnestly from the heart in Jesus' name.

I will not allow any type of pride being lifted of myself for
the purpose of being noticed or paid attention to.

In Jesus name I decree and declare that not only will I take
to him everything in prayer but will believe that those prayers
will be answered in Jesus' name. No worries, fears, doubts,
or unbelief and no lack of FAITH but as a grain of mustard
seed faith will be in continual motion growing inside of me,
in the mighty name of Jesus it is so; So, let it be done.

I decree and declare in the name of Jesus that the Lord will
hear and answer my prayers after hearing them and seeing
my heart of thanksgiving without an attitude of immaturity,
angered outburst upsets ill wills or ignorance of any kind
but will have gratitude in Jesus' name so it is done.

I decree and declare that I'm making my request be made known to my
LOVING LORD & SAVIOR JESUS CHRIST now, take out some time just

to pause and speak what it is that you want to speak or write it down and follow the instructions and apply what you have just read, and you will see the manifestations of GOD's spoken words in your life in Jesus name.

Philippians 4:13 · I can do all things through Christ which strengtheneth me. These words and decrees before the Lord with this eth are continual or continuously unceasingly or interrupted happening and taking place all at the same time.

I can do all that the Lord said that I can do, so I'm putting it into full action full swing, full momentum that will revolutionize my whole life of living and breathing, speaking to these things.

Speaking now to my mind, my will with good sound choices, and my emotions, which is my feelings. My soul, my minds thoughts, my will, the choices that I make at the time. The Spirit of GOD THAT IS; is moving forward going full speed ahead none stop.

I can do what GOD said I can do and no fears, no phobias of any type.

I will not allow to hinder me, stop, or block, me, slow me down or offset my plans. These plans that has been put in place from the foundations of the world we call Heaven. No doubts unbelief which is not believing fully like I should; negative thinking patterns of feelings simply because our feelings change so rapid doing the course of a day. But I will always allow myself to get things to make things right in the mighty name of Jesus. Other things that I might be dealing with of any type, I will get rid of.

I will make efforts to keep all of things in order. So, now, and especially that it may not cause any hindrances or setbacks in my life for my upcoming future events.

I can do what GOD has designed and given me to do with no rationalizing with those thoughts that he gives me to do, and I will carry each one of them out in the mighty name of Jesus; it is So; and let it be done.

In Jesus name it is so that whatsoever I put my mind to do with careful thinking considerations proper planning counting up the cost which is my thoughts in action, I can and will accomplish, stay focused, moving forward, making progress, in all that I do this, and these are my standards are being set in place to make and mode my life into all that ordained to take place, that I set for myself to do and carryout in the mighty name of Jesus it is so let it begin and see the finished work.

Jeremiah 29:11 - For I know the thoughts that
I think toward you, saith the LORD,

Lord Jesus, you know all my thoughts so as of this moment
I think good thoughts that you have given me.

I think the very best of myself. It will be a part of my life assignment to follow through with this type of thinking. I do not let these other thoughts crowd or flood my mind. I will not allow them to cause me to think other things that are not wholesome, real, true, and honorable. I will make my life all that GOD has planned in Jesus name. My thoughts that are good, true and right, powerful that you have written about me in Jesus' name, it is so its. Granted taken place right this moment with activation motivation and explanation. To be able to understand it and able to teach others as well, it is so, so let it be done.

Thank you, Lord Jesus, for the thoughts that you think toward me, and I also think these wonderful thoughts that I think toward myself as well, so I just want to say thank you wonderful Lord & Savior Jesus Christ in Jesus name.

I decree and declare that I do not believe in any type of luck, this word comes from the devil and so I want to set the record straight in the mighty name of Jesus.

Lord forgives us for using some of these words that we know too little about and we do not know that we are cursing ourselves, so we recant these statements in the mighty name of Jesus, that I do not speak in any type of luck, do not wish in anything to be lucky or no kind in the mighty name of Jesus. I destroy this demon of luck in Jesus name.

thoughts of peace, and not of evil, to give you an expected end.

Thank you, Lord Jesus, for your peaceful thoughts that you have given me. I now speak what you are saying about me, and not my own or the devils or anyone else's thoughts about me if there not uplifting and bring strength, restoration, encouragement, and life to me, to my soul and spirit in Jesus' name.

I speak no evil of myself or others, but I expect a
great turn out for my life in Jesus' name.

I will not put myself or others in harm's way. I will not damage, or
having a none caring fruitless, heartless, callous, or cold-hearted life.
I really do care about others and their situations and ways that will
not bring dangers, or in situations that can cause calamities, chaos,
or may be in the end of a thing can cause destruction, death this and
these will not be my lot of happening in my life in the name of Jesus.

Ephesians 4:31-32 · Let all bitterness, and wrath, and anger, and
clamour, and evil speaking, be put away from you, with all malice:

Bitterness means unpleasurable, of dislikes, discomfort, uneasy, not liked,
feelings, and emotions of anger, with harsh words hostile feelings hurt
feelings, and a subpresses, state of mind, patterns of thinking, which
is repressed, concealed, hidden, and overpowered feeling of emotions.

I decree and declare that I am healed, set free and destroy
any type of spirit of bitterness in the name of Jesus.

I am free from holding any type of subpressed emotions, which is
concealed, hidden or wounded feelings, deep hurts be healed, right now in
Jesus name. Evil patterns of thinking that's not right, I get rid of you and
throw you out in Jesus name. Overpowering thoughts that are devilish,
dark words, or repressed ideals I bind you in Jesus name. Anything that
is within that do not belong, I release, you and them in the name of Jesus,
and I uproot them and tilled them up, how to till up these roots, by letting
go of the feelings, forgiving, releasing them back to the enemy and letting
go. Asking the Lord to heal you and help you to overcome this type of
mindset. Cast out, the thoughts, cover yourself in the blood of Jesus and
stay out of those areas of darkness. Cast those demons in the abyss, hades,
and into the tormenting fires to be destroyed and cremated in Jesus name.

Wrath is in meaning strong vengeful feelings emotions wanting to release
indignation of revenge anger, and some type of punishment to others.
This wrath that they are dealing with brings some type of hurt and pain.
They want to get back at others for what they have done or said. These
things that have been said, it certainly stirs up your emotions to get
back at someone. This is ignorance by their unawareness, inexperience's

or their illiteracy or just uninformed about information. It could well be that others are really, not interested making them none caring, we are talking about people with little to no emotions of feelings, they just do not care what they say. These kind of none caring in their actions, this causes a cold or callous, meaning they are hard, with no feelings or just do not phase them with what they say to others or about others.

So, this we call being disrespectful not counting the cost as to what they are doing and all the mess they are causing with their mouths. The consequences that will follow, by the seeds they have planted with all the repercussions that takes place. Its longer than they have anticipated. It cost more than their willing to pay and stay into longer than imagined. This is what the tongue, the mouth, speaks out with and cause all types of troubles. The message is we need to watch our words around everyone we speak to and make sure were speaking life into others not death or destructions or even a curse.

Clamor is a loud noisy outcry yelling demanding in voice harsh rude or out of control at times, uproar, demands, & shouts.

Evil speaking; speaking evil of someone without no after thoughts or remorse,

I decree and declare that I will not be one that wants to hold suppressed anger be accessibly angry loud in voice out of control and let my feelings get the best of me in Jesus' name.

Lord Jesus, please help me to control my emotions so they will not get out of control and offend hurt slander crush wound or retaliate against others in any way shape form, or fashion in Jesus' name.

I decree and declare that I will not let jealousy hatred anger, wrath bitterness, yelling out at others, ruin or rule me. Not to allow the enemy to use me to embarrass, humiliate or misrepresent my Lord and Savior Jesus Christ in anyway in Jesus name.

I decree and declare that I will not succumb, meaning to yield to, or give in, to anything that's not good and uplifting. But I will submit to whatever is happening at the time. I will be aware to the things of this flesh and not allow or let myself fall into these emotional traps. That the enemy may set snares for me to fall into. But I will be wise enough to catch them and rebuke and stop them from happening in Jesus' name, and it is so.

In the mighty name of Jesus I bind all evil forces. Binding down not up every evil force meaning to stop them from advancing forward into, our lives. Stopping them and cut them off, throw and strip away all their accesses to all that they have caused in my life at this point. These Open accesses are no longer open for them to come in to wreak any type of trouble, problems or situations that will cause myself or others to be in danger. Restrictions are placed on them, that they cannot cause inflict or create havoc anymore with all their witchcraft attacks. Witchcraft attacks have to do with men or women whether they are in the church or out in the world. These types of people are sometimes greedy for power and control. Witch is both male and female. A warlock is both male and female, they simply like to control others in ways that are evil. They are doing this type of work for the devil, knowingly or unknowingly, either way its pure evil. Their motives and intentions are very manipulative, coming up against, you and me with hidden schemes and plans that will persuade others to do something that's evil in nature... Evil suggestions and works in my feelings to get me distracted, off course, hindered, putting objects in my way to cause me to become sidetracked or to lose focused will stop in the name of Jesus right now.

I command it and I continue to speak against them and to remain, alert on guard watchful and aware of the enemies' tactics skills, strategies, and schemes. He will strive to set into my life. The devil is a defeated foe, lost the war, and is losing the battle ongoing in my life because I am Triumphant in every area of my life. Meaning in all that I will do all that I put my hands to perform for the Lord while in this life I AM VICTORIOUS IN ALL AREAS OF MY LIFE, in JESUS NAME.

Matthew 21:22 - And all things, whatsoever ye shall ask in prayer, believing, ye shall receive.

I believe when I pray AND know that the Lord GOD hears my prayers; with no doubts, fears unbelief, terror, no side effects, or anything that the enemy will strive to form against me will not prosper in the name of Jesus. All tongues that rise against me in judgment I condemn, and I know this without any doubt whatsoever because I come to him in confidence boldly before the throne of grace to find help in time of trouble and need in Jesus' name.

I believe when I open my mouth in the morning noonday midday and evening and all through the day the Lord Jesus hears my voice, prayers, heart cries, and petitions. They will come up before him and I will receive the answers that I have requested from him In Jesus name.

I pray asking in faith I believe no doubts at all, therefore I receive whatsoever I have prayed for, because I ask according to his word in Jesus' name.

I don't ask selfishly to impress anyone.

I don't ask in vain or for nothing.

I don't ask because I don't know what I'm asking for.

I don't ask to be seen or heard.

I don't ask because I want attention.

I don't ask because I'm ignorant, foolish silly or just plain old dumb; no, I ask for specific reasons and purpose with meaning, intentions progress, furtherance of the destiny that is set before me in the mighty name of Jesus it is so.

I don't ask because I'm insecure, or I'm suffering from low self-esteem. Which is lacking in self-confidence; the ability GOD has put on the inside of me before the foundations of this world. Begin or even self-worth that is lacking or loss of Identity, because I don't know who I am, not so in this case I know who I am and what I believe and know is truth and true...

I ask in faith, not wavering at all whatsoever

I ask in total victory that it's just a matter of time before I get what I have ask for.

I never ask in fear, doubt, or without realizing what I'm saying In Jesus name.

I ask with purpose; reason hope and help for me and others.

I ask because he says I can ask whatsoever I ask it shall be given me without; that is with without being persuaded other ways contrary to the word of GOD no wavering in Jesus' name.

I ask because I love my HEAVENLY FATHER and desire to do his will.

I ask with a heart of thanksgiving.

I ask without becoming selfish with what I am asking, because it has purpose for its asking.

I ask because I simply believe what GOD'S word says that I can have in Jesus' name.

I simply ask because I love the Lord Jesus

I ask because I need him depend on him serve him adore him be obedient to him.

I simply ask because he told me I can ask whatsoever I would be believing and doubt not in my spirit or my feelings I can have whatsoever I say.

I decree and declare that I will be patient and wait on the lords' answers, information, and instructions as I wait in prayer for my Lord and Savior, my rescuer, redeemer, helper and protector king of Love, KING OF KING in Jesus' name.

Matthew 15:11 - Not that which goeth into the mouth defileth a man; but that which cometh out of the mouth, this defileth a man.

I Decree and declare that I will not let my mouth allow me to utter anything out of my mouth that will defile, corrupt, pervert, delay, deny or hinder my blessing for the now, which is present now and for the future.

I decree and declare that I will pray and ask the Lord to help me to control my thoughts, actions, feelings, and my words so that I don't speak anything out that's bad or give the enemy an entrance way into my life.

I decree and declare that which will come out of my mouth will bless, encourage enhance, build up, restore, edify, and bring life to others in the name of Jesus wonderful name.

I decree and declare that what will come out of my mouth will produce life health and strength, healing, deliverance, victory steadfastness, unmovable and unshaking results that will produce some thirty, some sixty, and some one hundred-fold of return in JESUS WONDERFUL NAME, AND IT IS SO RIGHT NOW.

My mouth is a mouth that can speak things into existence therefore I will speak life.

Romans 12:2 - And be not conformed to this world: but be ye transformed by the renewing of your mind, that ye may prove what is that good, and acceptable, and perfect, will of GOD. I will not be conformed to this world or the system that's running this world and all that's behind it. I will not allow myself to squeezed in a mold just to conform and or act like everyone else.

I will not allow the world to get me off course when it comes to the word of GOD But My Mind is and will be continue to be renewed, transformed, and made into the will of GOD DAILY.

Lord Jesus, thank you for not letting me be conformed to this world.

Thank you, Lord Jesus, for not letting me be squeezed into the molds of this evil world; and I will not allow myself as well to conform to what others are doing.

I will not copy, repeat, act out look at, imitate, mimic, what everyone else is doing in their individual lives.

Thank you, Lord Jesus, for calling me out of this world.

Thank you, Lord Jesus, for transforming me into your wonderful image. Thank you, Lord, for given me your likeness, that has already given me dominion over all the things of this life. I have been given this power to subdue, that is take authority or reign over it and maintain until you come back again and receive me unto yourself in Jesus' name, thanks and I love you dearly.

I decree and declare that my mind is renewed by the word of GOD; GOD's word which is SPIRIT & LIFE in Jesus name. St John 6:63

My mind is renewed with what GOD is saying that I can have and speak also perform, receive to be partakers of his divine plan.

I walk in his word each and every day. Doing whatever he has commanded me to do in Jesus' name. It will always be according to his statues, laws, precepts proverbs, information, instructions.

I do follow them and walk in them and speak, confess, meditate on them and in them each and every day.

They are life to my flesh and health and healing to my bones and every part of my body in JESUS NAME AND IT IS SO NOW.

My mind will think good things; things that are lively, and progress my life forward in advance adventures, realms levels and dimensions in Jesus' name.

I will not think evil things in my mind about others, my mind is not a trash dump for the enemy to sit in and suggest things, of evil unpleasant, things about others as well as myself.

I walk in the power of my thoughts, that breeds resurrection power creativity, exploits, marvels, in the spirit and with the SPIRIT of GOD LEADING AND GUIDING ME in Jesus name.

My mind is the seat of all activity, activities that flows through, this great mind. Thoughts that I have tapped into and connected to the mind of GOD. Out of it, his great mind flows great ideas, inventions, blessings, words of encouragement, strategies, well built, skillsets to create things and cause things to come together, successfully. Along with abilities to draw up and create blueprints for brand new, never seen or heard projects before. This is what the power of activity, with patterns of great thinking, from the mind of GOD, can do. All of this and much more, this is just some of many.

Blessings, blessings come in many shapes forms and sizes, as well as colors, levels dimensions and realms, this is just a few mentioned to get started.

money Ideas inventions, skills, tactics, and strategies against the enemy in Jesus' name,

These words mentioned here are so very powerful, I am not
going to dive into each and every one but use your imagination
and create some of your own, in the mighty name of Jesus.

My mind harbors a life support of life creations, world empires, kingdoms,
and all types of land masses that I have access to, so therefore I choose
to think, and react very carefully the choices that I make, the great
and awesome things that my mind will sit down and come up with. For
whatever the mind can create it will make it happen, in Jesus' name.

My Mind that the Lord has given me is a mind full of great plans. My
mind has the ability to guide me into and give me great directions and
has the ability to listen, to navigate across great plains, oceans, and
over huge mountains of rocks. To the voice of my Lord and SAVIOR
which is my rescuer, redeemer, and liberator, WHEN he is talking
to me. I'm paying close attention to whatever he is saying and I'm
following all his wonderful divine plans to the letter and not adding to
it or taking away from it, because HE, is my lifeline in Jesus' name.

My Mind is a bank of wealth thinking, reasonings
with decisions of importance.

Mind is a mind of GEMS of diamonds, gold silver platinum, and
all types of precious jewels and stones that's readily available
for me and too me in Jesus' name, and it is so now.

My mind is a storage of database, and wealth of information deep
within the recesses of my soul mind, thoughts patterns of thinking,
will to make great choices that will change my future forever.

MY MIND IS THE SEAT OF ALL THOUGHT LIFE, ANYTHING
THAT I CAN THINK OF CAN BE ACHIEVED, CONSTRUCTED
PUT TOGETHER MADE, MANIFEST, BUILD AND REBUILD
PRODUCED, BLUE PRINTED WHICH WILL BE MADE
ALIVE CAN BE AND BROUGHT TO LIFE JUST BY THE
THOUGHTS INTO THE DEEP RECESSES OF THE BRAIN,
MIND THOUGHT PATTERNS OF GODS ALMIGHTY WORD
DWELLING ON THE INSIDE OF THIS GREAT TEMPLE.

My mind can create such a monstrosity that will
astound the world and all that are a part of it.

My mind is very powerful full of thoughts, that can bring, breed, add
multiply, and advance life for many, years to come and that will listen,
in and apply the information and instructions in the name of Jesus.

The mind has made the world and all its structure's, buildings,
Businesses, plans, foods & drinks and whatsoever the
mind can think of. It can produce, our minds have so many
abilities: that it can come up with many answers and in
mass quantities; with qualities in the name of JESUS.

WE will go no further than we allow the lord to instruct our thoughts.

Our Ideals and things that he has put on the inside of us are endless.

Whatever we do we cannot put limits on what the
mind that we have with no restrictions.

But we must seek him to get these things out of us and start putting
them into action with applying them on a regular basis giving
him all the GLORY HONOR AND REVERENCE DUE TO HIS
AWESOME NAME IN THE MIGHTY NAME OF JESUS.

We must believe that when he imparted these things
on the inside of us that he has already made away for
us to carry them out throughout our lives.

So, we need to get busy seeking, searching, and researching, finding
out what it is that the Lord had deposited on the inside of us.

These things are just sitting dormant locked up in the storage thoughts,
in a huge warehouse of wealth knowledge, waiting to be opened, and
start producing all that GOD ALMIGHTY has planted insides of these
minds' wills and emotions. Others are waiting as well and the Lord
Jesus, for a great return on the deposit that has been sowed into us.

So, I will say I will not keep the LORD WAITING ANY LONGER.

I will begin to seek him for MORE.

I will seek more ways to bring all that I have on the inside of me to pass.

I WILL WORK ON AND ASK HIM TO HELP ME TO
BRING ALL THAT HE HAS PLANTED SEEDS ON THE
INSIDE OF ME TO CAUSE THEM TO GROW.

I DESIRE TO HAVE WINGS TO FLY AND SOAR IN THE
SPIRIT TO PRODUCE A GRAND WORLD HARVEST
THAT WILL NOT STOP UNTIL THE WORLD ENDS.

AND WE ARE INTO THE WORLD HE HAS PREPARED
FOR US IN JESUS NAME, AND IT IS SO.

RIGHT NOW, THIS MINUTE AND ITS HAPPENING AS I SPEAK.

MORE DECREES & DECLARATIONS:

Proverbs 15:1 - A soft answer turneth away wrath:
but grievous words stir up anger.

I will practice, to be mindful of my words, so that I will turn away, and
prevent these strong emotions of anger, wrath, and not let my words be
grievous, or regretting, Things. But be grateful in life toward others, also
remember to be careful with my thoughts, my words, and my actions. That
they will not come back to cause consequences, shame, penalties, fines,
and all unnecessary actions and situations in the mighty name of Jesus.

Hebrews 13:6 - So that we may boldly say, The Lord is my
helper, and I will not fear what man shall do unto me.

The Lord is my helper, and I will not be afraid of anyone that's
walking on the face of this Earth, but I will respect each and
every one on the face of the earth and not let these situations
overtake me at any giving time in the mighty name of Jesus.

I am bold as a lion and I walk in the Lord as he has
commanded me to speak, walk, and progress, to cause my
life to be enhanced on every level, in the name of Jesus.

The Lord is my Helper, and he helps me in all my situations.

Because I allow him, I need him to do so. I want him to because, I am submitted to his will. All his plans over my ENTIRE life in the mighty name of Jesus forever.

The Lord is my helper will I boldly declare the decree and to never walk in any type of fears, phobias but have a sound mind in thoughts and thinking in Jesus name.

Hebrews 13:5 - Let your conversation be without covetousness; and be content with such things as ye have: for he hath said, I will never leave thee, nor forsake thee.

I am content with such things that I have, but I will continue to seek the lord for more of a higher level in all things that he has for me. These things, like a more higher and deeper prayer life in the spirit.

A deeper walk into to the word of GOD with revelation knowledge.

In studying his wonderful, powerful word, seeking the Lord, in fasting and much cleaner life of purity, sanctification, and consecrations as well as sacrifices offerings in the mighty name of Jesus.

I am content with all that the Lord has given me, and he has cause me to spread my wings to fly, to flourish in all that I do and undertake in this life.

I have sheer supernatural supersonic excelling power in the Lord in the mighty name of Jesus Christ, NOW.

Thank you, Lord Jesus, for never Leaving me nor forsaking me.

I will do the same for you as well, that is; never leave you nor forsake you, for something else, which is nothing else out there that can compare, or even come close to match you.

So, I will continue to stay, and be steadfast unmovable, that is unmoved, never effected by others, that are not GODLY, always with you my Lord in Jesus name, all the days of my life.

John 14:27 - Peace I leave with you, my peace I give unto you: not as the world giveth, give I unto you. Let not your heart be troubled, neither let it be afraid.

Thank you, Lord Jesus, for your peace you have left me
while in this world and I except it and walk in all the days
of my life in the mighty name of Jesus and it is so.

Thank you, Lord, that my heart is not troubled at all in no situation,

I will not let my heart be troubled at home,

I will not be troubled on the job,

I will not be troubled in ministry,

I will not be troubled in the fellowship with the Saints, Sons of
GOD and Ambassadors' Envoys, Diplomats alike in Jesus name.

In the powerful name of Jesus I will not allow myself to be afraid,
fearful, or be dismayed, meaning to be distressed in anxiety at things
that are unexpected or unprepared in the name of Jesus. But I will pray,
deal with it, and ask the Lord to help me to go through these situations
so I will be triumphant, that is victorious in every area of my life.

I don't walk in the peace that the world is talking about, because
it's not the peace that will keep me in times of trouble. But the
Peace that the Lord has given me, I receive it and I am content and
stable in my mind, and my thinking patterns in Jesus' name.

Matthew 12:33-37 - Either make the tree good, and
his fruit good; or else make the tree corrupt, and his
fruit corrupt: for the tree is known by his fruit.

In the name of Jesus I'm making the tree good, with all that goes with
that; planting, and eating of the fruits off the tree and to allow the
Lord to prune and purge the tree so it will bring forth more fruit.

I will not make the tree evil or do evil things.

I will not walk in corruption, or other ways that isn't planned
by the will of the Lord for my life. I will not cause perverted
twisted fake phoniness, things that are not, real.

His Kingdom is within me so therefore I will produce fruits on the tree that he has planted in me, on the inside to bear, much fruit and that my fruit will remain and will attain more fruit.

I will be who GOD called me to be in the name of Jesus.

I will be fruitful and multiply and replenish what GOD has given me and duplicate it and give my GOD all the Glory in the name of Jesus.

Proverbs 18:21 · Death and life are in the power of the tongue: and they that love it shall eat the fruit thereof.

Death and life are truly in the power of my tongue therefore I will be very careful as to what I say coming out of my mouth in the mighty name of Jesus.

I decree and declare that I will not speak death out of my mouth but will speak life resurrection power, to bring back to life those things that might be dead and in need of life spoken back into it for the furtherance of life and health in Jesus name.

I decree and declare that my tongue will be used to speak those good things to produce more life in the name of Jesus Christ.

I decree and declare that my tongue has the power to create life, into others. Words of healing, words to build, Word to enhance and advance, to encourage, speak life of restoration, deliverances of all types. There's no limit to what the tongue will speak to utter and help others in the name of Jesus.

I decree and declare that my mouth and tongue working together has the power and force to bring relationships together.

Speak to the Lord in Prayer, help others when they are struggling to say or express themselves in life. Words to build friendships, relationships, that will last for a very long time to come, this is the power of the tongue, and even a lifetime.

The tongue has many uses, but we must be careful what we say and how we say it to others.

Our mouths or tongues are not speaking hard words that hurt.

To crush others, or even to pronounce a curse on someone else's life.

But we are to speak, life, speak in love, speak health, speak
those things as Christ Jesus spoke and is still speaking
in love to his creation on many levels of love.

Jesus is striving to reach out and support, aid many
in dire, terrible, urgent awful need. To help those
that have no way out or can see any way out.

The tongue can create words that will mend broken hearts.

The tongue has the power to put, or bring one's back to life, just
by saying a kind word to help build and give someone Hope.

These lives that was bruised, broken, and battered. Wholeness
being complete, full of strength it takes some time. We
must be aware of others when we are saying, or speaking,
from our mouths or should I say with our mouths.

The mouth as the ability to make sound, create words that can
make things happen in the lives of others without ever knowing.

If were not careful with our tongues, these tongues can cause bad,
harmful words. If we're not, careful with our tongues, we may find
ourselves saying things that can cut deep with the tongue.

The tongue can cause wounds, that will lodge deep in the soul, of man and
the wounds will stay longer if they will not or do not know where to get
some type of help and get some healing for their emotional hurts. As we
know from time to time the soul has been broken down as the mind, will
and emotions and we know this by now, of men & women. These wounds
can stay their lodge for a very long time without anyone noticing it.

All of this comes from our lips, that can speak things into existence and
make something happen, in a way of sound, words forming, making
things, come alive in the lives of others as well as ourselves, good, bad,
ugly, or indifferent. We need to be aware of what we are saying. By us
saying these types of things speaking things into the atmosphere we
have just created some pain and hurts for others just by opening our
mouths and speaking things that we not aware of what we have done

to others. We want to give and speak life strength, to be a blessing to others in many ways as possible representing the Lord Jesus Christ.

Now that you have come far to this point of READING STOP for a moment and focus, meditate on these nuggets of truth. You can quote them to memory, say them out loud, repeatedly, until you have them memorized in the mighty name of Jesus.

The tongue is talked about in the book 8 of James 3:1-1. With the mouth we can speak life, wisdom health healing, strength, and words of knowledge to support and assist others in describing things in life. The tongue has the ability to make someone love you with their words of kindness as well as make you very angry. We must be very careful the words we're speaking out of our mouths. Life or death-speaking force that can hurt, demolish, assassinate, kill, murder, or slay a person, beings, and bodies. Our mission in life is to build good character, support and help others to establish self-character with the power of our words making sounds coming from out of the mouth of each and every individual if we're not careful and sensitive will bring hurt harm, and even danger.

We can with our mouths bite off more than we can chew and that is not very nice. Nor is it a very pleasant for the ones on the other end of the spectrum, so people leaders' men women boys' girls... and all who read this book just be very mindful of our words, for ourselves and others as well. Words spoken out of the mouth with sound the tongue and bring and a lot of hurt mentally, socially. It is because of the mouth that wars start, relationships break up groups either come together or depart and start a mini war or long-lasting relationships throughout our lives.

Listen in and read what James has to say about our words and the tongue, all that it entails, involves, causes, and implies and can do for us, and to us if were not careful and aware of what we are saying to others, as well.

James 3 :1-18

I will not betray myself to be many master's to others.

I will not receive the greater condemnation on an account of what I did and did not do, or whatsoever I have spoken.

Words are made for creating and helping. I strive to build up others with words of comfort, in Yeshua name it is so.

I'm striving not to offend in any areas of my life to others, but I will tell and speak the truth in love and lie not.

I'm making efforts, that is labors, some work energy toward making things happen in a good way as possible, with exertions, attempts to bridle my tongue, not condemn others, and striving to become mature or perfect in the knowledge of the Lord as he continues to groom me with the leading of his spirit, called; THE HOLY SPIRIT. I do not boast great things but will watch my words and what comes from these lips, mouth, and tongue that make up sounds and the use of words and speech uttered forward from what the lord has given me and allowed me to speak or say.

With my mouth and lips and tongue I will learn to bless others, speak life, encourage, and pray for them even those that might be used by the enemy.

I will make efforts to tame my tongue asking the Lord to help me to do so and strengthen and purge my conscience from dead words and works.

I will speak a good conversation, right, and rich encouraging to support others in need.

THESE WORDS & SOME PHRASES ARE FORBIDDEN IN MY VOCABULARY AND LIFE.

The word **_try_**; thoughts on try example is I say I will try to make some money and if I keep on trying until I get tired and have not at any at this time so I say to myself well I have tried, trying is an excuse to fail and I will not do excuses to fail, this is what I call setting up myself to failure and this is not in my vocabulary.

❖ When we say I DON'T KNOW, we should never say we don't know what we can say is I'll get back with you, let me find out for you. But never I don't know. These thoughts will follow you in your life. Be careful what words come or proceed out of your mouth.

❖ I cannot say I can't, we do not say we can't, either we don't want to or we're not able to, but we don't say we can't

❖ Never assume something,

❖ Stop guessing things out but research and know for sure!

❖ Do not stand or sit somewhere and just out and out tell a bald-faced lie. You can pick up a lying spirit. You tell one lie your prone to tell another and it will keep on if you don't stop it.

❖ I quit, is not a good word to keep on repeating throughout my life. Never quit something when you were given a task, job, or responsibility, charge, obligation, or called to do a job. SO JUST DO IT.

❖ THERE ARE MANY MORE THIS IS JUST A FEW OF THEM. MORE WILL BE WRITTEN IN MORE OF MY BOOKS AND SERIES TO COME.

CHAPTER 3

EXPLOSIVE OUTCOMES INTENSIFIED WITH IMPACT, PART 3

WARFARE, WEAPONS, ARMOR, & TOOLS TO FIGHT OUR ENEMIES

WAGING THE WAR ENGAGED IN BATTLE.

We are Saints of GOD, and we have WEAPONS
of war in the spirit. Not fleshly wars,

Let me first of all say this statement, what the weapons is to the natural world with all of their explosive powers and damages that is designed for, that is to destroy break up get rid of dominate, and wipe out entire cities, states, and countries is what the Spirit is to the spiritual world to break up, destroy, wipe out and get rid of and cremate demonic spirits, evil and unclean and dark works of the devil, is what this book are mainly about in all of its content and information instructions and all that is in the pages of this writing. Ephesians 6:10-18

10 Finally, my brethren, be strong in the Lord,
and in the power of his might.

11 Put on the whole armour of GOD, that ye may be
able to stand against the wiles of the devil.

12 For we wrestle not against flesh and blood, but against principalities, against powers, against the rulers of the darkness of this world, against spiritual wickedness in high places.

13 Wherefore take unto you the whole armour of GOD, that ye may be able to withstand in the evil day, and having done all, to stand.

14 Stand therefore, having your loins girt about with truth, and having on the breastplate of righteousness;

15 And your feet shod with the preparation of the gospel of peace;

16 Above all, taking the shield of faith, wherewith ye shall be able to quench all the fiery darts of the wicked.

17 And take the helmet of salvation, and the sword of the Spirit, which is the word of GOD:

18 Praying always with all prayer and supplication in the Spirit, and watching thereunto with all perseverance and supplication for all saints;

For spiritual warfare to fight the battle against Our enemies. To drive out, to smite, is a way to hit our enemies with the word of GOD. The sword of the word will put to flight aliens of the darkness.

Armies' of fallen angels from Heaven, that is demon spirits, dark spirits of corruption, perversion. These demonic spirits, that have no bodies, desire to use our mouths, temples, and body parts to degrade the Holiness and Honor of GOD.

Those would be demons, evil entities, dark agents of the unclean spirit world, hybrids, super soldiers, clone demons made to look like a real man or women. The spiritual world of wickedness to cease its treacheries, evil plans, schemes, all his diabolical devious acts, plans, strategies, and all that he attempts to do while in our world. To stop all that the enemy does on a moment to moment, daily, weekly, monthly, quarterly, and yearly, decade, and beyond, our earthly existence before our world as we know it to be.

These attacks are designed to disturb what GOD is doing on the inside of each one of us that calls on the mighty name of Jesus, those that are living for him, striving to stay focused to fight the good fight of faith, desiring to make to heaven as it is our final resting place eternally forever without end. Where in the land of the living kingdom of GOD.

THERE ARE only two kingdoms, the KINGDOM OF GOD, and the kingdom of the devil, as you may have noticed GOD kingdom words are CAPITALIZED. The devil's kingdom words are not because there is only ONE true GOD, and his name one. The devil or his continual fallen state and regime of a so-called kingdom. We are depending on the Lord for all that we need in this life we're living.

One may ask what is warfare and how does it affect me? Good question. It started affecting us the minute, we were born into this world and the real fight in the spiritual warfare starts when we joined, in with GOD, receiving the plan of salvation, GODS redemption plan that came through Jesus Christ.

When we came to invite Yeshua the Christ into our lives. We are redeemed out of a sentence of death. So now that we come to GOD WE ARE CALLED, THE; saved and repented of the sins, that came as a result of our ancestors, our lineage, our genetics. So now that we are saved, we need to be filled with the Spirit of GOD. This gives us power over sin and teaches us how to fight.

Invited the Lord into our lives and excepted him as our Savior. We Said yes to all his will, and yes to all his plans for our lives, whatever that is, in the mighty name of Jesus.

We then Start living for him from that moment on.

Because Lucifer rebelled in Heaven and deceived one-third of the angelic sons of GOD.

What happened after that is the result of our invisible war. You see lucifer have gotten removed from heaven, thrown out, cast out on this earth, after his rebellion, going against what GOD wanted him to do and landed on the earth and became at that time and for all eternity the enemy of GOD ALMIGHTY.

So, if he is the enemy of GOD, and GOD is our eternal Father in Heaven, he is also our enemy as well. It enters us, automatically into a grand, spiritual warfare fight against all that he stands for. Isaiah 14:12-20 and Ezekiel 28:1-19 please take out some precious time to read the story and digest the content of the story and familiarize yourselves with what took place.

What took place in that time when lucifer, the light bearer rebelled against the plans of our GOD, this is a result of our world being in the conditions it is in at this present time in which we are now living. It is called a fallen world and system.

Warfare is stated to be spiritual conflicts, oppositions, fights, wrestling's and wars against opposing forces, opposites, rival opponents. These fights, and warfare are against GOD ALMIGHTY, and his heavenly host, the angelic forces, and the Saints of GOD on the earth. So, we are all joined into this great battle against the darkness of this world.

There are only two sides light or darkness, good or bad, right, or wrong. You have either righteousness or wickedness or just plain evil, and hateful deeds and acts of the devil, we are either in or out, going up to Heaven, or down to Hell. Both are eternal forever that never stops, without end.

We are either in GOD, and with him or we are working for the devil by not choosing to give Jesus our whole entire life, at a 100% rate until he comes to take us away forever, and again I say until then we are Living for him until he comes and take us away into HEAVEN.

We are either going up to be in HEAVEN FOR ETERNALLY or different one's are going DOWN TO A burning HELL FOR ALL ETERNALLY AND WILL NOT COME OUT EVER.!!!. these statements deserved to be repeated for remembrance of our mission while born on the earth and into an invisible war. For the definition of ETERNITY, WORLD WITHOUT END. Ephesians 3:21 states.

Unto him be glory in the church by Christ Jesus throughout all ages WORLD WITHOUT END, THAT'S ETERNAL. Psalms eight talks about, all our opposing forces is the devil, demons, evil agents of the darkness.

Unclean spirits, evil spirits, foul and spirits
of the marine kingdom of the sea.

Monitoring recording, demons that write down and keep up with, things that are going on in our lives. They report this info back to the devil. The devil cannot be everywhere all at the same time. He has limitations, that is why he is set up the way that he is. All those evil workers that pass through the sea, in the way of evil princesses, and queens of the south, prince of the oceans.

Those that are in the underworld, there are all types of demon's spirits, that work, that are around, that we might not be aware of; But our Lord Heavenly Father is revealing them to us in this season and time in our lives, across the globe in Jesus name. This is a time of Mysteries, secrets, ancient activities, and

ancient beings, being revealed to and for, us for awareness. Some of these things hidden, from us its being revealed to us in the mighty name of Jesus. We have all types of equipment, tools to use against our enemies, but we must know how to use what he has provided in the mighty name of Jesus.

There are other writings like the book of Enoch, the three books or so about Adam and eve information about the fall, the book of Jasher, Gad the Seer, the life and story of Jesus when he was a child coming up and the things that took place, and many more things that are being revealed in our lifetime like never before.

But this changes everything because if we, do not know how to use what our WONDERFUL LORD AND SAVIOR JESUS CHRIST, and GOD our FATHER, has given us.

It is not a good position to stand in a that time. But there is a way out and there are always ways we can get out from, under the traps of the devil. All we have to do is to submit ourselves to GOD and the enemy will flee or go away James 4:7.

Then if it's our family, we need to stand in the gap for our families and pray for them and let them know what they need to do about face, praying for a turnaround of GODS JUDGEMENT.

So that he would not destroy a generation, or our family through their sins. When we begin to intercede, stand into gaps, talking to the Lord on the behalf of our love ones; it will change the course of our lives. The lives of the family through prayer and intercessions with love, cares, and concerns for all. We must have a love for others if not it serves no purpose and no use, and it can be the difference between winning a battle or being defeated with powerful attacks, overwhelming deceptions.

Our enemy has many strategies that he attempts to use against us as children of GOD. The word of GOD declares that we are not ignorant of his devices. Manipulations, have you really thought about the word manipulations, what it is; and how and why do others use it on us to get what exactly they are after. I am here to answer this, Manipulation is the ability to use something either, a person, a place, or a thing to get what they want. It is a spirit of selfishness, greed, and lust all packaged into one scheme or trick.

They have the ability to shape, make, or form, and change something, say something, use something or make something for their own use and progress.

They know how to put together something that was not there, use things to their advantage. This is a trick from the devil. This is also deception, deceiving someone into thinking one thing and another thing has taken place. In other words, they have lied and used something and made it or said for their own use, this is deception and manipulation.

For example, you were working for a company selling Insurance or a banker; for example, the banker advertises $30 for all those who open a new account in the month of January, so the customers begin to pour in their money into the bank. The banker will not tell them they are using their money for loans for other companies and corporations.

These people may or may not get a return on their money, if the banker does not inform them about what is going on with their money. The people are thinking that they are opening an account for a savings. The banker begins to put $30 in each one of their accounts as promised. But what they do not know he is making hundreds and even thousands off their money and they get a little kick back. But the kick back and returns he is given them, makes their money looks likes crumbs in the corner. So, let us talk about for a few minutes the things of GOD.

. There are all kinds of deceptions and manipulations out here. We cannot mistake of who is who. We do not want to mistake the devils plan for our lives and think that our Almighty GOD & Father is doing or saying something when he is not at all. Due to ignorance, we need to pay attention to what the word of GOD is telling us and not to let the enemy use, trick or deceive us into things that is not of GOD.

Hosea 4:6 which says, My People are destroyed for lack of knowledge: because thou hast rejected knowledge, I will also reject thee, that thou shalt be no priest to me: seeing thou hast forgotten the law of thy GOD, I will also forget thy children.

So, in reading and seeing this passage as it reads.

There is an Indictments, judgments, and even curses put on other generations. Why? Because of the ignorance of our ancestor's. Not taking out quality time to find out or do research on a subject, even seek the lord for some right answers. Condemnations or in other words a curse, could be placed on the children, families of the ignorant, so now the children must suffer for the ignorance of their parents.

This is part of what warfare is all about. We have got to know what the Lord requires of us. We should know and inform others in the family what is going on, so ignorance will not take place on our watch. All the generations, lineages, and ancestors because of their lack of knowledge of not knowing. Because no one is taking out the time to find out what is going on around here.

They are not considering to be interested to seek the Lord get some real heartfelt directional answers that will save their families in the mighty name of Jesus, and the generations to come. This is not a great choice for what GOD has designed for us.

The Lord does not want us to be removed from positions and causing some to be abased or lowered to a lesser place but that the lessens will be learned at an early stage in life. We that are saved and know that the Lord requires need to set one's course in a charted path and reach the destination and fulfill all that he has been ask, written, or requested of us to carry out in the name of Jesus.

Knowing how to use our weapons back to this subject. When we are in an intense battle with our enemies and there is so much going on and others are involved there is no time to become slack, slow, lose or not knowing what to do and to stop, to take a break due to fatigued, exhausted, or even confused about what is going on and what just happened.

This teaching will help you to Identify with some of our weapons and how to effectively use them when in a heated battled, attacks, blockages may arrive hinderances try to appear its ugly head.

This teaching will help us, help you become aware of what is going on and who is behind these attacks. We first must always go before the Lord in prayer, I have said before, prayer is the first line of defense, meaning we should always be in a mindset of prayer, praise, worship, and thanksgiving to the Lord. This will help us out when the battle begins to raise its ugly head. Then we begin to take authority in the mighty name of Jesus. We lose the blood of Jesus against the devil, plead the blood, bind, down or tie down, restrict, the enemy's movement, all the hindering forces in the mighty name of Jesus.

Rebuke the demonic forces that is attempting to make head way into your affairs, from attacks, distractions or whatever may come our way in any form fashion or type that the devil would try to bring, stop it in the name of Jesus. This is warfare attacks and how to combat, and what to do when you are in the midst of this heated battle or battles.

Decree, and declare the word of GOD against evil forces, sing songs, pray, and get in the presence of GOD.

Quote, confess We must get to know our enemies and how they come and their **tactics, maneuvers, strategies, snares, and the traps** they try to set for us. I would ask or someone may ask what is the meaning of these words and how can I use this information effectively? Good question and it's good to find out before entering a battle of conflicts and fights; the first word we want to define meaning to is Tactics-

The art of arranging army agents of the military, soldiers or anyone that will be fighting and taking over something setting up forces to take over or overthrow the enemy and staging themselves for combat.

Maneuvers- what are they and how to set ourselves to maneuver against our enemies? before he tries to maneuver against us first, to plan and move in such a way of scheming manipulating against one's enemies as to bring a sneak attack and they don't see or hear it coming or hear anything coming for that matter at all; maneuvering with skill and a well thought out plan of attack.

Strategies- is a plan of Actions that are planned on how to move at what angle, weapons to employ, armies to do what at giving times a plan of attack on how to get drive out and overcome the enemy.

<u>Snares & Traps</u> are the same except a snare is when one is entangled by wires or cable of barbwires of some type, and a trap is planning to catch something with a device that holds one into a place that they cannot get free, that they make attempts to set up against us. We must be sharp on point when dealing with our enemies in these seasons of attacks or assaults from the forces. The demonic and all unclean spirits, foul in nature no remorse for the weak, ignorant, blind, and those that are unprepared.

Some in some cases will be learning firsthand, so they will be unskillful to combat his attacks. Sometimes it will be a surprise attack if he can, and he likes to catch us off guard if he can. So, we do not want to give or allow him to have that, kind of progress over us, to take advantage of us with that surprise tactic. All of this, information, may entails so we must be alert on guard on the wall and always watching. There is a never time in our lives or walk with GOD, that we should be taking for granted or neglecting that we can do all this by ourselves, not so.

Our enemy is very cunning, the word of GOD said in the book of genesis that the devil is the most subtle beast of the field, that is what the word cunning really means. and wise as he can be when it comes to setting up things to ensnare one into bondage, prison, capture and hold them against their will.

Our weapons are designed to help aid us in counter attacks knowing how to attack, do some damage to the kingdom of darkness. knowing his motives, and who will be a target and how are they become a target for the enemy and how. So, our weapons, which are also gifts of the spirit, give us the advantages above and beyond what the devil and his agents have. If we know how to use them very effectively such as for example, when we're in prayer and we're developing a great and grand relationship with the Lord, he will let us know through this time of prayer and communion that an attack is coming. We need to get ready, and the Lord begin to tell us how to prepare ourselves for the battle.

Prayer to accompany with GOD's word is the first line of defense. Meaning when things happen to us or may take place, in our lives. The very first things we are supposed to do is pray to begin to use the word of GOD AS A SWORD to cut slash our enemies into pieces without mercy at all. Whatsoever because he is a devil that has no feelings. Listen the devil don't care about you and me at ALL. Warfare prayers and counter attacks using in this invisible war. IS ONE OF THE HIGHEST FORMS OF FIGHTING.

When things take place in the lives of believers, what is the first things that they do; get on the phone or talk and tell someone, that knows the Lord, and can get through to him, so their situation can be resolve or solved, handled and dissipate or go way, but it's not going to do that of its own free will.

We must learn how to fight the enemy at some time in our lives, and not depend on everyone else to do all, the hard work for us. We must learn how to fight the good fight of faith. This is another part of what this book is all about, knowing how to Identify the enemy and how to stop him before he tries to destroy us and our families. The way we handle our battles is to fall on our knees and cry out in prayer to the Lord. We are in training when these begin to happen. These battles and fights are designed to help us to become skillful, sharp, armed, ready, and dangerous to the devil and all his tactics.

The Lord already sees and knows all things beforehand and can answer right away. When he see fit to do so THIS is what prayer and standing on and in the word of GOD is all about. The use of the word of GOD, PRAYING in Tongues, is a very powerful weapon.

This is a secret weapon because it builds us up and our faith. Also praying the perfect prayer, the will of GOD, bringing strength and strengthening us while were in prayer.

The enemy don't know what we are praying as well as ourselves. The greatest things we need to know about this is our prayers are being lined up properly. Because the Spirit of GOD is making intercessions for us through his Spirit with groanings that cannot be uttered.

Romans 8:26 take some time to read it and meditate on it. Spend some time hiding it in your hearts in the name of Jesus. Spend some time praying in tongues on a regular basis. Praying and crying out to the Lord in times of need is what takes place. Relationship with our Lord and Savior Jesus Christ. Our Chief Corner Stone PRECIOUS.

The devil strives to weaken us through lack of desires, laziness, procrastination, confusions, strife, lack of Passions. Please let me say right now, these are ways he attacks us.

Lack of desires to keep going forward and begin to lose ground, that has already been gained through spiritual attacks against our enemy. When we are in prayer, it gives us the fortitude to take back what he has stolen. Fear is another type of way he tries, to get us caught up in, through our thoughts. Not being sure of yourself, suffering from types of insecurities. Identity is out of reach or do not know who you are. These are ways the enemy can come to attack you, or I, because he sees a weakness lingering, through monitoring demons, that study our lives, to report weaknesses and other areas that can come under attack.

He makes attempts, puts forth efforts to get at us or tries to speak, suggest, his evil thoughts in our minds. He the devil or any evil spirit wants to try, or test. These attacks are to see previously to see if we're going to take the bait or if he can plant a seed in our field of the thoughts of our minds.

Later, he can wait patiently for a return for his coming harvest. IF we let him and we're not wise enough to catch all the signs to his attacks strategies and this is exactly what warfare is all about. If he can get or catch us off guard, then there maybe be a chance he can set up and go in for the kill. We're not, or don't suppose to be ignorant of his devices 2 Corinthians 2:11.

So, we must be wise as serpents and harmless as doves to people, but dangerous against our arch enemies and rivals. GOD has given us a POWERFUL SKILLSET OF things to fight and withstand against our enemies in the mighty name of Jesus. The devil and all his cohorts like to steal, kill and to destroy, in St John 10:10 he the devil comes to steal, kill, and destroy, or damage and or do away with us if he had his way. But he simply does not because we belong to the Lord. If we belong to the lord Jesus, and we do, without doubt. We are the children of GOD. Then we need to leave the devils mess alone.

Close all types of doors, entrances, access points, portals, ways the enemy can get in, needs to be blocked, locked down and sealed up. Let me say this while we are on this subject, if we have anything that belongs to the devil, in the way of evilness, games, toys, dolls, figurines, things that are like witchcraft practicing materials, and the likes, books about magic, clothes, just a few things to mention the list is great.

Give it back to him, meaning throw it away and whatever you do please do not give it to anyone else. Get rid of it, and not to possess his stuff and things.

It's our responsibility to know what is right and wrong, good, and bad evil or right. We must begin to do research, there's much we can do to do our part in this matter. If we have any of his objects in our possessions, we need to expose them and never ever again buy, receive anything evil from others. Let me say this for this time while you are reading this wonderful material, when we part take in with the mess, such as books and other products of the devil, we open up ourselves to an impartation to receive a spiritual part from the enemy, and do not even know it. Lets not be ignorant of his devices, we do not need the enemies stuff, such as; souvenirs, ornaments, objects, and so forth, they do carry a spirit with it. A spirit MAY could very well be apart of it. A spell can be attached to it, for lack of a better word, materials, trinkets, lockets, stuffs, rings and other things that he has to offer us if were not wise enough to recognize, these things can bring a curse on your life. What is going on, because our LORD is a very Jealous GOD. LET'S SEEK HIM FOR ALL THAT WE HAVE NEED, BECAUSE HE HAS AND ALL HE WANTS US TO DO IS ASK. SEEK, AND, KNOCK, IN YESHUA NAME.

HE has every right to be because, he is the only ONE True GOD, Which was, and he still is, which is, and always will be and which is to come, I want to say He is always present, but this is talking about Him coming to take us away for good, that is our Savior Jesus, that has not happened yet why?

We are still here and where not done with what he has given us to do. He is the ALMIGHTY GOD Rev 1:8 able to back up anything he has said or spoken to us about, and it's our job to believe it. The Lord does not want us to possess any of the enemies' things such as clothing wear, jewelry, reading artifacts, statues or even speaking any of his mess out of our mouths to ourselves or other for that matters period.

Enough to be said about this so if I said in these writing before and I said it again the important are being brought out for everyone to know.

Why because knowledge is power, and this book is about POWER, DECREES, AND ATOMIC POWER, and SPEAKING THINGS OUT, WITH OUR TONGUES. Knowing about this will bring you into more abilities. It will cause you to be able to use the power more efficiently and effectively.

Ephesians 6:10-18

Finally, my brethren, be strong in the Lord, and in the power of his might. QUESTION: have you ever ask yourselves or others, how do we carry all this out.? When all things around us seems to be in a chaotic confused, topsy Turvey, situation. Being strong in the Lord and in the power of his might, this is how we carry this out. First, we carry all this out in Prayer.

Which I have said before, the first line of defense along with
GODs word, is when we take it to him in prayer, this is our
line of COMMUNICATION ON EVERY LEVEL.

Quoting, confessing, feeding, and nourishing our spirit. As we feed and
nourish our flesh with natural food and water. Quenching our thirst is
the same way as it is done in heaven so it is done on the earth and insides
of these earths and temples that belongs to the Lord GOD ALMIGHTY.

We are bought with a price therefore we suppose to glorify GOD in our
bodies which are GODS. 1 Corinthians 6:14-20 take out some time to
read the precious word of GOD to get all that he has for YOU; strength
to fight and do battle against the devil and his cohorts to defeat him
successfully with praise and worship. Speaking to ourselves with songs
and spiritual melodies with tunes making sound or giving thanks to
the Lord. Throughout the time we are going through our situations.

Fights attacks and trials and even temptations. Submitted to GOD resist
the devil, and he will flee. Not to ever forget to humble our souls and
always be ready to repent of any, and all sins. Because GOD will not
answer prayer with sin in our lives. Unconfessed sins, wrong doings,
offenses. Never to forget trespasses, doing things we ought not to be
doing or going. Transgressions, going against what he said not to do.

These words and definitions are according to his laws, commandments,
promises, we may have caused to others. I can hinder, my (our) progress,
and take away from what he has promised us. So, if we have hurt,
wounded someone. Bites, and want to destroy one another like a fox or
wolf dog or other types of things happens. When one is suffering from
an open wound. Listen while on this subject when we hurt or offend one
another it's like we just bit our brother or sister. But the one question
should be in our minds did we realize that we hurt their feelings?

This is calling bit by the sheep or sheep bitten. Have you ever been bit by
a sheep? in the fold? If you have you must forgive them, like right, now

since you know about this information. Are We paying attention to their reactions and ask questions. It's one thing to tell them what the Lord has given to you to tell them. But it's another thing to go off, on someone and give them a piece of how you felt, about what they have done or said. With intentions to hurt or wound, them that's a bit into their soul. They feel that it takes some time to heal if they don't let it go now. Give to the Lord, asking for help, it goes on to fester, the seed is planted and if not dealt with to let go it will grow and become, much bigger in their lives.

This is a wounded soul, and they take on a wounded spirit, that spirit begins to attach himself to that person and they become a person with self-pity. These spirits come aboard a person because they are open and vulnerable, weak, and their defenses are very low if up at all. Currently, they Begin to live those offences, out more than one or even a few. We must get all this right, before we can expect the Lord, to do anything, worthy for us through his grace and mercy on our behalf. Setting our platforms free and our conduits with a free flow meaning everything that might have been in the way prior to these situations taking place in our lives, clearing out of the way of the lord; so, he can grant us mercy, peace and help us without any hinderances in the mighty name of Jesus.

Now we should at this time have more of a better understanding about spiritual warfare and how it takes place. What to do while in the midst of all the activities going on with us, and our family members. Sometimes it can be coming from unsaved household, like our children, siblings in the house or out of the house makes no difference nevertheless it has happened or may happen, so we know what we need to do to prevent these unnecessary battles to come against us without being aware. So, we need to practice the laws of prevention, and it says if we prevent it from happening, we don't have to deal with the repercussions and make no mistake about it; there are repercussions from the actions that brought reactions and these are the repercussions, that have showed up.

They don't just go away automatically, so this causes us to be careful what we do and why we do such things because of the things we have sown.

REMEMBER IN previous chapters of this book we talked about sowing and reaping, take out some time in this book, go back over and review.

2 Corinthians 10:3-4

The weapons of our warfare are not carnal but mighty through GOD to the pulling down of strongholds.

For though we walk in the flesh, we do not war after the flesh:

4(For the weapons of our warfare are not carnal, but mighty through GOD to the pulling down of strong holds;)

5 Casting down imaginations, and every high thing that exalted itself against the knowledge of GOD, and bringing into captivity every thought to the obedience of Christ.

6. And having in a readiness to revenge all disobedience, when your obedience is fulfilled.

GODS WORD AS THE SWORD OF THE SPIRIT. SPEAKING THE WORD OUT LOUD with power, strength, passion, and energy.

Desires to see and feel things that will take place not to forget when we speak the word of GOD; the Angels of GOD are harkening to the voice of his, (GOD'S) words to perform and bring it about for us in our lives.

Psalms 144:6

Cast forth lightning, and scatter them: shoot out thine arrows, and destroy them.

I destroy all my enemies with my arrows that I shoot out against him as a great archer and I will hit my targets all the time in the name of Jesus.

I will shoot out my arrows against my enemies that fight against me day and night, my enemies will be wounded by my firing out of these arrows of purpose.

I will continue to shoot out arrows of attack to drive back the devil to cripple him with arrows that will severely hurt damage, wound dismantle, and even slow him down with my arrows in the name of Jesus.

2 Samuel 22:15

And he sent out arrows, and scattered them;
lightning, and discomfited them.

I continue to send out bolts of lightning upon my enemies and bring attacks discomforts, hurts blow to my enemies in the name of Jesus.

I will continue to send out my arrows of attack as the archer to always site in on my enemies and scatter, disrupt, drive back send back and push back these tactics that he the devil and all his agents come against me with and I will not fear at all but will continue to be bold in the name of Jesus.

Job 28:26

When he made a decree for the rain, and a way
for the lightning of the thunder:

Zechariah 9:14

And the LORD shall be seen over them, and his arrow shall
go forth as the lightning: and the Lord GOD shall blow the
trumpet, and shall go with whirlwinds of the south.

Jeremiah 51:20

Thou art my battle axe and weapons of war: for with thee will I break in pieces the nations, and with thee will I destroy kingdoms.

Lord GOD use us as your axe as a weapon to bring a death blow to our enemies as an instrument of war. To hurt wound and bring terror, confusion to all of them; them being evil demons, unclean spirits, that what they are evil and unclean and we must keep ourselves clear of this type of activity. Their main function is to fine ways about us that are weak. Launch an all assault & attack and make attempts to bring fear, of all types. He the devil love to bring disruption, what's peaceful, distraction to the kingdom in the name of Jesus if he can.

Lord GOD use your weapons of war to fight against those that fight against us, and scatter and destroy all those that, want to scatter and destroy us, and make attempts, on our lives, to pursue us, or chase or go after us for attacks to bring all kinds of hindrances, I speak in the mighty name of Jesus this will not happen but strength will come and give me rest in the name of Jesus, and it is so.

Isaiah 13:5

They come from a far country, from the end of heaven, even the LORD, and the weapons of his indignation, to destroy the whole land.

Lord uses your weapons of indignation against our enemies, to destroy and stop the workings of the enemy in Jesus name.

Ecclesiastes 9:18

Wisdom is better than weapons of war: but one sinner destroyeth much good.

Heavenly Father thank you for giving me some wisdom to out think my enemies, my rivals, all evil forces, and all evil attacks, that may come my way from time to time in Jesus name.

Isaiah 42:13

The LORD shall go forth as a mighty man, he shall stir up jealousy like a man of war: he shall cry, yea, roar; he shall prevail against his enemies.

The Lord is going forth before me as a mighty man of war stirring up jealousy like a man of war roaring and prevailing against our enemies in the mighty name of Jesus.

Lord thank you for going against our enemies, getting rid of our enemies that they will not, be able to prevail, or over take or over power us, or stand against us, in the mighty name of Jesus and it is so.

Deuteronomy 21:10

When thou goest forth to war against thine enemies, and the LORD thy GOD hath delivered them into thine hands, and thou hast taken them captive.

Psalms 44:5

Through thee will we push down our enemies: through thy name will we tread them under that rise up against us.

As warriors and soldiers we must stand our grounds against all the forces of hell in the mighty name of Jesus. The devil is defeated in our lives as we continue to rebuke the works, strategies, assaults and all that he throws at us at any given time.

Numbers 10:9

And if ye go to war in your land against the enemy that oppresseth you, then ye shall blow an alarm with the trumpets; and ye shall be remembered before the LORD your GOD, and ye shall be saved from your enemies.

Psalms 27:3

Though an host should encamp against me, my heart shall not fear: though war should rise against me, in this will I be confident.

Lamentations 3:46

All our enemies have opened their mouths against us.

When the enemy has opened his mouth against me then will I speak and tell our enemies to shut his mouth.

The mouth of the enemy is shut up against me, his words are not affecting me because I have spoken to shut the mouths of my enemies in the name of Jesus.

The enemy has been silenced through his mouth, being shut that he cannot utter any words to bring hurt, harm, or danger in the name of Jesus.

WE MUST LEARN HOW TO SILENCE THE MOUTH OF OUR ENEMIES.

The devil is defeated the enemy is a loser, the devil is on his way down and I'm on my way up in the name of Jesus.

In the mighty name of Jesus I silence the mouth of the enemy,
and I command him and all of his demonic activity to cease
and desist, meaning to stop, cease, or discontinue.

Psalms 108:13

Through GOD we shall do valiantly: for he it is
that shall tread down our enemies.

Lord, thank you for treading, overcoming, keeping the enemy
under my feet, with the authority that you have given me in Jesus
name. and not letting him get up, stepping on his neck with my
foot, rending him helpless, harmless, and ineffective against me,
I continue to keep him down all in the mighty name of Jesus.

THANK YOU, LORD, FOR TREADING DOWN OUR ENEMIES IN THE MIGHTY NAME OF JESUS.

But now you have given us the power and authority to overcome and
tread upon all our enemies and we're in Training to master this part of
our lives in the mighty name of Jesus our Christ, and we cannot expect
the Lord to do everything for us when he has come down and defeated
the devil and taught us how to do the same thing in the mighty name of
Jesus. His name that's above EVERY name that at the name of Jesus
each and every knee shall bow, not might not maybe but will bow to
the name of Jesus, and my BIG question to you all out there is are you
going to bow now willingly or be made to bow without a choice.???

Psalms 60:12

Through GOD we shall do valiantly: for he it is
that shall tread down our enemies.

THROUGH GOD WE shall overcome weakened every devil,
every demon, every trial, every, assignment, every soul that has
been given. Destine by our Lord and Savior Jesus the Christ,
nothing shall by any means will overpower us to take us out.

THROUGH GOD WE SHALL come into all of our blessings and nothing and nobody shall be able to stop us from achieving our GOD GIVEN GOALS IN THIS; time we are living in., We are MILLIONAIRES, BILLIONAIRE'S, AND EVEN TRILLIONAIRES IF WE STANDFAST IN THE FAITH AND CONTINUE TO BELIEVE AND TRUST IN HIS ALL MIGHTY HAND IN THE NAME OF JESUS CHRIST AND OUR GREAT AND AWESOME EMPEROR THAT'S GOD ALL MIGHTY ALL POWERFUL AND HAS ALL KNOWLEDGE AND HE IS ALL WAYS PRESENT ALL THE TIME BECAUSE HE IS OUR ETERNAL GOD SELF EXISTING.(((**THAT'S MIND BLOWING ALL BY ITSELF OK**)))

Psalms 136:24

And hath redeemed us from our enemies: for his mercy endureth forever.

<u>REDEEMED</u>- meaning brought back into right standing, brought back into what he has planned, given, written, penned, predestinated or preplanned before the foundations of the world begin, Ordained, sanctioned, released, giving us access and destined in all of his riches and abundance for us that love his and waiting for his appearance to be with him though out all ETERNITY THAT NEVER ENDS, NEVER STOPS WITHOUT TIME, ENDLESS. (Period) end of conversation OK

I am redeemed from my enemies, out of the hands of the snares and traps of the devil and all his workers of darkness because in all things we, you and I have the VICTORY IN EVERY AREA OF OUR LIVES ALREADY IN THE MIGHTY NAME OF JESUS.

Psalms 106:27

To overthrow their seed also among the nations, and to scatter them in the lands.

All Our enemies are Overthrown, shutdown, shutout, shattered & scattered in the mighty name of Jesus Christ of Nazareth.

Their seeds are overthrown amongst all the nations and shame is their portions in the name of Jesus.

Psalms 92:9

For, lo, thine enemies, O LORD, for, lo, thine enemies shall perish; all the workers of iniquity shall be scattered.

All the workers of Iniquities that are set up against us shall perish and all their works are scattered across the land and never to come together ever again in the mighty name of Jesus.

2 Timothy 3:15

"All scripture is given by inspiration of GOD, and is profitable for doctrine, for reproof, for correction, for instruction in righteousness:" 2 Tim 3:16

FASTING TO MORTIFY THE DEEDS OF THE FLESH. TO HEAR GODS VOICE MUCH CLEARER, AND TO RECEIVE DEMONSTRATIONS OF THE POWER OF GOD. Isaiah 58:1-14

Fasting, which is abstaining from certain ways, things, food and drinks, places to kill out, squash, put to death, the deeds of the flesh, with the affections and lust. Those strong feelings, that are not dead yet, that have grabbed us, through lustfulness, or some kind of temptation. These are works of the flesh they are deeds, that are in controlling the fleshly desires need, to be dead, or die out, without life.

The type things I am referring to works, Through open doors, portals, entrances to be invited to come in and take over, or on the dark side, evil practices, evil and horror movies, sexual pictures, magazines, all of these open the doors for evil spirits to come in and get settled into your feelings, appetites, desires, passions, doing things for the enemy Giving the devil permission to come in and to do whatever he likes, are all lustful works, flesh on display for the devil and being used, with voluntarily, or through not knowing, or simply being rebellious, just do not care.

Living a carefree life, doing, and going wherever they please. Which is a spirit of ignorance. Which is the kingdom of the devil, all evilness belongs to the enemy. What are these things that seems to be too strong lust of the flesh, lust of the eyes, and the pride of life 1st John 2:15-17 TAKE OUT SOME TIME TO READ IT DIGEST AND SOAK IT IN YOUR MEMORY, MEDITATE ON IT

AND IN IT. It does seem to be too strong to handle when it comes to temptations, try, or give you a hard testing of your faith.

This is your answer because we, or you have open up your emotions, which is your feelings your soul which is your mind the seat of all thoughts, your will or choices, the actions you follow after listening to your own or someone else, like the devils thoughts because of carnal thoughts, ideas, suggestions, or your so called friends associates, family like husbands, wives co-workers boy or girl friend or people you hang out with.

But somebody nevertheless has influenced you or is still influencing you. You may be too weak to do something about it or they are controlling you through witchcraft. To do something that you know little or nothing about get you in trouble. So, what you do, you open yourself to all these activities and let the devil or unclean spirits, demons of all types, come in. They begin to take over getting you deeper into this thing you have been caught up in or invited, to participate with, or gotten yourself way over your head in it. Pretty soon you are so deep you cannot even see the top or the bottom because you've been doing it for so long.

Listen at this time you do not know how to get out, you are in deep trouble, so you are TRAPPED AND ON YOUR WAY DOWN AND NO WAY TO ESCAPE you're in a snare, which means as explained before your all tangled up into some type of web and you begin to become very fearful, scared that's your thoughts at the moment. So, you begin to come to your senses and begin to ask for and cry out for help. That's when Jesus comes and begin to help you out of your situation. So, let's do a little recap on fasting. Fasting helps you to see clearly, gives you peace, causes you to hear GODs voice better, understand his words through Revelations.

There is a lot of things fasting helps us as Saints of GOD. But we must use it to our advantage, OFTEN, much as we can, never stop fasting even after 50 years. Keep going, so much for that enough cannot be said, because fasting helps us get out of the snares and traps and gives us insight, oversight, hindsight, and foresight enough said for now. NOW READ!

THESE ARE THE BLESSINGS OF WHEN ONE GOES ON A COMPLETE FAST ABSTAINING FROM ANY TYPE OF FOOD. Listen in as the prophet begins to get the word of GOD AND TELL THE PEOPLE.

Isaiah 58:1-14

Cry aloud, spare not, lift up thy voice like a trumpet, and shew my people their transgression, and the house of Jacob their sins.

Fasting causes us to seek the Lord daily while we are turning down our plates so we can obtain a faster accelerated level in the Lord.

We must have a right approach when coming to our Heavenly Father. We must approach him with respect, with reverence, honor, and value all his attributes, principles, of holiness, and honor his character traits.

This is a time when we afflict our souls in humility as of a humble state depending on the Lord in all that we are endeavor to do, seeing that we are weak and need to depend on his strength.

The Lord sees and knows our intentions for fasting and they must be pure and without corruption or manipulation trying to get the Lord our Heavenly Father to do something for us that has been a promise to us if we meet his criteria's.

We do not fast to be seen or heard, whatever we do, it is for the glory of GOD our father to come and present ourselves before him without spot, blemish, wrinkles or any such things and the Lord will receive us unto himself, that whatever we ask of him it shall be given to us.

This is the time that we have chosen or the Lord has chosen for us to fast and seek his face in secret and the Lord which sees in secret will reward us Openly, but we must have the right motives and intentions in our spirit. Just as a side note heart and spirit here are primarily the same.

Our fast must be acceptable to the Lord and not for open show for others or telling others we are fasting to get the pity and rewards from man, as the word of the Lord said in the gospels, they have their rewards, from man because they have openly announced what they are doing in front of man and not to GOD in secret.

We want to fast to loosen wickedness from us, break and destroy bondages of spirits off our lives, the heavy loads, yokes that GOD did not put on us. Evil things we have open up do to having a spirit of ignorance. We may have things in our lives that needs to be dead like our sexual lust spirits that may have been open through pornography, and other means of sexual doors and portals if evilness.

We are to feed ourselves with the word of GOD both naturally and spiritually by taking care of ourselves and reading and studying, memorizing, declaring & decreeing his awesome words in our spirit or heart, which is mentioned throughout this book. Many things are mentioned in this book that will help us but we must apply these principles to our lives each and every day so we can grow spiritually.

We fast to be led by the spirit of GOD, to hear his voice and to follow his planned that has been laid down for us.

Feeding the poor, closing, and providing a haven for those that are hungry, and homeless.

Then when we begin to do these things, then the light of GODS spirit will begin to shine through us and out of us that the others may be able to see that the Lord is doing all that is going on.

Our health will be blessed through fasting, our strength, our skin will become a lot brighter and more enhanced through fasting.

We are also become more sensitive to the move of GOD and his spirit in our midst.

The many blessings that will come from fasting, when we begin to pray, he will hear when we call on his wonderful name and answer us on a speedily basis in the mighty name of Jesus.

If there were any darkness in our lives it will be removed, our minds will be clear and peaceful of any type of tormenting thoughts in the mighty name of Jesus.

When we fast, we shall be guided by his awesome presence, and there will be no failures when it comes to what the Lord wants to do in our lives, if we continue to follow his divine plans.

We shall have fruitfulness in our lives when fasting takes place, there will be many repairs, in areas that has been either destroyed or damaged. It and they will be restored and made new again.

WHAT IS PRAISE?

Its Praising him for what he has done for you and I, praising him all through the day and night, giving thanks to him loving him with words of expressions of our thoughts, and he loves those thoughts that comes from a humble and sincere emotions. Praise will keep us in the right frame of mind and keep us from having a wrong type of attitude as to what going on at the time. We are to praise him with the breath that he has giving us. Giving him Honor Respect, showing some gratitude toward him for all the things that he has done for you and I showing our appreciation, thoughtfulness, gratefulness for all the great things he has done for you and me.

Psalms 150:1 - 127:6 - Praise ye the LORD. Praise GOD in his sanctuary: praise him in the firmament of his power.

Hebrews 13:15 - By him therefore let us offer the sacrifice of praise to GOD continually, that is, the fruit of our lips giving thanks to his name.

Psalms 100:1-5 - Make a joyful noise unto the LORD, all ye lands.

Psalms 99:3 - Let them praise thy great and terrible name; for it is holy.

Psalms 147:1 - 127:20 - Praise ye the LORD: for it is good to sing praises unto our GOD; for it is pleasant; and praise is comely.

Psalms 109:30 - I will greatly praise the LORD with my mouth; yea, I will praise him among the multitude.

Psalms 106:1 - Praise ye the LORD. O give thanks unto the LORD; for he is good: for his mercy endureth for ever.

Psalms 148:1 - 127:14 - Praise ye the LORD. Praise ye the LORD from the heavens: praise him in the heights.

1 Peter 1:3 - Blessed be the GOD and Father of our Lord Jesus Christ, which according to his abundant mercy hath begotten us again unto a lively hope by the resurrection of Jesus Christ from the dead.

WORSHIP

Adore him and tell him how great he is how we feel about him and he loves that. smiles to GOD Jesus & the Holy Spirit. This is where we need to spend a lot or time in his awesome presence of GOD. Soaking up his wonderful presence and letting him know how much we do indeed love him. Not always what we want from him, asking him what can we do, to serve him better?

Psalms 150:1

Praise ye the LORD. Praise GOD in his sanctuary: praise him in the firmament of his power. Praising GOD IS A WEAPON against our enemies.

I will continue to praise him not only at home, out in the marketplace; but also in the sanctuary, where all the saints are gathering to fellowship with our loving Lord Jesus Christ, our Heavenly and loving Father, and the Holy Spirit, when we think about it all, of our lives, we owe it to our GOD, our Heavenly Father, that loves us with an everlasting love.

This love that will not change, and yet is never at the end of what he has or will do for us. Sometimes song writers put in their writings he has not failed me yet like they are looking for him to fail.

Listen everyone how can a GOD, with all power, all might and dominion, omni presents, has all power, and has all knowledge where is failure in that kind of ability. So, we need to stop using these terms and putting him in other or all categories, as we put all others. We need to stop using these terms and start seeing him as a GOD that has no limitations, only if we believe him.

I will continue to talk of his wonderful goodness, out wherever I might be amongst others in the mighty name of Jesus.

Lord GOD I will exalt your awesome name because of who you are, with my appreciation, and gratitude, with a humble heart or spirit.

Psalms 138:2

I will worship toward thy holy temple, and praise thy name for thy lovingkindness and for thy truth: for thou hast magnified thy word above all thy name.

I will praise your name speak of your fantastic, enormous, incredible, and amazing ways of who you are and all your unlimited abilities, but will speak to them others also.

FATHER GOD, I will worship you in Spirit and in truth and adore you with all your tremendous ways.

I will worship him in spirit and in truth in the heights, while in high places that the lord takes me, I will praise him every chance I get lifting his Holy and precious name in the name of Jesus,

Praise ye him, all his angels: praise ye him, all his hosts.

CLAPPING OUR HANDS TO THE LORD; FOR HIS GOODNESS & FOR THE LORD. AS WEAPONS OF WAR THROUGH WARFARE, TO DRIVE OUR ENEMIES BACK IN THE NAME OF JESUS.

PRAYER OF COURSE IS ONE OF THE GREATEST WEAPONS OF WAR; IT IS AT THE TOP OF THE LIST along with GOD's WORD.

St Luke 18:1 And he spake a parable unto them to this end, that men ought always to pray, and not to faint.

Which means for us not to give up, or feel like giving up or sinning or abandoning our post or defecting to the enemies' side. Just because things aren't going the way we would like for them to go. Not caving in or throwing in the towels speak. That means to stop, it's not a time to stop, back away slow down, or get sidetracked by the enemies' tactics.

That is what he tries, or make attempts on our lives, to make us do, is to give up, giving up should never be in our thoughts when it comes to serving our Lord. When we have not prayed like we should, Prayer should have been our very first and foremost thought automatically. Because at this time we have left a door opened for the devil.

In fact, our enemy will come in and that he did, he does not only, have a plan. He wants to Come in and set up camp with his helpers with him suggestions, started to control and cause thoughts of confusion, fears, doubts, despair, which is lack of hope, hope is nowhere in sight, lost, gone, and not to ever come back. Trapped thoughts and Ideals to do sinful acts or actions.

Words, deeds or go places we, you, or they, have no business going i.e., which means that is going to a bar to drink, liquor, strong mixed drinks, called spirits, or mineral spirits, have you ever heard of them or such? Or going over a female or males house that is not saved. I want to add saved as well; because the saved still have emotional, sexual feelings, as well let's not allow the devil to trick, or deceive us; into thinking that: just because they are saved and we are also saved that nothing will happen.

They might even be a leader in the body of Christ, that's not an excuse to still go without someone else, going with you male or female, the word of GOD, says let not our good be evil spoken of, Romans 16:23.

Indulging in other sexual or ungodly behaviors, and activities is forbidden. GOD would not be pleased out of any of us, that we have allowed such sin to pull us in due to strong sexual affections and may I add lust strong desires that is excessive, this kind of desires comes from the devil. This type never gets enough of having sex, with men or women. Both or dealing with a spirit of LUST OR A LUST demon. Which is a spirit of an angel that has fallen and looking for a body to fulfill that passion of lust..

Us wanting to have sex with that person, and lust is not done away with, or even delivered from a lust demon of some kind.

I am sure all that, are reading this kind of information, can identify with what is being said hear, we have done, this at sometime in our lives. If this happens confess, your sins openly to one another, pray and asking the person that you were with, or involved to pray and ask forgiveness, for each other, repent, and turn, striving, be clean before the Lord.

Then ask the Lord to forgive you all and stay out and away from this kind of temptations, and may have to stay away from each other as well, read what the book of James 1:12-16 has to say about temptations, these scriptures are very important to read.

We have lost the fear of the Lord at this time, or currently to some degree. Have you ever been there or done that or are you still doing this or that right now? IF SO, YOU NEED TO STOP IT, before Jesus crack those EASTERN SKIES. Even interact with others all of this would be for the devil carrying out what he has put into or planted these thoughts, seeds suggestions, temptations, and intentions and if we do not learn to keep praying. As ambassador or Christ, we must be aware of the devil's devices.

We will be always falling in these types of traps of sin and trespassing, even transgressions against the words of GOD. THIS is what happens to some of us when we stop praying. We must continue to research, studying the word of GOD, reading, applying, his instructions, information, with what we have, learned. Doing all these many years and times we have been saved. It will tell on you, about your walk.

Whether you have really been developed in the spirit with spiritual growth or not. Some have had growth, but many are still in need of some more, a little is not enough to be aware of the devils' tactics, schemes, and tricks. They are all the same we need to learn this and get our degree into fighting the enemy and win over. All of his aims, and targets, are at our lives, to do whatever he can to stop, block, or even hinder us if he can, but in the mighty name of Jesus Christ, He do not have a fighting chance when we are dressed for war, with all of our weapons, tactics, knowledge, tools and our equipment in the mighty name of Jesus, it is so.

1 Thess 5:17 Pray without Ceasing. Don't ever stop praying don't have to be on your knees all the time or all day but thing is to PRAY!!!!

Thank you Lord and Master of my life My GOD for being with me and not turning me over to the will and desire of mine enemies, your mercy is forever and I will talk about you to all those that will listen and take heed to your word in the name of Jesus, YOUR SIMPLY GREAT AND WORDS JUST CAN NOT DESCRIBE THE WAY I FEEL ABOUT YOU JUST TO SIMPLY I LOVE YOU WITH ALL, EVERYTHING.

USING THE BLOOD OF JESUS

BLOOD IS THROUGHOUT SCRIPTURE, BUT WHAT DOES CHRIST'S BLOOD MEAN TO US?

Behold, when we come into the land, thou shalt bind this line of scarlet thread in the window which thou didst let us down by... and whosoever shall be with thee in the house, his blood shall be on our head if any hand be upon him. Joshua 2:18-19

The blood of Jesus is a PROTECTION against the enemies.

The blood of Jesus is our weapon of war and can be loosed against the enemy to defeat, destroy, stop, barricade him, bind up all of his works and his words from doing any type of damage to our lives if we use it right and continue to do as we're told to do. We must be found in right standings in using the blood of Jesus, against our enemies because GOD WILL not do wrong for wrong but we must submit ourselves to GOD and him satan, beelzebub, the devil, which is Lucifer will flee.

The blood of Jesus is a power that will cleanse us from all of our unrighteousness and present us faultless before the Lord in Jesus name.

The blood of Jesus is a redeemer it will get us or bring us to him and allow him to have mercy on us do to our repentance, our regrets, sorrows or our remorse and forsaken the sins we have committed before the lord or Our GOD.

The blood of Jesus can cover us, our homes businesses, and our families, as well as the Ministries he has given to us to carry out while on this earth, in Jesus name and it is so.

The blood of Jesus is a force, a power, weapon as stated before, cleansing agent, protection, and as we discover more it will be added to the list so we can get all the Lord has for us in Jesus name.

Rahab, the woman spoken to in this passage, was a harlot in the city of Jericho. As the Israelites came to possess the land, her city was destined for destruction — and she along with it. But she was delivered, and her life transformed, simply by tying a scarlet cord in her window.

This cord represented the blood of the Lord Jesus Christ, and it pointed toward the Lamb of GOD that takes away the sin of the world. In fact, all of the Bible is about Jesus Christ and His blood redemption, and you will find this scarlet thread throughout the Word of GOD.

From the very beginning of human history, it is revealed. When Adam and Eve sinned, GOD shed innocent blood to make them clothes from animal skins (Genesis 3:21). This is a picture of the covering of righteousness that we receive when the Lord Jesus Christ died for us.

Then, GOD wanted to deliver His people from bondage in the land of Egypt. On the night of the Passover, GOD instructed each house to slay a lamb and put the blood on their door. GOD said in Exodus 12:13, "When I see the blood, I will pass over you."

And in the tabernacle and later in the temple, thousands upon thousands of sheep, oxen, and turtle doves were killed and their blood spilt as sacrifices for sin.

And finally, the Lord Jesus Christ died upon the cross. His death was the fulfillment of all the prophecy and promises. Revelation 13:8

proclaims that He was slain before the foundation of the world. He came to die; He planned to die; He lived to die; and He was born to die.

As we've seen - the blood of Jesus is throughout Scripture. What does the Blood of Jesus mean for us today?

THE POWER OF THE BLOOD OF JESUS

His blood redeems us. There was a price against us that we could not pay, but the blood of Jesus redeemed us. 1 Peter 1:18-19 says, "Forasmuch as ye know that ye were not redeemed with corruptible things.... But with the precious blood of Christ, as of a lamb without blemish and without spot."

His blood brings us into fellowship with GOD. According to Ephesians 2:13, "But now in Christ Jesus ye who sometimes were far off are made nigh by the blood of Christ." Without the blood of Christ, man is a long way from GOD.

His blood makes peace with GOD. Man, by nature, is at war with GOD; and we can only come to GOD on His peace terms — the blood atonement. The Bible says in Colossians 1:20, "And, having made peace through the blood of His cross, by Him to reconcile all things unto Himself...."

His blood cleanses. Not only does it remove the punishment of sin, but it also removes the pollution. I don't care what sin you've committed; "the blood of Jesus Christ His Son cleanseth us from all sin (1 John 1:7).

His blood gives power over the devil. It's the blood that satan fears. Revelation 12:11 says, "And they overcame him [satan] by the blood of the Lamb...." The devil doesn't want you to learn about the blood. He hates it!

Before this planet was ever swung into space, GOD had determined in His heart that He would send His Son to die upon the cross. How wonderful it is to trace the scarlet thread of the blood of Christ woven throughout the Bible! How much more wonderful to experience its redemption personally. Praise GOD for the blood of His Lamb!

THE NAME OF JESUS

Acts 4:12 - Neither is there salvation in any other: for there is none other name under heaven given among men, whereby we must be saved

Philippians 2:9-11 - Wherefore GOD also hath highly exalted him, and given him a name which is above every name:

John 14:13 - And whatsoever ye shall ask in my name, that will I do, that the Father may be glorified in the Son

John 14:6 - Jesus saith unto him, I am the way, the truth, and the life: no man cometh unto the Father, but by me.

Luke 10:17 - And the seventy returned again with joy, saying, Lord, even the devils are subject unto us through thy name.

Romans 10:13 - For whosoever shall call upon the name of the Lord shall be saved

Matthew 1:21 - And she shall bring forth a son, and thou shalt call his name JESUS: for he shall save his people from their sins.

1 Corinthians 6:11 - And such were some of you: but ye are washed, but ye are sanctified, but ye are justified in the name of the Lord Jesus, and by the Spirit of our GOD.

Acts 2:38 - Then Peter said unto them, Repent, and be baptized every one of you in the name of Jesus Christ for the remission of sins, and ye shall receive the gift of the HOLY SPIRIT.

Mark 16:17 - And these signs shall follow them that believe; In my name shall they cast out devils; they shall speak with new tongues.

Acts 3:12-16 - And when Peter saw it, he answered unto the people, Ye men of Israel, why marvel ye at this? or why look ye so earnestly on us, as though by our own power or holiness we had made this man to walk?

Jeremiah 10:6 - Forasmuch as there is none like unto thee, O LORD; thou art great, and thy name is great in might.

John 16:26 - At that day ye shall ask in my name: and I say not unto you, that I will pray the Father for you:

Acts 8:12 - But when they believed Philip preaching the things concerning the kingdom of GOD, and the name of Jesus Christ, they were baptized, both men and women.

Isaiah 9:6 - For unto us a child is born, unto us a son is given: and the government shall be upon his shoulder: and his name shall be called Wonderful, Counsellor, The mighty GOD, The everlasting Father, The Prince of Peace.

DECREES AND DECLARATIONS

ISAIAH 10:1

Woe unto them that decree unrighteous decrees, and that write grievousness which they have prescribed.

DANCING AS A WAY OF PRAISING THE LORD AND LOOSING YOUR SELF FROM BONDAGES AND EVIL spirits that may HAVE ATTACKED or attached themselves.

CHAPTER 4

GODS CREATIVE POWER, SPOKEN THROUGH HIS DIVINE, VOICE.

IN Genesis we read about our Heavenly Father,
speaking our world into existence.

Genesis 1:1-31 READ.

In the beginning GOD created the Heaven and the earth. And the earth was without form and void: and darkness was upon the face of the deep. And the Spirit of GOD moved upon the face of the waters. And GOD said, let there be light: and there was light. And GOD saw the light, that it was good: and GOD divided the light from the darkness. So here we read about what the Lord GOD has Created.

Because he is Our Great Creator. Through speaking his divine word in existence. It is whatever he has spoken, it will appear. Whatever GOD SPEAKS it was and will be very good. GOD is the ONLY ONE TRUE GOD. He has ALL POWER to speak anything into existence out of nothing. GOD can speak making it into whatever HE wants it to be. Let's talk about this just for a few moments in time.

There is only One GOD. When we think about this there cannot be another GOD, I want all to notice that GOD is in all capital letters, signifying that there is only one true GOD. All others are hand made from stones, wood, marble, or rocks, iron of whatever materials they have made them, still our GOD was not made with the hand of man. GOD is a Spirit and you or I cannot make a spirit with our own hands, I just want to explained this is the behalf of my GOD, he deserves this value and truth for him. Why? it will & would be confusing. Think about this; if it were another or more than only one true GOD THAN he cannot be sovereign to do whatever he wants, and don't have to answer to anyone else absolutely.

I am writing this, information about GOD, to clarify, some biblical issues that was lingering in the past about who GOD IS. First, of all, like I have said before there is but one GOD. He is sovereign, meaning he can do exactly what he wants to do.

The title GOD is said to knows all things, has all power, and he is everywhere, all at the same time. It is also said about GOD, that he can create anything out of nothing, as we no to be nothing.

All things from nothing came out of him to become something, for us of him.

He is everything. GOD is the only one that can do this kind of creativity, that qualifies him as, THE ONLY ONE TRUE GOD. Then we have the Savior of the whole world, which is Jesus, The Christ.

The only begotten SON of GOD, out of the bosom, of Our Heavenly Father, GOD, has declared him. St John 1:18 and he is full of grace and truth St John 1:14. Because there are those that believe that there is more than one GOD.

Think about this just for a moment in time again. no one else, would give his son for the sins of the whole entire world, to go through all that Jesus has gone through for all of mankind.

This we are referring to, past, present, and future sins of the world, laid down his life, and have the power to pick it back up again and rose on the third day as Jesus did because, he is BECOME OUR SALVATION. So, there are three, THE FATHER, FATHER GOD, the father in creation, our heavenly father, the father of us all.

Then we have Jesus the Son of GOD, the redeemer, the one that was slain for the sins of all, our Savior, the one we go through to be saved, from our sins and continue to live a sinless life, or a life, not sinning willfully. So now we are going to talk about the HOLY SPIRIT, the comforter, that was sent in the name of Jesus. He (Jesus) through his LOVE for his FATHER, gave his life, for us all and has delivered our souls from the pits of hell. This all started in the beginning of genesis, due to what Adam did and did not do. Adam gave his Authority over to lucifer or satan, the fallen angel from Heaven at the time. Lucifer is called the anointed cherub that covereth. Ezekiel 28:14 while in Heaven. These three are ONE,

1 Timothy 3:16

And without controversy great is the mystery of GODLINESS: GOD was manifest in the flesh, justified in the Spirit, seen of angels, preached unto the Gentiles, believed on in the world, received up into glory.

But in the garden of Eden. This is where all the transferring, and deception of the serpent, that old devil deceived the woman, Eve, but Adam, being a Son of GOD GIVEN over his rights and authority to satan. But Jesus REDEEMED US BACK IN THE RIGHT STANDING WITH GOD. When this took place, we lost our sonship and authority due to sin. Read in Genesis the story what happen. So, picking up the story from where we left off from, JESUS is the word made into flesh and dwelt amongst us. St John 1:1-14 READ THE REST ON YOUR SPARE TIME. IN the Beginning was the word, and the Word was with GOD, and the WORD was GOD. All things were made by him; and without him was not anything made that was made.

GOD is The ONLY Creator of all things, as far as making something out of nothing. No one else can claim to be a GOD, like unto Our great, GOD. GOD when written is always capitalized, that qualifies him as the one true GOD, Lord & KING. THE ONE MAJESTIC ONE CALLED OUR GREAT EMPEROR, which is our sovereign ruler and Monarch. GOD has done and is Doing something no other so called god with a little g can do which is no god or no other god, or gods, but that is another subject for another day and time. IN this world and the world called HEAVEN in the third realm far above all principalities, powers, might and dominions and the rulers of the darkness of this world, and above spiritual wickedness in high places.

What is the main function of what is being said here is that GOD is our Creator and he made everything that was made by speaking these things into existence by speaking with his creative power. Let me say this; we also have power to speak life or death as well. Proverbs 18:21 because we are made in the image of our GOD. Image and likeness, has the ability to do some of the very same things that our Heavenly FATHER did. GOD SPOKE in Genesis 1:26 And GOD said let us make man in our image after our likeness and let them have dominion over the fish of the sea, and the fowls of the air, and over the cattle, and over every creeping thing that creepeth upon the earth.

Just remember each and every word we speak out of our mouths is in the form of creativeness. It will either produce, or create positive OR negative, life or death, good or bad right or wrong that's corresponds with our thoughts. These things that are in our minds at the time were thinking these things. Never forget our outlook and experiences that comes along with this, so please whatever you or I do take in consideration our words. OUR WORDS are words of creation, creativeness, speaking things into existence. We have power to speak thing with our mouths. We have power to create just like our heavenly father in heaven, spoken AND THEY CARRY WITH THEM POWER. Let me say this about this book, THIS IS ONE OF THE MOST POWERFUL, books that have ever been written.

I am not saying this to boast or brag. I am saying, this because it's very true. Just like our HEAVENLY FATHER ELOHIM, and so much more. Proverbs 18:21 death and life are in the power of your tongue.

This book and information have the power to change your life forever. Its contingent, and hangs on the time and effort that is spent applying all of this info into your spirit, soul, and watch it manifest or be seen in and through your physical body.

Death and life are in the power of the tongue: and they that love it shall eat the fruit thereof. Proverbs 18:21

I have the power to speak life, therefore I will speak life to my situations, and cause life, to manifest and be seen as well as heard, not for show, form or fashion, but to give GOD all the Glory, due to his HOLY name. Who is worthy of all the Glory in JESUS name, and it is so, so let it be done.

I have the power to speak life to my finances, my tithes, offerings. My giving's and all that the Lord has granted me to get and receive in Jesus name. I continue to speak growth into my checking accounts. I continue to speak interests, dividends, and unexpected deposits, to appear through speaking life to my monies. I speak bonuses, money coming to me from places unexpected. Places I was not aware of, or did not know about. I proclaim; all that is owed to me; I receive it. I am getting back all that the devil has stolen, and have taken away, things that have dwindle down to almost nothing, has come back to life again in the mighty name of Jesus. I REPEAT AGAIN, I SPEAK ALL THAT HAVE BEEN STOLEN, LOST, TAKEN AWAY, BE PAID BACK TO ME WITH INTEREST, from THIS TIME ON in the mighty name of Jesus. All types of finances that is supposed to come to me, I command it to come in Jesus' name now! let it come, and appear, let it begin to show up in my accounts, and manifest now the mighty name of Jesus Yeshua, the Christ, be put into my accounts in the name of Jesus.

I speak all the money that is owed to me, from past situations, that different ones, companies, have missed, did not give to me, all types of money, that is owed to me be given back in the name of Jesus. Banks, jobs, and family members; Those that borrowed money and promised to pay back. Those that have cheated me, stolen, lied, taken from me. Those that have mishandled my money. I command and I speak it to come to me in the mighty name of Jesus, with interest, and restitution, be given back to me in Yeshua's name and it is so..

I NOW, SPEAK RELEASE NOW IN THE MIGHTY NAME OF JESUS,my money freedom, liberties in CHRIST, Healings, and deliverances of all types, are my portion. I receive all that GOD has given, spoken, and written for me, to receive in the name of Jesus. You can also speak other things that may not be mentioned in this book or chapter this is just some of them. SO MAKE A LIST OF THINGS THAT WAS STOLEN AND START DECREEING AND DECLARING, WHAT BELONGS TO YOU.

I am a good steward of the money, finances, checks, benefits, businesses, and all that is put into my trust, that GOD has entrusted, commended, delegated, granted to me. I will give my tithes, of all that I owe my Lord and Savior, my 10% and even he asked me to give more that will I do.

I will pay my bills honestly and innocently to my perspective creditors. All that I owe them according to contracts and agreements' that I have made, agree to, or signed, as a promise, in the name of Jesus.

I will not ROB GOD in tithes or Offerings Malachi 3:8-11 but will give and it shall be given unto me good measures pressed down and shaken together and running over shall men give into my bosom, St Luke 6:38

Isaiah 55:8-11

When it comes to the Lord and the way he thinks, our thoughts are so much farther from his thoughts so that's why its very important that we seek his face and ask, seek, and knock, for the things that he wants us to have, in the mighty name of Jesus.

His ways does not compare to our ways, his words declared as the heavens are so much higher than the earth, so are his ways, and thoughts, actions, plans, and responses are higher and deeper, broader, longer than any of our ways.

GOD's power is much more powerful than the atom. The nuclear blast and any type of bomb that man has ever built or erected, put together because he is the CREATOR of all such. Hebrews 4:12

For the word of GOD is quick, and powerful, and sharper than any two-Edged sword, piercing even to the dividing asunder of soul and spirit, and of the joints and marrow, and is a discerner of the thoughts and intents of the heart.

Warfare meaning;

An engagement in spiritual conflicts with our enemies, called the devil, demons, unclean spirits and fallen angels.

Conflicts a strong disagreements and very serious disputes, quarreling: not to forget arguments & clashes. AS MENTIONED EARLIER

IN THIS TEACHING SO, GO BACK OVER IT, Remember to PONDER SOAK IN THE CONTENT INFORMATION TO: GET ALL THAT'S THERE FOR YOU TO TAKE ADVANTAGE OF IT, all that is has to offer BECAUSE IT IS WRITTEN FOR THAT PURPOSE IN THE MIGHTY NAME OF JESUS, AND IT IS SO.

Power Romans 13:1 Let every soul be subject unto the higher powers. For there is no power but of GOD: the powers that be are ordained of GOD. all the power belongs to GOD ALMIGHTY *UNLIMITED ENERGY & POWER.*

Our Prayers is backed up by GOD's SPIRIT or energy flowing through our vessels that's considered to be a place like a pipe. Specifically, we are the temples of GOD. A vessel where the spirit of GOD dwells in, a place were GOD SPIRIT, in resides, stays, occupies, and houses himself inside of us. Abide and stay, We are considered a wire pole, or highways of transporting ENERGY that carries or can be considered a vessel for transporting or housing powers to destroy and annihilate the works of the enemy. Our enemy is evil and already defeated. Satan has lost the war because Jesus has triumphed over him well over 2000 years. He's on his way to the lake of FIRE; THAT BURNETH with fire and BRIMSTONE FOR EVER AND EVER. in the name of Jesus. *(The eth has as a word that means continual still happening)*

OUR WORDS: BEING SPOKEN out of our mouths, CARRIES & HAS POWER TO CREATE BOTH GOOD OR BAD, RIGHT & WRONG LIGHT & DARKNESS so begin to speak life to our, (your) present situation and watch the manifestation come to pass in Jesus' name.

Speaking, out of our mouths;

Out of your mouth using your tongue_proverbs 18:21 death and life in is the power of the tongue: to speak out loud St Matthews 15:11 [11] It is not what goes into the mouth of a man that makes him unclean *and* defiled, but what comes out of the mouth; this makes a man unclean *and* defiles or make *them dirty, polluted or impure* [him]. kjv[11] Not that which goeth *(continually going in)* into the mouth defileth a man; but that which cometh out of the mouth, this defileth a man.

THE word of GOD Spoken into the atmosphere the power, energy, and Spirit of GOD's unending supply of supernatural flow ALL IN THE NAME OF JESUS, being spoken out of our mouths will create, either life or death, blessing or cursing right or wrong, Job 6:25

HOW FORCIBLE ARE THE RIGHT WORDS!

James 3:2-18

We must be careful with the words that come out of our mouths. We want to only be speaking life to ourselves and others

Our part is simply just believing it and watching it all come to pass, after speaking it into existence, as if GOD himself is speaking it out of his mouth, this is what, take place when we speak the words of GOD, the downloaded thoughts of GOD ALMIGHTY OUR OF HIS MOUTH, this is like, THAT so we need to just start doing it, be very careful, not to speak things that will harm, or bring a curse to others, and we need to start speaking these things according to the words of GOD, for long periods of time and see the results in the name of Jesus.

11 Now faith is the substance of things hoped for, the evidence of things not seen. Heb 11:1 2 Cor 5:7 ⁷ For we walk by faith, not by sight.

Speaking wisdom into my life.

WISDOM IS A KEY CONTRAST

What is the biblical definition of the word wisdom.

WISDOM: wisdom is the GOD given ability to use, understand, interpret, and work with knowledge effectively, in such a way as to bring about goods, information, fullness, positive results, facts, manifestations of the spoken results, truths and ways to best carry out any kind of plan, sufficiently, adequately, satisfactorily and suitable, affective, affordable, and comprehensively by applying instructions, information, effectively, bringing great results. This wisdom has the ability to produce the knowledge that has been provided, to be put to full use to the maximum, and to maximize, all the potential, that can be mustered up at that time.

WHAT IS CONTRAST?

A state of being strikingly different from something else. Or differently from others; so. We also want to look at the word comparison, comparing for example, apples to oranges totally different but they are both fruits, but they are not the same, fruit. Nevertheless they are in the fruit category, so contrasting is knowing the different between what is, and what is not. In this GODLY wisdom is quite different from the world's wisdom; 1 Corinthians 2:6

Howbeit we speak wisdom among them that are perfect: yet not the wisdom of this world, nor of the princes of this world, that come to nought:

Ecclesiastes 9:16

Then said I, Wisdom is better than strength: nevertheless, the poor man's wisdom is despised, and his words are not heard.

I proclaim that I am not poor but my words will be heard throughout the land in the name of Jesus and give GOD all the GLORY, HONOR & PRAISE due to his name in Jesus name.

My words will not be despised, those that are hated and looked down on without remorse but used to train the unlearned, uneducated, & uninformed.

1 Kings 4:30

And Solomon's wisdom excelled the wisdom of all the children of the east country, and all the wisdom of Egypt.

Thank you, Lord, for letting my wisdom that you have given to excel worldwide, which is universal, international and all-inclusive in Jesus name.

I love the wisdom of the Lord GOD ALMIGHTY and I want to flow in it and master it, grow in it, learn it and be able to use it effectively

Proverbs 4:7

Wisdom is the principal thing; therefore, get wisdom:
and with all thy getting get understanding.

Ecclesiastes 7:12

For wisdom is a defense, and money is a defense: but the excellency
of knowledge is, that wisdom giveth life to them that have it.

1 Kings 4:34

And there came of all people to hear the wisdom of Solomon,
from all kings of the earth, which had heard of his wisdom.

1 Corinthians 2:7

But we speak the wisdom of GOD in a mystery, even the hidden
wisdom, which GOD ordained before the world unto our glory:

1 Corinthians 2:6

Howbeit we speak wisdom among them that are perfect: yet not the
wisdom of this world, nor of the princes of this world, that come to nought:

1 Corinthians 1:21

For after that in the wisdom of GOD the world by wisdom knew not GOD,
it pleased GOD by the foolishness of preaching to save them that believe.

Ecclesiastes 1:16

I communed with mine own heart, saying, Lo, I am come to great estate,
and have gotten more wisdom than all they that have been before me in
Jerusalem: yea, my heart had great experience of wisdom and knowledge.

Proverbs 8:5

O ye simple, understand wisdom: and, ye fools,
be ye of an understanding heart.

Proverbs 24:3

Through wisdom is an house builded; and by
understanding it is established:

Job 12:12

With the ancient is wisdom; and in length of days understanding.

Proverbs 8:14

Counsel is mine, and sound wisdom: I am understanding; I have strength.

Proverbs 1:2

To know wisdom and instruction; to perceive the words of understanding;

Ephesians 1:8

Wherein he hath abounded toward us in all wisdom and prudence;

Proverbs 10:23

It is as sport to a fool to do mischief: but a man
of understanding hath wisdom.

Proverbs 23:4

Labour not to be rich: cease from thine own wisdom.

Proverbs 1:20

Wisdom crieth without; she uttereth her voice in the streets:

Job 28:20

Whence then cometh wisdom? and where is the place of understanding?

Proverbs 5:1

My son, attend unto my wisdom, and bow thine ear to my understanding:

Colossians 2:3

In whom are hid all the treasures of wisdom and knowledge.

James 3:15

This wisdom descendeth not from above, but is earthly, sensual, devilish.

Proverbs 8:1

Doth not wisdom cry? and understanding put forth her voice?

Colossians 4:5

Walk in wisdom toward them that are without, redeeming the time.

Proverbs 13:10

Only by pride cometh contention: but with the well advised is wisdom.

Proverbs 8:12

I wisdom dwell with prudence, and find out knowledge of witty inventions.

Proverbs 8:11

For wisdom is better than rubies; and all the things
that may be desired are not to be compared to it.

BEGIN TO READ THESE WORDS, AND THOUGHTS
OF GOD OVER AND OVER OUT OF YOUR MOUTH,
AND THE RESULTS WILL BE ASTOUDING.

CHAPTER 5

HUMILITY; THE STARTING POINT

Humble, what is it? And how do I become like this?

not proud: not thinking of yourself as better than other people, being lowly in heart, not being boastful, bragging about one's abilities, not lifting up yourself, trying to make yourself look like you are all together in all manners, not bringing attention to yourself as one that's in need of being heard, or noticed about anything. Not doing something and want to let everyone see and hear what you have done or have to say.

James 1:19-20 Wherefore, my beloved brethren, let every man be swift to hear, slow to speak, slow to wrath: For the wrath of man worketh not the righteousness of GOD.

I am swift to hear, slow to say my words, and slow to get angry

And whosoever shall exalt himself shall be abased; and he that shall humble himself shall be exalted.

I Decree and declare that I not only will but continue to humble myself in the Lord and he will exalt me in due time. - But now ye also put off all these; anger, wrath, malice, blasphemy, filthy communication out of your mouth.

I now put off all these anger wrath malice blasphemies filthy communication will not proceed out of my mouth. - With all lowliness and meekness, with longsuffering, forbearing one another in love; I speak evil of no man, I am not a brawler, but gentle, shewing all meekness unto all men.

For by grace, I am saved through faith; and that
not of Myself : it is the gift of GOD:

- I confess My sins, he is faithful and just to forgive Me of
my sins, and to cleanse Me from all unrighteousness.

Wherefore I lay apart all filthiness and superfluity of naughtiness, and I
receive with meekness the engrafted word, which is able to save My soul.

I Humble Myself therefore under the mighty hand
of GOD, that he Will exalt Me in due time:

Take my yoke upon you, and learn of me; for I am meek and
lowly in heart: and ye shall find rest unto your souls.

Whosoever therefore shall humble himself as this little
child, the same is greatest in the kingdom of heaven.

A fool uttereth all his mind: but a wise man keepeth it in till
afterward. I don't give all my words as a fool but am wise in all
things- Thy word is a lamp unto my feet and a light unto my path.

As newborn babes, desire the sincere milk of the word, that ye may
grow thereby That I may know him, and the power of his resurrection,
and the fellowship of his sufferings, being made conformable
unto his death; But be ye doers of the word, and not hearers only,
deceiving your own selves. For all have sinned, and come short of
the glory of GOD - Not of works, lest any man should boast. Obey
them that have the rule over you, and submit yourselves: for they
watch for your souls, as they that must give account, that they may
do it with joy, and not with grief: for that is unprofitable for you.

But why dost thou judge thy brother? or why dost thou set at nought
thy brother? for we shall all stand before the judgment seat of Christ.

But sanctify the Lord GOD in your hearts: and be ready always
to give an answer to every man that asketh you a reason
of the hope that is in you with meekness and fear: Study to
shew thyself approved unto GOD, a workman that needeth
not to be ashamed, rightly dividing the word of truth.

HUMILITY

Let nothing be done through strife or vainglory; but in lowliness
of mind let each esteem other better than themselves.

But he giveth more grace. Wherefore he saith, GOD
resisteth the proud, but giveth grace unto the humble.

For whosoever exalteth himself shall be abased; and
he that humbleth himself shall be exalted.

- By humility and the fear of the LORD are riches, and honour, and life.

Humble yourselves therefore under the mighty hand
of GOD, that he may exalt you in due time:

And whosoever shall exalt himself shall be abased; and
he that shall humble himself shall be exalted.

For I say, through the grace given unto me, to every man
that is among you, not to think of himself more highly
than he ought to think; but to think soberly, according as
GOD hath dealt to every man the measure of faith.

Put on therefore, as the elect of GOD, holy and beloved, bowels of
mercies, kindness, humbleness of mind, meekness, longsuffering;

He must increase, but I must decrease.

When pride cometh, then cometh shame: but with the lowly is wisdom.

Likewise, ye younger, submit yourselves unto the elder. Yea, all
of you be subject one to another, and be clothed with humility:
for GOD resisteth the proud, and giveth grace to the humble.

Humble yourselves in the sight of the Lord, and he shall lift you up.

With all lowliness and meekness, with longsuffering, forbearing one another in love; Thus saith the LORD, Let not the wise man glory in his wisdom, neither let the mighty man glory in his might, let not the rich man glory in his riches:

Boast not against the branches. But if thou boast, thou bearest not the root, but the root thee.

HUMBLENESS

We know that Jesus died for our sins and our human faults. This was done to reestablish our relationship with GOD. But there's an important step each of us must still take to *access the mercy and grace* that His death affords us.

That step is to practice humility. Scripture says, *"GOD resists the proud, but gives grace to the humble"* (James 4:6).

But what does it mean to be humble?

To be humble is to realize how weak we are, and how helpless we are to change the course of our lives in our own power. It's to ask GOD for His forgiveness and to trust Him for His guidance. That's what He wants to see abiding in our hearts.

He wants us to realize and confess our helplessness, our sinfulness, and our complete need for Him in our lives; and we can do exactly that, regardless of the depth of the flaw, since we know GOD will never reject those who come to Him with a humble spirit:

"The Lord is near to those who have a broken heart, and saves such as have a contrite spirit" (Psalm 34:18).

Even if we believe we're being humble, it's often difficult in our current society to show as much humility as the Lord would like. Culturally, we've moved further away from GOD's ways and instead placed focus on the world's ways. Humility is not seen as a positive trait—it's seen as a weakness—and in a lot of cases, humility is seen as a flaw that should be avoided at all costs.

Just think about your own social or professional life. How often do you hear someone around you admit they were wrong or made a mistake? When was the last time *you* admitted such things?

These days, people are afraid to admit wrong or unveil a weakness, and instead let themselves move to a position of pride. Once there, it's easier to lie, make excuses, or ignore personal issues rather than face them in humility. And in GOD's plan, pride becomes an obstacle that halts His mercy.

To put pride aside and receive GOD's full blessings, we must come to GOD, through Jesus, confess our need and weakness, and ask Christ to cleanse and receive us. We must ask Jesus to take control of our lives and *guide us every step of the way.*

It's then that pride will be put aside and the doors opened to receive His full blessings. Remember this passage as you turn your back on your old ways:

Let the wicked forsake his way, and the unrighteous man his thoughts; and let him return to the LORD, and He will have compassion on him; and to our GOD, for He will abundantly pardon (Isaiah 55:7).

Even if you've already confessed your weaknesses and asked Christ to receive you, doing it is not a one-time thing. It's ongoing and should be a part of your daily prayer life.

If you've never acknowledged that you're a sinner, confessed your sins, repented for your sins, and declared your belief that Jesus is GOD's Son who died to save you, use the link below to pray for Him to come into your life.

We must live out our lives as humble ambassadors of CHRIST just as JESUS did while on earth and he humbled himself and became obedient even to the death of the cross.

There is much to be said about humility in this passage. including the way that it frames our understanding of the relationships between husbands and wives in Ephesians 5. But at present, we will attend to the role of humility in the divine life.

"Perhaps there is more to be said about GOD's humility."

SUBMIT OURSELVES TO GODS PLAN

"Subordinate, obey, subject to, submit, surrender, to come under the rulership of another in following, applications instructions, being humble staying in our places of duties, obligations.

The biblical concept of submission is to place oneself under the authority of another.

1. To let down; to cause to sink or lower.

2. To yield, resign, or surrender to the power, will, or authority of another.

Wives, submit yourselves to your own husbands. Eph.5:22

Submit yourselves to every ordinance of man. 1 Pet. 2:13

I will continue to submit to the law's rules and regulations according to GODS divine plan for my life in Jesus name amen.

3. To refer; to leave or commit to the discretion of judgment of another; as, to submit, give oneself to for a worthy cause.

SUBMIT"; To surrender; to yield one's person to the power of another; to give up resistance.

To be subject; to give in acknowledge, to embrace, take in, apply, accept, receive leadership, in the authority as the head even in following in the steps of Christ Jesus our Lord and Savior.

To be submissive; to yield without murmuring. I will yield myself to the plans of the Lord without murmuring or speaking

out sounds of discontent I will strive to keep these thoughts
to myself or just do not think of them altogether.

Colossians 3:18

Wives, submit yourselves unto your own husbands, as it is fit in the Lord.

James 4:7

Submit yourselves therefore to GOD. Resist
the devil, and he will flee from you.

I submit myself to GOD and I will resist the evil one, the devil, my arch
enemy, and all unclean spirits that's foul in nature in Jesus name amen
and I command these spirits to flee, go away, do not come back ever again.

If we want to see victory in our lives, then it all starts with lower
ourselves to the rule's laws, commandments of the Lord, by submitting
which means we will follow everything to the letter to avoid further
troubles, unforeseen situations, lowering our attitudes, thoughts,
ideas, and ways actions that we might be thinking to carry out.
Put all these things aside get rid of our own actions and ways.

Ephesians 5:22

Wives, submit yourselves unto your own husbands, as unto the Lord.

Men or women, we will submit ourselves, to come down with our thoughts
and whatever may get us out of line, is disallowed, so with this said we'll
stay in line and do what is necessary to abide by GOD's rules so we can be
pleasing in all that we do because he is watching all that we do and speak.

1 Peter 2:13

Submit yourselves to every ordinance of man for the
Lord's sake: whether it be to the king, as supreme.

Thank you, Lord Jesus, for helping me to follow and submit to
marketplace rules and regulations without griping or making
or even thinking other things that might get us in trouble.

I will strive to do my part to abide by certain guidelines
to be pleasing to my Lord and Savior Jesus Christ.

CHAPTER 6

JUST SIMPLY BELIEVE, NO DOUBT IT WILL HAPPEN.

Why is it so hard for us to believe what our Lord and Savior has promised us? Why is it so hard for us to accept what GOD HAS done, spoken or will perform for us while on this earth? Why do we doubt so much? Disbelieve, not accept, do not cling to hold on to? embrace the words, promises, decrees, declarations, and other prophecies that has been given or spoken to us, by GOD, or through his prophets, in the body of Christ. Do we really take GOD at his words literally? Do we really walk by faith and not by sight? or is it just words we hear and think that we are doing what he requires of us to do? These questions are often asked during our lifetime and we need to dig in and get some real answers from the word of GOD. What do the word of GOD says about belief, believe, believing.

Always Believing GOD; ALWAYS

Words to ENCOURAGEMENT FOR ENHANCING YOUR LIFE.

Why do we have problems believing what GOD has said to us? Spoken or promised that he will do for us? Why do we struggle with these statements? words that have been uttered to us by others or some of the thing's GOD has said to us? in our minds, through the patterns of thoughts, that we're thinking, or our spirit, emotions, and most of all our actions shows it with vivid evidence, these and many other answers will be discussed and resolved so we can reach our destiny and quit doubting, being filled with unbelief, lacking in full faith in Jesus name and blaming & accusing.

WHAT IS BELIEF?

Having a state of mind set to believe that something is true, worthy of leaning on, relying of information that has dependency, value, that is truth and confidence as to whatever is spoken can be backed up and can be substantiated, with value, validated verified and authenticated by the works not only previously but at all times by the power of Honor with the character that speaks of whatever is being said. Having a firm persuasion. Believing GOD means coming to him acting on whatever he has said without asking a whole lot of questions and rationalizing, pondering thoughts in our hearts or mind through our thinking, but just simply follow through with, and do it just like he said to do and not let anything interfere with our focus carrying out this great plan in Jesus name being triumphant which is victory in every area of our lives.

> But without faith it is impossible to please him: for he that cometh to GOD must believe that he is, and that he is a rewarder of them that diligently seek him. Hebrews 11:6

So, what are some of the reasons we doubt, have lacking faith, to simply believe and run with it. But will not simply believe? what is true, or truth? Spoken, and act on it by faith. Trust broken, hurts internally, insecure lifestyles, feelings, and emotions, that have been damaged through previous relationships. There are a lot of reasons why and we need to make a list and start looking at it, to see where we fit in on the list, not the Lord Jesus or our Great Father GOD; but we tend to taking it out on them; GOD, our Heavenly Father, JESUS, YESHUA THE CHRIST, & THE HOLY SPIRIT. Because simply we do not understand, we are ignorant of knowledge, limited to research and it could very well be that we are just, plan olde lazy. By blaming, sometimes blaming and accusing can be much easier than to see ourselves, what part we played in the matter when it comes to choices, that we have made. Many times we try to justify ourselves, and excuse that we have done. Because, we feel like they have the power, to do something about it and seems like they did absolutely, nothing and just let it happened. This is not a true statement and I'm letting you all know that is reading this information, and training manual, WE NEED TO PUT THE BLAME WE IT BELONGS, and that is to the devil, our adversary, right here and right now that the devil is the accuser of the brethren, and I must say that I've could have been guilty of that, but not anymore because the Lord really does love us with an everlasting love, with a loving humbleness of thoughts; eyes of nothing but pure true love that is overwhelming to him about us.

Think about this who we are, HIS (GOD) highest creation which is his highest prize possession that's who we are. OK, except it, embrace,hang on to it, think about it, and don't let it ever go from your thoughts. Let me say this because if you do you will find yourselves blaming and saying Lord; why did you let this happen to me. That statement is not right toward him, so stop it and don't find yourself letting or even allowing these words, to come from your lips in Jesus name. So quit blaming the Lord of Glory, for things he was not responsible for, it was not his doing. That is putting yourself in a dangerous, place to be in the seat of blaming GOD. For what our enemies, devils, unclean spirits, devil worshippers, occult practices, witches, warlocks, wizards, those in the world of darkness. Working for the devil are responsible for, .these types of actions and maybe even our own selves could be responsible for some of these activities, that has taken place in our lives, and not really think about it or recognize,that we think that we have not had a part in at all, we need to rethink this again and put the blame were it belongs..

THE LORD GOD ALMIGHTY WANT TO SAY TO US ALL. I HAD NOTHING TO DO WITH THIS TRUST IN ME WITH ALL THINE HEART AND STOP LEANING TO YOUR OWN UNDERSTANDING. IN ALL OF YOUR WAYS ACKNOWLEDGE ME AND I WILL DIRECT YOUR PATH. **PROVERBS 3:5-6**

We need to ask forgiveness and renounce these blames, guilts, accusations, fault findings, condemning, condemnations and feelings, of guilt trips like; the Lord has done you wrong, not so. The bible says the devil is the accuser of the brethren accusing us before him, the lord that is day and night. Rev 12:10" I heard a loud voice saying in

Heaven, Now is come Salvation and strength, and the Kingdom of our GOD, and the Power of his Christ: for the accuser of our brethren is cast down, which accused them before our GOD, day and night".

WE ARE LIVING IN A FALLEN WORLD & SYSTEMS, RAN BY THE devil:

By the way, I do not capitalize satan or the devils' names or titles. So if you see it capitalized, it is by the beginning of a sentence or paragraph.

Well when we live In a fallen world of negativity, where we are taking advantage of one another, along with the devil and all his evil cohorts of hell. All of this evil around us on TV, the media, on the Job, in the home and everywhere we turn. There seems to be negative information, evil seems to be on the uprise. Someone getting hurt terrorized by some group, individuals, the government, people in the home and out of the home whether it's on the job out in the streets or whatever situations are happening everywhere. Our world is continuing to be in a decreasing in a fallen negative vicious cycle that's what it seems like but that's not always the bonafide truth their things we do not see behind the scenes of life.

GOD is at work and a lot of us as the creation of GOD, don't even recognize what is taking place because. We are too busy doing our own things, selfishly and not paying attention to what is going on in our world, at home,or elsewhere for that matter, because most of us, or should I say a lot of us in this world; really do not care, as long as it doesn't affect us or dock at our doorsteps. But this is sinical thinking, one day will come, when things, you have read about, or looked at on the TV, may find itself in your reality, then what are you going to do about???

So now we are going to take a moment in our lives and repent for accusing and blaming our Lord for things he was not responsible for. We need to put the blame on the devil or may even ourselves for allowing these things to take place in our lives and not be watchful to stop it from happening or taking place through not being sober minded, alert on guard or whatever may have been the case.

A SINCERE PRAYER OF REPENTANCE FOR BLAMING YOU FOR MY CHOICES:

Now my Loving Lord and Savior, I'm coming to you on my behalf; asking you for your forgiveness, of all my sins of blaming, and accusing you of things that happened to me that you did not do, but helped me to see and recognize them, opening up my blinded eyes, so please forgive my faults, blaming, accusations against you GOD, JESUS CHRIST & THE HOLY SPIRIT for my negligence, I now humble my soul under your mighty hand and ask you to cleanse me, wash me purge me and purify my thoughts, my spirit, soul, mind, will and emotions would be healed set free and made whole and complete from this point on into ETERNITY; AND I will be very careful to always give you the praise.

I will adore you in worship and give you all the GLORY due to your wonderful name in the name of Yeshua JESUS Christ my LORD. Redeemer and sanctifier it is so.

In the name of Jesus I bind the works of all my enemies at work against me, I rebuke you in Jesus name.

I take authority over you against my thoughts, thinking, my feelings.

I take authority over all of my emotions and command you to stop your activity against me in the mighty name of Jesus.

I bind restrict all your monitoring, recording demons. I restrict all your movement toward me in any way, shape, form, or fashion.

I command the WARRIOR ANGELS OF GOD, to handcuff, and restrict these demons from their activities in the mighty name of Jesus, and to be cast into the fires of HELL, the abyss, the Gehenna, hades, the burning inferno of fires in the mighty name of Jesus, to burn forever, never to come against me ever again in the mighty name of Jesus.

Also as well My loving FATHER to cover all my family members until you bring them in, to be saved. THANK YOU for covering all of them under your powerful BLOOD JESUS, and I personally thank you for doing this for all of our family, in YESHUA NAME; SO LET IT BE DONE NOW!

If we cannot believe simply what GOD has done for us how can we perform his work? We will be like a ship without a charted course, not navigational compass, no goals aim in life no meaning because we refuse to believe in the only begotten of the FATHER full of grace and truth St John 1:14 And the Word was made flesh, and we beheld his Glory, the Glory as of the only begotten of the Father, full of Grace and truth.

John 14:12-14 - Verily, verily, I say unto you, He that believeth on me, the works that I do shall he do also; and greater works than these shall he do, because I go unto my Father.

Gracious Father; thank you for letting me do the greater works, giving you the Glory out of my life. Walking in your Glory healing all manners of sicknesses and diseases, making no matter how difficult it may seems. It's not me doing the work but your Spirit in me performing and carrying out all of these operations, with signs wonders, miracles, and marvels in the mighty name of Jesus Christ of Nazareth. I expect it to happen each and every day, I'm looking for an opportunity to allow it to take place in the mighty name of Jesus.

In the mighty name of Jesus I expect to raise the dead. Cast out nasty demons, commanding them to GO in the mighty name of Jesus. Seeing the blind receive their sight again, the lame to walk, the dumb & deaf to be able to understand and speak. Expect money in large amounts to show up in our accounts. All of our bills miraculously amazing astoundingly and astonish, surprised paid off without lifting a finger and receiving a bill that states $0, Balance and closed out.

These are things that I expect the Lord to do for me
and others in the name of Jesus. And it is so

Each and every day I look for the Lord to do something for me and my family and the ministry to give GOD all the Glory in Jesus name.

I am a firm believer in his word, teachings, and all that he
has spoken to me and not doubt at all in Jesus name.

I live in believing whatever his word said to me
that will I carry out in Jesus name.

John 20:29 - Jesus saith unto him, Thomas, because
thou hast seen me, thou hast believed: blessed are they
that have not seen, and yet have believed.

Lord thank you that you have made a believer out of me, and I yet believe
your awesome words of life to come to pass in my life in the name of Jesus.

John 3:16 - For GOD so loved the world, that he gave
his only begotten SON, that whosoever believeth in him
should not perish, but have everlasting life.

I believe and I will not perish but believe that I have ETERNAL
LIFE ABIDING WITHIN ME, my hope is in the Lord.

IF WE DO NOT BELIEVE WHAT GOD HAS SPOKEN AND SAID TO US, THEN HOW FAR CAN YOU MOVE AND GROW IN GOD???????

A lot is hanging on what we believe. Everything we, and everything
we say hangs on what we believe. If we believe a little we will receive
a little. If we believe a lot WE WILL RECEIVE A LOT. THE LORD
SPOKE TO ME AND GIVEN ME THIS FOR ALL OF THOSE THAT
HAVE THIS BOOK THIS IS FOR YOUR USE. TAKE AND START
PRACTICING IT. THIS IS ONE OF THE PRINCIPLES THAT
THE HOLY SPIRIT TEACHES THROUGH ME. OUR TRAINING
CLASSES AND TEACHING SESSIONS CALLED ELITE WARRIORS
TRAINING CENTER. FOR MORE INFORMATION. EMAIL ME
AT ATOMICWARRIOR100@GMAIL.COM. ALL IN SMALL CAPS.
Please leave your information such as your name your calling,title
and what do you expect to get out of this training. THIS TRAINING
WILL START REAL SOON. This training is for warriors that
want to go further into who they are, and beyond in Jesus name

THANK YOU. Prophet Carl A Burden Teacher & instructor.

Mark 16:15-16 - And he said unto them, go ye into all the
world, and preach the gospel to every creature.

John 14:1 - Let not your heart be troubled: ye
believe in GOD, believe also in me.

Lord, I believe in your word of truth, and my heart or spirit is not
troubled because of anything I have seen or heard in the name of Jesus.

Romans 10:9-10 - That if thou shalt confess with thy mouth
the Lord Jesus, and shalt believe in thine heart that GOD
hath raised him from the dead, thou shalt be saved.

Exodus 6:6 - Wherefore say unto the children of Israel, I am the
LORD, and I will bring you out from under the burdens of the
Egyptians, and I will rid you out of their bondage, and I will redeem
you with a stretched-out arm, and with great judgments:

Mark 9:24 - And straightway the father of the child cried out,
and said with tears, Lord, I believe; help thou mine unbelief.

Romans 10:14 - How then shall they call on him in whom they
have not believed? and how shall they believe in him of whom they
have not heard? and how shall they hear without a preacher?

Job 2:3 - And the LORD said unto satan, Hast thou considered
my servant Job, that there is none like him in the earth, a perfect
and an upright man, one that feareth GOD, and escheweth
evil? and still, he holdeth fast his integrity, although thou
movedst me against him, to destroy him without cause.

James 2:22 - Seest thou how faith wrought with his
works, and by works was faith made perfect?

John 3:16-18 - For GOD so loved the world, that he gave
his only begotten Son, that whosoever believeth in him
should not perish, but have everlasting life.

Romans 8:38-39 - For I am persuaded, that neither
death, nor life, nor angels, nor principalities, nor
powers, nor things present, nor things to come,

1 John 4:1-2 - Beloved, believe not every spirit, but try the spirits whether
they are of GOD: because many false prophets are gone out into the world.

Colossians 3:17 - And whatsoever ye do in word or deed, do all in the name of the Lord Jesus, giving thanks to GOD and the Father by him.

Romans 5:8 - But GOD commendeth his love toward us, in that, while we were yet sinners, Christ died for us.

John 1:12 - But as many as received him, to them gave he power to become the sons of GOD, even to them that believe in his name:

2 Timothy 2:15 - Study to shew thyself approved unto GOD, a workman that needeth not to be ashamed, rightly dividing the word of truth.

Believing is more than just confessing that we believe. Belief comes with actions, commitment, obligation, and steadfastness in what has been delivered to me, or you. We must be loyal in what is said and heard. Do not be moved by anybody else's words other than what GOD has spoken or told, revealed, or promised to do for you. This must be without wavering, unshakable, undeterred by circumstances, actions, incidents, situations, or anything that will come or go with resilience.

Do not be moved, by your feelings, thoughts, words or actions if it's not motivated by the BREATH OF GOD OR THE THOUGHTS ON HIS MIND. Let nothing be uprooted and anyway, shape, form or fashion being persuaded that the truth will set and make you free in Jesus name. By the way, if anything that is not of GOD WE NEED to get rid of it. Let go abort it out of your life. A lot of thoughts that we think and act upon need and should have been gone by now. This is how we renew our minds with what GOD has said and throw the rest of the mess that we have learned out the window and shut it tight. Listen we need to stop picking up stray information that leads to traps and snares which gets us in a lot of trouble.

ALL RELATIONSHIPS ARE BUILT ON TRUST RELYING ON WHAT THEY HAVE SAID AND PROMISED. THESE RELATIONSHIPS BUILD CONFIDENCE OVER TIME. PLEASE REMEMBER THIS; BECAUSE THIS IS ONE OF THE MAJOR KEYS TO BEING USED BY GOD. IN ALL OF OUR LIVES.

Also believing in GOD's word requires confidence in the Lord because that is RELATIONSHIP that is built on trust, dependency, relying leaning on and a strong sense of confidence to carry out promises, commands ordinances, and all the like. Relationships must be built and continue to grow and to develop an unbreakable bond with the Lord that is second to none.

When we develop an intimate relationship with our Lord and Savior Jesus Christ, and so not forgetting our HEAVENLY FATHER as well than this relationship will take on affection, trust what is said with dependency and strong belief without wavering. Or being persuaded, sidetracked, loss of focus, remembering his words, promises, whatsoever, this is, what it means to believe or have belief in our hearts or spirit, trusting the words of our Lord and KING: because he cannot lie and he has the power to back up EVERYTHING; that he has spoken or said he would do for you and me, in Jesus name, and it is true.

Hebrews 4:12 - For the word of GOD'S is quick, and powerful, and sharper than any two-edged sword, piercing even to the dividing asunder of soul and spirit, and of the joints and marrow, and is a discerner of the thoughts and intents of the heart.

2 Timothy 3:16 - All scripture is given by inspiration of GOD and is profitable for doctrine, for reproof, for correction, for instruction in righteousness:

Matthew 24:35 - Heaven and earth shall pass away, but my words shall not pass away.

Amplified Bible.

16 All Scripture is GOD-breathed [given by divine inspiration] and is profitable for instruction, for conviction [of sin], for correction [of error and restoration to obedience], for training in righteousness [learning to live in conformity to GOD's will, both publicly and privately—behaving honorably with personal integrity and moral courage]; The Word of GOD, is the thoughts and plans of GOD. The things on his mind that he wants to say to his children. The plans, blessings, inheritance, laws, rules commandments and promises that he wants us to know about. He has put them into a written form so we can digest it.

Proverbs 4:20-22 - My son, attend to my words;
incline thine ear unto my sayings.

Proverbs 30:5-6 - Every word of GOD is pure: he is a
shield unto them that put their trust in him.

John 1:1 - In the beginning was the Word, and the
Word was with GOD and the Word was GOD.

Psalms 119:105 -. Thy word is a lamp unto
my feet, and a light unto my path.

Isaiah 40:8 - The grass withereth, the flower fadeth:
but the word of our GOD shall stand for ever.

John 12:48 - He that rejecteth me, and receiveth not my
words, hath one that judgeth him: the word that I have
spoken, the same shall judge him in the last day.

Colossians 3:16 - Let the word of Christ dwell in you richly in all
wisdom; teaching and admonishing one another in psalms and hymns
and spiritual songs, singing with grace in your hearts to the Lord.

Proverbs 3:1-35 - My son, forget not my law; but
let thine heart keep my commandments:

John 6:63 - It is the spirit that quickeneth; the flesh profiteth nothing:
the words that I speak unto you, they are spirit, and they are life.

John 17:17 - Sanctify them through thy truth: thy word is truth.

John 6:68 - Then Simon Peter answered him, Lord, to
whom shall we go? thou hast the words of eternal life.

John 1:14 - And the Word was made flesh, and dwelt among us, (and we beheld his glory, the glory as of the only begotten of the Father,) full of grace and truth.

John 16:13 - Howbeit when he, the Spirit of truth, is come, he will guide you into all truth: for he shall not speak of himself; but whatsoever he shall hear, that shall he speak: and he will shew you things to come.

I BELIEVE and know what Jesus has already done for us.

I believe in the Apostle's doctrine, that Jesus Christ. Came to earth through the virgin birth of Mary's womb overshadowing her by the HOLY SPIRIT, lived and taught, instructed, raised up mentored, trained, and coached the 12 disciples he handpicked. Ministered to the lost, raised the dead, healed the lepers, fed the poor, opened the eyes of the blind, healed the lame, so they could walk again, the dumb were able to speak again. He was crucified, beaten and whipped, taking on his body, stripes, with a whip of cords, or it was said a cat of nine tales with metal sharp pieces attached, that when he was whipped,torn his flesh and done all of this for our healing and deliverances that is 39 stripes saved one.

Died and buried in a borrowed tomb it was said. No one has taken his life: he laid it down, and had the power to pick it back up again. On the third day, before that; going into the lower parts of the earth. It is called hades, hell, Gehenna, the place of the damned. The souls that did not retain or live for the Lord. Those that did not invite the Lord into their lives for a change. Those that lived in sin, practiced sin, those that were sinners. Those that did not get saved from or out of their sins. Those that did not receive the SALVATION PLAN OF GOD. Those that did as they were grown enough to do and live, how they wanted to. This is their punishment, ETERNAL DAMNATION TO A BURNING HELL OF TORMENTS; THAT NEVER STOPS. IT IS FOREVER AND FOREVER A WORLD WITHOUT END, IS ETERNITY. THOSE THAT ARE USELESS, WASTE. THOSE THAT ARE CONSIDERED TO BE TRASH, TO GOD. RUBBISH, DID NOT PRODUCE RIGHTEOUS FRUITS. THOSE THAT LIVED UNTO THEMSELVES AND WILL DIE FOR WHAT THEY HAVE DONE FOR THEMSELVES AND NOT FOR GOD, BUT LIVED FOR THE devil. Those that did evil and wicked, and evil things to others. Those that lied, cheated and stolen goods, and services and did not repent and ask the Lord into their lives. Those that was not sorry for what they have done, and said to other without remorse or asking forgiveness. Those that served the devil and done his work while on this earth. MUCH IS SAID ABOUT THIS SUBJECT; BUT FOR NOW WE WILL MOVE ON. But JESUS, descended to the lower parts of the earth, to Tae the keys, of death, and to strip satan from the powers that he previously had. To take away from the devil satan that old evil demon, that is forever fallen and part of his punishment will be that he will be fallen on a continual basis thoughtout eternity, without end. But Jesus rose again (he) Jesus ascended up on high to sit on the right hand of the FATHER OF GLORY, representing power and all authority in his awesome and powerful name, sprinkled his sinless blood, on the mercy seat, and pleased the FATHER; TO BE BRUISED, FOR ALL OF OUR SINS: for our redemption, REDEEMING us back in right standing, as at the first as if it has never happened, in the name of JESUS CHRIST; THIS IS A GREAT MYSTERY WITH GOD, JESUS YESHUA AND THE HOLY SPIRIT AS ONE, with separate distinct, manifestations but yet is one Lord One faith and one lordship of Christ.

AS a lamb slain before the foundation of the world, once and for all, sacrificed for the sins of the whole world, for our past, present, and future sins of the whole entire world. He has done it all because he so loved us, not forgetting that HE JESUS DIED AND REDEEMED US ALL FOR THE PLEASING THE FATHER GOD ALMIGHTY BECAUSE OF HIS LOVE In JESUS NAME AND IT IS SO WILL CONTINUE.

I believe in paying tithes Malachi 3: 10

I believe in fasting abstaining from for a period of time to make more room for other things in the spirit so I can grow and be fed in the name of Jesus.

I believe in submitting to Heavenly and earthly leadership.

I believe in the power of prayer and praying in tongues as the spirit of GOD has given the utterance better known as the HOLY SPIRIT.

I believe in repenting of all my sins daily and dying out to my old ways and living a new life through CHRIST Jesus.

I believe in supporting other Ministries with the money, that the Lord has provided for me, finances and other ways of support along with prayers and supplications, and helping out anyway that I can for the cause of JESUS CHRIST.

I believe in GOD'S WORD, His SPIRIT, HIS BLOOD, HIS GIFTS, HIS ANOINTINGS OF ALL KINDS AS WELL AS HIS MANTALS, and his spoken words being taught under the unction of the HOLY SPIRIT WITH FIRE.

I believe in giving in the OFFERING.

I believe in daily devotions reading studying the word of GOD, PRAISING WORSHIPPING, SINGING AND making melody in my heart for the Lord and all the things that he has done and will do for me throughout my life in the name of Jesus and it is true.

I believe in consecrations, all night prayer vigils, shut ins, for the continual seeking the Lord, calling on his name, crying out for his will to be done, in the mighty name of Jesus. Soakings, in GOD's presence with the Saints in meditations, of his words, decrees, and declarations, along with confessions, will help my life in Christ Jesus to gain spiritual ground in the spirit. Waiting on the Lord, for answers and confirmations in the Spirit in the name of Jesus.

I believe in intercessory, and intercessions of prayers. Intercessory and intercessions of prayer is a ministry all by itself. Interceding, standing in the gaps, as a mediator between death and life eternal, for all of mankind.

This comes with passions, desires, a burden, which is a deep stirring of sincerity, desires, and hunger to see the lost saved, those that are in captivity to be set free, and for those that are in any type of bondages, to be broken and destroyed, to stay out of these areas, and to help those that are in trouble; to be set free in the name of Jesus. Meditations, healings of all type's deliverances, casting out demons, which is a fallen spirits, or angels that lost their first estate in heaven, was thrust down to earth.

I believe in being a witness for the Lord in Jesus name.

THIS BELIEVING AND BELIEF TAKES US TO ANOTHER LEVEL AND REALM IN THE SPIRIT.

CHAPTER 7

TRUST IS A TRUE TEST.

What is TRUST?

Trusting, RELYING ON TO LEAN FOR DEPENDENCE. Help, support.

Depending on relying on and in something or someone; leaning
and depending on for support, protection and safety that would
be GODS word and GOD himself, OUR ETERNAL FATHER
IN THE HEAVENLIES; AND HIS final truth that will not
be denied. GOD is truth, and he is the first, & final way truth
and life and the light that gave mankind life and still is.

GOD has given all of that to Jesus, being the way, to be saved, the
truth, to stand on and abide in and speak, and the life to live before all
the world. GOD CREATED EVERYTHING and he knows the hairs on
everyone's head all at the same time, NOW CONSIDER THIS JUST
FOR A MOMENT. GOD CREATED ALL THE PEOPLE in the world;
let's say from Adam to all the people that will be born, after Adam from
his time, in the pass, the presents in which we are now living, and the
future, when we might not be here on earth, but children and people
are still being birth here on the earth, what a thought about how much
our Heavenly Father knows. All of mankind till Heaven and earth
pass away so give or take according to GOD'S word. For the sake of
using an even number 100 BILLION people on the face of the earth,

I was saying from Adam till Jesus comes and take us away into Heaven
for all eternity, GOD CREATED EACH ONE OF THEM, AND HE
KNOWS THE HAIRS ON EACH & EVERYONE OF THEIR HEADS,

they are all numbered, which means they are counted, and he only and alone knows how many, ALL AT THE SAME TIME. While you and I are struggling to keep count of our penny's nickels and dimes.

GOD knows the count of all of our hairs that he has made and created and the hair is still growing, as we read & speak, so my point is; that GOD knows: each and every hair on our heads, being many all at the same time. WHY DO WE HAVE A HARD TIME TRUSTING HIM FOR SOMETHING AS LITTLE AS BELIEVING THAT HIS WORD IS TRUTH?

Trust in the LORD with all thine heart; and lean not unto thine own understanding. In all thy ways acknowledge him, and he shall direct thy paths Proverbs 3:5-6

Trust in *and* rely confidently on the LORD with all your heart and do not rely on your own insight *or* understanding. In all your ways know *and* acknowledge *and* recognize Him, And He will make your paths straight *and* smooth [removing obstacles that block your way. AMP

Psalms 56:4

In GOD I will praise his word, in GOD I have put my trust; I will not fear what flesh can do unto me.

GOD is exalted alone with word, name, in all the world. Our GOD HE REIGNS SUPREME in my life. In GOD HE IS THE FIRST THE ONLY AND THE BEST IN ALL THE WORLD PERIOD.

My trust is leaning on you for everything, that I ever need, Lord you have supplied my food, clothing, a warm shelter, over our heads for me and my family, and all that concerns me through my entire life. So I will not and, I say again I will not, worry about ANYTHING, AT ALL NO MORE ; ANYMORE FOR ANYTHING AND THAT'S MY FINAL ANSWER, IN JESUS, YESHUA NAME, AND IT IS SO.

I REFUSE TO WALK IN ANY TYPE OF FEAR OR FEARS

OR PHOBIAS IN JESUS name.

All fears comes when we do not practice believe, confess and know what He GOD has said to us in his word, what he has spoken to us. We simply bypassed what he has said he will do for us and have taken our own ways and we have hit a brick wall. WE AS PEOPLE LIKE TO PLAY WITH FIRE, this is what the LORD IS SAYING TO ME NOW. Proverbs 6:27 . Can a man or woman take fire into their bosom and not be burned? certainly not they will be burned because they are playing with hot fiery gases and it will burn them severely. When we do not stand read and study confess, decree, and declare what he has spoken to and what he want for us. What has been given to us in a way of his wonderful not guessing, promises that will be fulfilled promises. Fears comes in many shapes forms and fashion types by words, feelings, thoughts and our actions. We certainly and surely do not want to forget about our attitudes that play a big part in what we do and say. It displays, or tells us we are not taking GOD at his word. OUR actions are speaking for us telling us you did not believe what your HEAVENLY FATHERS' WORDS AND PROMISES HAVE TOLD YOU and have told us. SO THIS is WHAT YOU GET IN RETURN FOR WHAT YOU HAVE BELIEVED IN FOR YOUR EITHER REWARD OR CONSEQUENCES. Fears or fear comes when we ourselves try or tries to do something on our own with out his help. The troubles comes and we then want to invite the Lord into our situations after we have made a mess of things. We want the Lord GOD to fix our chaos, turmoil or knotts, entanglements and so forth. What we need to do is too seek the Lord and ask seek and knock to find out what it is that the Lord our GOD, AND HEAVENLY FATHER want me to do or direction he desires for me to take. Instead, we set off on a course of collision and when that crash comes then we are crying, hurt emotionally and sometimes physically as well depending. Fear is first of all comes from the devil himself. When we are not confidence within what has been given or said to us. Fear comes in to distort sidetrack and bring with it distractions. Before we know we have opened a door or window of opportunity to invite the enemy in and he IS HAVING A FIELD DAY. A FIELD DAY IS A MILITARY TERM THAT SIMPLY MEANS HE CLEANS AND CLEAR OUT EVERYTHING. Nothing left of any good. Your have been ROBBED of your goods. You have allowed the thief to come, and he has stolen everything and now we are sad, hurt confused and blaming someone else for the actions we have made prior to this. Not counting up the cost of our decisions, through taking on the spirit of fear. The spirit of fear belongs to the devil and we have stolen the spirit of fear and also have trespassed on the devils property and allowed something that he possessed, now we have taken ownership of that thing. This is what we call a theif and a robber.

I BIND AND RESTRAIN ALL FEARS THAT TRY TO COME INTO MY LIFE THROUGH MY THINKING, SUGGESTIONS, IDEAS OR EVEN MY ACTIONS.

I WALK BY FAITH AND NOT FEARS OF ANY KIND IN JESUS NAME, AND IT IS SO.

NO ONE CAN DO NOTHING TO ME WHEN I'M DOING WHAT I AM SUPPOSED TO BE DOING; BEING SOBERMINDED, WATCHFUL, ALERT ON GUARD, AND ATTENTIVE TO MY ASSIGNMENT IN JESUS NAME.

I DON'T WALK IN ANY TYPE OF NEGATIVE THOUGHTS OR MINDSETS THAT ARE NOT WRITTEN IN THE WORD OF GOD;

I WILL NOT ALLOW BAD THOUGHTS, TO BE PLANTED IN MY MIND OF THOUGHTS, THAT WILL HELP ME BUT HURT ME, AND I'M NOT ALLOWING ANYTHING TO CAUSE ME TO BE PERSUADED ANY OTHER WAY OTHER, THAN WHAT GOD'S WORD HAS GIVEN, SPOKEN, INSTRUCTED ME, OR INFORMED THAT I SHOULD OR SHOULD NOT DO; SO I COMPLY WITH ALL OF HIS WAYS AND HIS WORDS IN JESUS NAME, AND IT IS SO.

Proverbs 30:5

Every word of GOD is pure: he is a shield unto them that put their trust in him.

GODS WORD IS A SHIELD FOR ME, SO I'M LEANING ON HIS EVERLASTING ARM AND STRENGTH.

Psalms 18:30

As for GOD, his way is perfect: the word of the LORD is tried: he is a buckler to all those that trust in him.

GOD IS MY PROTECTOR, THE WATCHER OF MY SOUL
AND I TRUST IN HIM AT ALL TIMES NEVER DOUBT HIS
ABILITIES, STRENGTH AND POWER IN JESUS NAME.

2 Samuel 22:31

As for GOD, his way is perfect; the word of the LORD is
tried: he is a buckler to all of them that trust in him.

I TRUST IN HIM AT ALL TIMES EACH AND EVERYDAY IN ALL
SITUATIONS THAT I MAY ENCOUNTER FROM TIME TO TIME,
SO THEREFORE MY FULL TRUST IS IN MY LORDS CARE,
CONCERNS, BLESSINGS FOR MY LIFE AND HIS DECISIONS
THAT HE BRINGS ME THROUGH IN JESUS NAME.

Psalms 119:42

So shall I have wherewith to answer him that
reproached me: for I trust in thy word.

LORD JESUS, I TRUST IN YOUR WORD AND ON YOUR WORD TO
PERFORM ALL THAT IS NEEDED IN MY LIFE IN JESUS NAME.

1 Thessalonians 2:13

For this cause also thank we GOD without ceasing, because, when
ye received the word of GOD which ye heard of us, ye received it not
as the word of men, but as it is in truth, the word of GOD, which
effectually worketh also in you that believe. GRACIOUS FATHER
THANK YOU THAT YOUR WORD OF POWER IS WORKING
FOR ME EVERYDAY AND NIGHT IN JESUS NAME.

But it is good for me to draw near to GOD: I have put my
trust in the Lord GOD, that I may declare all thy works.

I AM AND CONTINUE TO DRAW NEAR TO THE LORD, FOR
ALL THAT HE HAS FOR ME. SO THAT I DECLARE ALL THE
WORKS OF MY HANDS TO BE SUCCESSFUL IN JESUS NAME.

Psalms 16:1 Preserve me, O GOD: for in thee do I put my trust.

THANK YOU, MY LORD, FOR PRESERVING ME THROUGH MY TRIALS AND TEST AND ANY TRIBULATIONS THAT I HAVE GONE THROUGH IN VARIOUS TIMES IN JESUS NAME.

2 Corinthians 3:4

And such trust have we through Christ to GOD-ward:

1 Thessalonians 2:4

But as we were allowed of GOD to be put in trust with the gospel, even so we speak; not as pleasing men, but GOD, which trieth our hearts.

I SIMPLY TRUST IN YOU LORD WITH ALL MY HEART, AND PLEASING TO YOU IS MY DESIRES TOWARD YOU IN ALL THINGS.

Psalms 52:8

But I am like a green olive tree in the house of GOD: I trust in the mercy of God for ever and ever. HEAVENLY FATHER I TRUST IN YOUR MERCY AND GRACE FOR EVER IN JESUS NAME.

Psalms 56:11

In GOD have I put my trust: I will not be afraid what man can do unto me. (So, I will not allow anyone to put me in any type of fears, phobias, which is fears, terrors and dreads or in a panic mode of any kind in the name of Jesus.)

I AM NOT AFRAID BECAUSE MY TRUST IN TRULY IN GOD AND HIS POWERFUL WORDS OF COMFORT.

John 1:1

In the beginning was the Word, and the Word was with GOD, and the Word was GOD.

I trust his word from the beginning and will follow it until the end in Jesus name.

Psalms 91:2

I will say of the LORD, He is my refuge and my fortress: my GOD; in him will I trust.

Thank you, Lord, for being my fortress a hedge of protection around me, a refuge which is a safe place to dwell in knowing that I am secure safe and well taking care of in the mighty name of Jesus.
I receive your level of trust in the name of Jesus, it is so.

Psalms 62:8

Trust in him at all times; ye people, pour out your
heart before him: GOD is a refuge for us.

I trust in at all times; and will get this in my memory, not to forget ever that you are with me always even throughout the ends of the earth.

Psalms 141:8

But mine eyes are unto thee, O GOD the Lord: in
thee is my trust; leave not my soul destitute.

2 Corinthians 2:17

For we are not as many, which corrupt the word of GOD: but as of sincerity, but as of GOD, in the sight of GOD speak we in Christ

Psalms 25:2

O my GOD, I trust in thee: let me not be ashamed,
let not mine enemies triumph over me.

Psalms 20:7

Some trust in chariots, and some in horses: but we will
remember the name of the LORD our GOD.

1 Timothy 4:10

For therefore we both labour and suffer reproach, because we trust in the living GOD, who is the Saviour of all men, specially of those that believe.

Psalms 71:5

For thou art my hope, O Lord GOD: thou art my trust from my youth.

Psalms 36:7

How excellent is thy lovingkindness, O GOD! therefore the
children of men put their trust under the shadow of thy wings

Isaiah 12:2

Behold, GOD is my salvation; I will trust, and not be afraid: for the LORD
JEHOVAH is my strength and my song; he also is become my salvation.

2 Samuel 22:3

The GOD of my rock; in him will I trust: he is my shield,
and the horn of my salvation, my high tower, and my
refuge, my saviour; thou savest me from violence.

(AMP)

Hear this, all peoples; Listen carefully, all inhabitants of the world,

He will not fear bad news; His heart is steadfast, **trusting**
[confidently relying on and believing] in the LORD.

The reverent fear of the LORD worshiping, obeying, serving,
and **trusting** Him with awe-filled respect prolongs one's
life, But the years of the wicked will be shortened.

Charm *and* grace are deceptive, and superficial beauty is vain, but a
woman who fears the LORD reverently worshiping, obeying, serving,
and **trusting** Him with awe-filled respect], she shall be praised.

When the people [instead of **trusting** God] say to you, "Consult
the mediums [who try to talk to the dead] and the soothsayers who
chirp *and* whisper and mutter," should not a people consult their
GOD? *Should they consult* the dead-on behalf of the living?

"Behold, you are **trusting** in deceptive *and*
useless words that bring no benefit.

Immediately they left their nets and followed Him [becoming His
disciples, believing and **trusting** in Him and following His example].

Immediately they left the boat and their father, and followed Him [becoming His disciples, believing and **trusting** in Him and following His example].

And blessed [joyful, favored by GOD] is he who does not take offense at Me [accepting Me as the Messiah and **trusting** confidently in My message of salvation].

and said, "I assure you *and* most solemnly say to you, unless you repent [that is, change your inner self—your old way of thinking, live changed lives] and become like children [**trusting**, humble, and forgiving], you will never enter the kingdom of heaven.

Jesus answered him, "If you wish to be perfect [that is, have the spiritual maturity that accompanies godly, with no moral or ethical deficiencies], go and sell what you have and give [the money] to the poor, and you will have treasure in heaven; and come, follow Me [becoming My disciple, believing and **trusting** in Me and walking the same path of life that I walk]."

Immediately they left their nets and followed Him [becoming His disciples, believing and **trusting** in Him and following His example].

Immediately Jesus called to them; and they left their father Zebedee in the boat with the hired workers, and went away to follow Him [becoming His disciples, believing and **trusting** in Him and following His example].

As He was passing by, He saw Levi (Matthew) the son of Alphaeus sitting in the tax collector's booth, and He said to him, "Follow Me [as My disciple, accepting Me as your Master and Teacher and walking the same path of life that I walk]." And he got up and followed Him [becoming His disciple, believing and **trusting** in Him and following His example].

Looking at him, Jesus felt a love high regard, compassion) for him, and He said to him, "You lack one thing: go and sell all your property and give the money to the poor, and you will have [abundant] treasure in heaven; and come, follow Me becoming My disciple, believing and **trusting** in Me and walking the same path of life that I walk."

After they had brought their boats to land, they left everything and followed Him [becoming His disciples, believing and **trusting** in Him and following His example].

When Jesus heard this, He said to him, "You still lack one thing; sell everything that you have and distribute the money to the poor, and you will have abundant treasure in heaven; and come, follow Me becoming My disciple, believing and **trusting** in Me and walking the same path of life that I walk."

but these have been written so that you may believe [with a deep, abiding trust] that Jesus is the Christ (the Messiah, the Anointed), the Son of GOD; and that by believing and **trusting** in and relying on Him, you may have life in His name.

I have been crucified with Christ [that is, in Him I have shared His crucifixion]; it is no longer I who live, but Christ lives in me. The *life* I now live in the body I live by faith [by adhering to, relying on, and completely **trusting**] in the Son of God, who loved me and gave Himself up for me.

But My righteous one the one justified by faith shall live by faith [respecting man's relationship to God and **trusting** And if he draws back [shrinking in fear], My soul has no delight in him.

Blessed (happy, prosperous, to be admired) are those who wash their robes [in the blood of Christ by believing and **trusting** in Him—the righteous who do His commandments], so that they may have the right to the tree of life, and may enter by the gates into the city.

CHAPTER 8

PRAYERS & CONFESSIONS WILL IGNITE YOUR DESIRES.

What is PRAYER?

It's communicating, talking to GOD our Heavenly Father with passion for the one (we) I LOVE, enjoying spending time that's quality and Intimate spilling out our heart's thoughts and ideals, waiting to hear him speak to us about others as well as ourselves for various things we may need at the time.

Seeking His wonderful face for the things in ministry, family, and so on, the list is ENDLESS it also establishes a long loving, and living relationship while in his awesome presence, with thanksgiving, praise, WORSHIPPING Him Adoring HIM (GOD) JESUS AND THE HOLY SPIRIT and all that he has done, speaking to us, saying to us and will do for us, in the PAST, PRESENT, & FUTURE, concerning our destinies.

PRAYER IS SPENDING Quality time with the Lord just enjoying all his goodness AWESOMENESS, his Graciousness, the since of SECURITY, SAFETYNESS, PROTECTION. ALL of GOD'S ETERNAL BLESSINGS; THAT COMES with being ENGULFED, BY HIS ETERNAL PRESENTS, GLORY BRIGHTNESS, FRAGRANCE, SPIRIT, ENERGIES, UNLOADING ALL OF OUR CARES, UPON OUR HEAVENLY FATHER; THAT LOVE US WITH AN AGAPE; UNCONDITIONAL LOVE, AS OUR HEAVENLY FATHER, WATCHING OVER us DAY & NIGHT as his children, sons of GOD, Ambassadors of Christ while on this earth.

THE LORD'S PRAYER.

ST MATTHEWS 6:9-13

[9] After this manner therefore pray ye: Our Father
which art in heaven, Hallowed be thy name.

[10] Thy kingdom come, Thy will be done
in earth, as it is in heaven.

[11] Give us this day our daily bread.

[12] And forgive us our debts, as we forgive our debtors.

[13] And lead us not into temptation, but deliver
us from evil: For thine is the kingdom, and the
power, and the glory, forever. Amen.

GRACIOUS AND HEAVENLY

FATHER IN THE ONLY POWERFUL NAME ABOVE EVERY
OTHER NAME; IN HEAVEN AND ON EARTH IN THE NAME
OF JESUS. THANK YOU FOR ALL OF YOUR MERCY, GRACE,
FAVOR, LOVE, and UNDERSTANDING. ALL THE THINGS YOU
HAVE GIVEN us I just want to say THANK YOU FOR WATCHING
OVER us BOTH DAY AND NIGHT. ALL THE TIME. YOU NEVER
SLEEP NOR SLUMBER OR GET TIRED, WEARY OF TAKING
CARE AND HEARING YOUR CHILDREN'S CRIES. Thank you
for hearing our PRAYERS COMING UP BEFORE YOU ALL THE
TIME. THANK YOU FOR SUPPLYING ALL OF OUR DAILY
NEEDS THROUGHOUT THE DAY AND ALL THE TIME WHILE
ON THIS EARTH YOU HAVE PLANTED us IN AND CREATED
us TO DO AND TO BE AS YOUR CHILDREN IN JESUS NAME.

As we all come before Your HEAVENLY presence, we're asking
you to please forgive us for all of our transgressions and trespasses
against your laws rules regulations statutes commandments and
ordinance's _(decrees orders and rules to go by or follow)_. Please

forgive us for all of our sins that we know to do right but for some reason failed to do so, as well as omitting things that we should have paid attention to and give more time effort and heart passion and desire to help out and support in the mighty name of Jesus.

TRUSTING IN THE LORD

11 In the Lord put I my trust: how say ye to my
soul, Flee as a bird to your mountain?

[2] For, lo, the wicked bend their bow, they make ready their arrow upon the string, that they may privily shoot at the upright in heart.

[3] If the foundations be destroyed, what can the righteous do?

[4] The Lord is in his holy temple, the Lord's throne is in heaven: his eyes behold, his eyelids try, the children of men.

[5] The Lord trieth the righteous: but the wicked and him that loveth violence his soul hateth.

[6] Upon the wicked he shall rain snares, fire and brimstone, and an horrible tempest: this shall be the portion of their cup.

[7] For the righteous Lord loveth righteousness; his countenance doth behold the upright.

Repetitive speaking brings breakthrough

Daily CONFESSIONS

THIS INFORMATION IS TO BE REPEATED FOR STRENGTH & ENCOURAGEMENT.

What are confessions and how can we apply it to our lives? & the RESULTS THAT WILL STEM, AND REAP, ALL THAT WE HAVE PLANTED TO RECEIVE A HARVEST.

It Means to own up to something, come out with the truth, declare the word as truth: a state of being upfront, decreeing what is right and truth, affirmations that gives the person strength, to move forward in his or her life. The power to strengthen one's personality, soul mind and thoughts, in return it will strengthen one's actions, and brings about good and great habits,in acknowledging with our mouths, speaking out what is right & TRUTH. Expressing the living truth that will set you free.

Restore, recover and revive your character, enhancing your personality. When we begin to confess the truth and believe what we're saying, and know it to be one hundred percent facts ; authentic, true, genuine, reliable, that we believe it so much so, that there is no doubts, or unbelief whatsoever, due to the experiences previously had and continue to have that's without questions or any other disputes.

Confessions of our faith is just that no second thoughts about this bonifide truth, that were walking in each and every day, of our lives because this is our lifeline of rescues, supplies, surplus and the likes. So when we begin to say a phrase, scriptures, that has life in it, and we really become to believe, what we're saying it; becomes a strength to our spirit, soul and eventually manifest in our bodies.

That's what breakthroughs are all about, repeatedly saying something that we really truly believe in and stick with it, not wavering whatsoever. It becomes like a muscle that gains strength and it becomes part of our lives,this is what constitute a breakthrough doing something over and over again, until it gets in the fibers of your soul and spirit to a point ; it becomes automatic in nature and doing it without thinking about it that's what breakthroughs are all about and seeing, feeling observing, sensing change that will get others attention asking questions.

the TRUTH IN THE NAME OF JESUS.

FAITH CONFESSIONS.

I CONFESS THAT I AM WHOLE, COMPLETE IN HIM JESUS.

Colossians 2:10

I confess that I am forgiven of all my sins, and cleansed by the blood of Jesus. 1 John 1:7 read it at your leisure.

I confess that I am free and liberated through Christ Jesus St John 8:36

I confess that I am cleansed, washed, and redeemed
with the precious blood of Jesus 1 Peter 1:18-19

I confess that I am rich, prosperous, healthy,
wealthy, in the name of Jesus.

I confess that I am disciple of Christ a follower when I continue
to do as I am instructed by the HOLY SPIRIT in Jesus name . St
John 8:31-32 his word also makes me free by knowing the truth.

THE 5 G FUNCTIONS IN THE BODY OF CHRIST,

BETTER KNOWN AS THE 5G NETWORK OF GOD.

I confess that I am an Apostle, of GOD sent out by his directions
and called to Govern the body of Christ. Bringing order where its
needed. Ordained and sanctioned by the SPIRIT of GOD, to bring
spiritual governing Teachings with the word of GOD, order, growth
and maturity to the house and the body of Christ in Jesus name.

I confess that I am a Prophet of GOD, hearing and speaking
whatsoever he speaks to me to give to the people. We that are
prophets are sent to Guide the Saints whether they are in the body
or in the nations around the world, in the mighty name of Jesus, to
build, exhort, encourage, and bring comfort in the name of Jesus.

APOSTLE'S & PROPHETS ARE NOT ELECTED IN THE BODY
OF CHRIST BY MAN BUT, CALLED BY GOD ALMIGHTY,

THEREFORE NO ONE BUT GOD CAN SIT THEM DOWN OR
DEAL WITH THEM AS HE SEES FIT. BUT GOD CAN SEND
OTHER APOSTLES AND PROPHETS TO TAKE CARE OF
HIS WORK AND TO DO WHATEVER IS NECESSARY.

I confess that I am a Evangelist of GOD, to be one that, has the ability, to Gather in the souls all for the cause of Christ Jesus, the reason he has died for all of mankind.

I confess that I am a Pastor of the Gospel of Christ Jesus sent to Guard the sheep, from the hirlings, foxes, wolves not sparing the flocks of GOD, not caring at all whatsoever who he destroys and take to hell for eternity.

I confess that I am a Teacher of the Gospel of Christ Jesus to Ground the people of GOD with his divine words of truth, teachings, foundational basics, apostolic prophetic sound doctrine that will feed, the flocks of GOD with the word to nourish and build, causing growth, duplication and sound in their walk. To empower the people, to be able to fight and stand against the wiles of the devils in the mighty name of Jesus.

— HOW TO ACTIVATE THE PROMISES OF GOD;

Faith is believing with your heart or your (spirit) HEART & SPIRIT are interchangeable) and confessing with your mouth the promises of GOD as you are led by the Holy Spirit. Faith is an act that brings forth (ACTIONS, APPLICATIONS, THINGS THAT MUST BE APPLIED TO WHAT GODS WORD HAS OR WILL SAY TO OUR SPIRIT). Faith acts on the promises until you are completely healed. Keep calling healing into your soul and body until your healing is complete. Always resist the devil by rebuking and resisting the symptoms and the disease in the name of Jesus until they are gone. Also remembering that is might be a spirit attached to a sickness or a disease, so we must cast out the demon as well to be totally healed.

So all that we do is by faith, as the word of GOD says, "But without faith it is impossible to please him: for he that cometh to GOD must believe that he is, and that he is a rewarder of them that diligently seek him. Praying in tongues enables the Holy Spirit to minister to our human spirit and heart through edification and the revealing of mysteries regarding the plan of GOD. Meditation on the Word increases our capacity for faith. It keeps us centered on the Word of GOD. And speaking the Word in confession, releases the power and anointing of God into the trouble spots of our lives.

It brings the answer to our petitions. Private worship will show us how much GOD loves us, and how to live and walk in His glory, and we will learn how to love GOD. I am to hold fast to my confession of the absolute integrity of the Bible. The Word of GOD is anointed. Faith does not produce healing; rather, it lays hold of the healing GOD has already provided.

I am to hold fast to my confession of the New Creation, of receiving the Life and Nature of GOD. I am to hold fast to the confession that GOD is the strength of my life. I am to hold fast to the confession that "Surely, He Jesus bare my sicknesses and carried my diseases, and that by His stripes I am healed"). These diseases are not mine, therefore I do not claim them, as if I own them. We as the Sons of GOD, need to stop claiming what is not ours. Start claiming what GOD said that belongs to us, to me to you and to the whole body of Christ in the awesome name of Yeshua. The anointing is on the Word of GOD to bring it to pass. Faith holds fast to the confession of the Word.

To receive means you take it, hold on to, claim it to be what you have been asking the Lord for, and most of all apply it to your lives. The words, that we speak, is power to perform whatever we may need to do, for us with believing, holds, fast to the confession of our faith until physical evidences manifest. This is what faith, is all about. Not doubting and unbelief, or wavering, or just do not simply believe it will happen.

I hold fast to my confession that GOD's Word is true, that by His stripes, I am already healed. That My GOD does supply all my needs. Jesus taught us an undeniable Biblical principle that things obey words. I will study the Word until I know what my rights are, and then hold fast to them with my confession.

I will stand by my confession through thick and thin, through good report and evil.

I know that my confession is according to the Word.

The substance from which our world is made is influenced and manifested by words.

I will hold fast to my confession in the face of apparent defeat. Ambassadors, & Saints is called "the Great Confession.

Confession is affirming something that I believe. It is testifying of something that I know. It is witnessing for a truth that I have embraced.

Confession holds a very, very large place in THE BODY OF CHRIST, THE CHURCH OF THE LIVING GOD. Jesus planned that this great Life and Love should be given to the world through testimony, that is, through the confession of our lips.

Our confession centers around several things:

first, what GOD in Christ has wrought, or worked out for us.

Second, what GOD through the Word and the Spirit has wrought, worked out, or brought out, in us.

Third, what we are to the Father in Christ. And last of all, what GOD can do through us, or what the Word will do in our lips.

"Wherefore if any man is in Christ, he is a new creation.

I am a New Creation created in Christ Jesus with the life of GOD, the nature of GOD, and the ability of GOD in me.

"If GOD be for us, who can be against us.

"Ye are of GOD, my little children, and have overcome them: because greater is He that is in you, than he that is in the world."

GOD is in me now; the Master of creation is in me!

I am filled with joy and victory because GOD my Father
has taken me over; He is fighting my battles.

I confess Jesus as my Lord, and I possess salvation. I confess
"by His (Jesus') stripes I am healed and I possess healing.

I confess "the Son has made me free" and I possess absolute freedom.

I confess "the love of God is shed abroad in my heart by the
Holy Spirit and I possess the ability to love everyone.

I am filled with the love of GOD and it flows through me continually.

I confess "the righteous are bold as a lion" and I possess
lion-hearted boldness in spiritual warfare.

I command all parasites to die and come out of me in the name of Jesus.

I confess "He will never leave me nor forsake me", and I
possess the presence of GOD each step I take. The Kingdom
of GOD lives in my spirit! I confess "I am the redeemed of
the Lord". I possess redemption benefits every day.

I confess "the anointing of the Holy One abideth in me" and
I possess yoke destroying results by this anointing.

I confess "in the Name of Jesus I can cast out devils and
I possess dynamic deliverances as a devil-master.

I confess "I lay my hands on the sick and they shall recover
and I possess positive healings for the oppressed...

I confess "I am a branch of the Living Vine, and
I possess Jesus' life wherever I go.

I confess "I am the righteousness of GOD in Christ"
and I possess the ability to stand freely in GOD's holy
presence, and in satan's presence as a victor!

I confess "I am a temple of the living GOD and I possess
GOD dwelling in me, and walking in me!

I confess "my GOD shall supply all my need" and I possess the
supply of every need. My words are the coins in the Kingdom

of Faith. My words snare me and hold me captive or they set me free and become powerful in the lives of others. It is what I confess with my lips that really dominates my inner being.

I confess that by Jesus' stripes I am healed; I hold fast to my confession and no disease can stand before me. The atoms in my soul and body know what I believe, hear what I say, and behave accordingly! It is when I confess the Word of GOD, and hold fast to my confession that I will see my deliverance. Our words beget faith or doubt in others. Our lips become the means of transportation of GODs deliverance from heaven to man's needs here on earth, We use GOD's Word.

I confess, "For whosoever shall call upon the name of the Lord shall be saved" and I possess know-so salvation for I have called upon the name of the Lord Jesus.

I confess, "The Lord shall preserve me from all evil" and I possess preservation from all forms of evil...

I confess, "Blessed are the pure in heart: for they shall see GOD" (and I possess the assurance I shall see GOD for the blood of Jesus has made me pure in heart.

I confess, "The Lord will give strength unto His people; the Lord will bless His people with peace" and I possess daily strength and an abundance of peace. I confess, "Blessed be the Lord, who daily loaded us with benefits", and I possess a life daily loaded with the benefits of the Lord.

I confess, "I am the light of the world: he that followed Me shall not walk in darkness, but shall have the light of life", and I possess light upon life's pathway for I am following Jesus.

I confess, "And GOD is able to make all grace abound toward you; that ye, always having all sufficiency in all things may abound to every good work and I possess all grace, abounding grace saving grace, healing grace, baptizing grace, all-sufficient grace.

I confess, "For with GOD nothing shall be impossible" and I possess impossibilities becoming realities, for I am linked up with GOD by divine birth.

I confess, "I will pour out of my Spirit upon all flesh" and I possess the Spirit out-poured upon my life daily, continually in the name of Jesus.

I confess, "As far as the east is from the west, so far hath He removed our transgressions from us"). and I possess the assurance that my sins are removed far from me in the name of Jesus, hallelujah!

Jesus walked in the light of His confession. Jesus was what He confessed. Faith follows in the footprints of our confession.

Our confession builds the road over which faith hauls its mighty cargo.

I have to understand that I will never rise above my confession.

I will never enjoy the riches of grace (GOD's ability in me) until I confess them My confession of what Jesus is, what Jesus has done for me and what I am in Jesus, always precedes Jesus' revelation of Himself.

Salvation follows confession. "For if thou shalt confess with thy mouth Jesus as Lord." Receiving the Holy Spirit follows confession.

Our healing follows our confession. I receive the baptism of the Holy Spirit, with the evidence of speaking in other tongues, as the Spirit gives me the utterance in the name of Jesus.

I will speak and pray in tongues every day, to edify me and build up my faith (Jude 20) in the name of Jesus.

I am filled with the power and anointing of the Holy Spirit.

Some people have to "hold fast to their confession" in the face of apparent defeat. They refuse to give in to sense evidences. Your confession is the thing that challenges the world. Saints and Sons of GOD is the great confession. I possess continual guidance for I confess "The Lord shall guide thee [me] continually.

I possess eternal life for I confess "My sheep hear my voice and I give them eternal life I possess the peace of GOD for I confess "The peace of GOD which passed all understanding, shall keep OUR hearts and minds through Christ Jesus our Lord.

I possess freedom from fear for I confess "I the Lord thy GOD will hold thy right hand, saying unto thee, fear not.

I possess bountiful blessings financially for I confess "He which soweth bountifully shall reap also bountifully".

I possess supernatural help in every situation for I confess "My help cometh from the Lord, which made heaven and earth.

I possess peace with my enemies for I confess "When a man's ways please the Lord, He maketh even his enemies to be at peace with him, the Key to solving every problem: In order to shrink the problem, you have to magnify the answer—magnify the Word, Jesus, for he is the answers for all the world today above, him there is no other for Jesus is the WAY. YES.

I possess wholesome, sound sleep at night for I confess "He giveth His beloved sleep".

I possess the assurance my labor in the Lord is fruitful for I confess "Forasmuch as ye know that your labour is not in vain in the Lord."

I possess as a faith man abounding blessing, for I confess "A faithful man shall abound with blessings.

I possess strength for my day for I confess "As thy days, so shall thy strength be".

I possess special honor from my Father for I confess "If any man serves Me, him will my Father honour" the Apostle and High Priest [Jesus] of our confession".

I confess the Word of GOD and Jesus as my High Priest until my confession is brought into manifestation.

I confess the promises from the Word of GOD in the name of Jesus. Ambassadores of Christ is called our confession, and in our confessions, we confess the word of GOD is true and we believe it and stand on it and meditate in his powerful words that gives us and brings deliverance in Jesus name. He tells us to "hold fast our confession.". Living a life of faith, confessing his words. Being true to who he called us to be in before the foundations of the world is a confession.

It is our open confession of what we are in Christ, of what Christ is in us.

Our faith is gauged by our confession.

We never believe beyond our confession. "It is not I that live, but Christ lived in me; and the life which I now live in the flesh, I live by the faith of the Son of GOD who loved me and gave Himself for me".

I confess Jesus lives in me! And the life I now live,
I live by the faith of the Son of GOD.

It is His victorious faith by which I really live. I confess that "Greater is He that is within me, than he that is in the world."

The Kingdom of GOD lives in my spirit.

I confess that "GOD hath not given me the spirit of fear,
but of power, and of love, and of a sound mind".

I have the spirit of power, of love and of a
sound mind in the name of Jesus.

I acknowledge that within me is liberty, for
the Holy Spirit lives in my spirit.

"Now the Lord is that Spirit, and where the
Spirit of the Lord is, there is liberty.

I confess that "I can lay my hands on the sick and they shall recover.

I realize the effect of my spoken word on my
own heart and on my adversary.

No Word from GOD is void of His power.

The Word of GOD has the power residing within it to bring
it to pass if I will speak and confess it continually.

GOD watches over His Word to perform it.

GOD our Father has divinely instructed us to "hold fast to
our confession. "Let us hold fast the confession of our faith
without wavering: for He is faithful that promised.

I will hold fast to my confession of faith the Word without wavering, until I am completely healed and set free in the name of Jesus. To hold fast, to my confession is to say what GOD has said over and over until the thing desired in my heart and promised in the Word is fully manifested, which is seen and brought to pass.

There's no such thing as possession without confession.
This is the procedure for receiving your healing.

When we discover our rights in Christ, we are to affirm these things constantly. Testify to them, Witness to these gigantic true facts. "The communication of thy faith becomes effectual by the acknowledging of every good thing which is in you in Christ Jesus" (Philemon 6).

If you don't acknowledge what is sealed in your spirit it will never manifest itself in your soul and body.

Affirmations of truth (GOD's Word) are to ring from our lips constantly.

The penalty for wavering in our confession is that we deny ourselves of GOD's Promise, blessings and the performance of it.

"But let him ask in faith, nothing wavering.

GOD is who He says He is.

I am who GOD says I am.

GOD can do what He says He can do.

I can do what GOD says I can do.

GOD has what He says He has.

I have what GOD says I have.

To confess that I am an actual New Creation created in Christ Jesus, that I am a partaker of the very nature and life of GOD.

I don't confess it once, but daily affirming my relationship to Him (GOD, Jesus, Holy Spirit), confessing my Righteousness, my ability to stand in His presence without the sense of guilt or inferiority.

I confess that GOD my Father allowed these, things to happen to Jesus, so that we by the licks with the whips of cords, represents, stripes to wipe away our sins, which is things our fathers have done to go against the laws and commandments of GOD. They have transgressed or went against, or ignored his commandments and brought on us the sins throughout the whole world. We are referring to what Adam did In the garden of Eden. Eating the forbidden fruit, caused the world to be taking over by, sin and death, and also corruption at that time lucifer which is an fallen angel from heaven thrusted down like lightning from GOD, for his rebellion and disobedience. Ruled and reign on earth. Adam lost his place and his authority to lucifer, satan,

the devil. Authority to satan the devil started all this mess that we are experiencing in our lifetime and world, that satan has no right to put, any sicknesses or diseases on us, and that, "by His (Jesus) stripes we are healed.

This is why confession is so powerful, saying and getting what GOD, and Jesus, the Holy Spirit has done for us alone with his angels watching over us day and night.

I live in the new realm above the senses, so I hold fast to my confession that I am what the Word says I am.

The power that is in me is the Holy Spirit; and I know that spiritual forces are greater than the forces in the sense realm. I am born into GOD's royal family.

I am a son/daughter of GOD.

GOD has created me now in Christ Jesus

. He has put new life into me.

I have been born from above, born of the Spirit. My spirit is sealed by the Holy Spirit, OF PROMISE.

I am in Christ, and in Christ I have been granted new life.

The old life is gone.

I am a citizen of a new kingdom. My citizenship is in Heaven.

My name is written in the, LAMBS Book of Life.

I am a new creation in Christ.

Created by GOD, His own workmanship.

GOD is now working within me both to will and do His own good pleasure.

GOD is building me up! Making me strong in faith.
How is He doing this? By His own Word!

I am the righteousness of GOD in Christ".

Jesus made me righteous through His blood. GOD has
made me righteous with His own righteousness.

I stand before Him with no sense of unworthiness.

I am complete in Christ.

I am redeemed from the kingdom of darkness and I have
been translated into the Kingdom of GOD's dear Son.

I have been delivered from sickness, fear, poverty, and failure
through the blood of Jesus. I say it boldly, "Goodbye sickness,
goodbye fear, goodbye lack, goodbye weakness. I am free!

I am an heir of GOD and a joint heir with Jesus Christ.

I am blessed with every spiritual blessing in
the heavenly places in Christ Jesus.

My Father loves me as He loved the Lord Jesus.

He loves me with an everlasting love.

Jesus said, "I am the vine and ye are the branches. The
same life, love, joy, peace, power, wisdom, and ability that
flows in the Vine (Jesus) flows into the branch (me).

Wherever I, the branch goes, the Vine-life flows! I have
the life of GOD in my mortal body right now.

I have what GOD says I have.

I can do what GOD says I can do.

I am what GOD says I am.

I confess that I have the money before it has arrived.

I confess perfect healing while pain is still in the body.

I rebuke and resist symptoms while they are still in my body.

I confess victory under all circumstances.

The Word is now, and I have faith now.

The Word is true in my case.

My heart acts and that will drive my lips to confess the Word of GOD.

A fearless confession comes from a Word-ruled heart.

My heart is filled with the power and anointing of GOD my Father in the name of Jesus. Always remember (heart and spirit is the same.)

When we know that the Word is GOD speaking to us now, it is not difficult to act upon it.

The Word is settled in my heart and no Word from GOD is void of fulfillment.

The Word has become more real to me than any word man has ever spoken.

A hesitant confession is a forerunner of failure.

A joyful confession a forerunner of victory.

When we fearlessly act upon the Word and joyfully cast our every care on Jesus, victory is as sure as the rising of the sun.

To agree with GOD is to say the same thing God says in His Word about salvation, healing, deliverance, peace, Holy Spirit, answer to prayer, and an overcoming life.

I agree with God that I am who GOD says I am: His heaven-born child.

A new creature in Christ.

More than a conqueror through Christ.

I disagree with the devil who tells me I am "no-good, a failure, and a weakling that I am going under.

"I AGREE with GOD and disagree with the devil!

I agree with GOD that I have what He says I have: His Name, His nature, His power, His authority, His love.

I agree that I have what GOD says—in His Word—that I have! I have the ability to do what GOD says I can do: witness with power, cast out demons, and minister His healing power.

"I can do all things through Christ.

I can do what GOD says—in His Book—that I can do.

It is the "confession of faith" that is my victory.

Daily I walk with GOD by agreeing with GOD my Father and His Word. Faith talks about the ability of the Father that is mine, and fills my lips with praise for answers to prayers that I have asked.

I keep my confession positive and in line with the Word of GOD.

I study about what I am in Christ and then confess it boldly.

Faith will demand the impossible.

Faith is never for the possible, but always for the thing that is out of human reasoning.

It is GOD who is at work with us, in us, and for us.

Faith refuses to take counsel with fear or to entertain a doubt.

By faith I hold fast to my confession and the Word was made good. By faith I confess my dominion over disease in Jesus' name.

I have authority over sickness and disease in the name of Jesus, and I command it to leave my soul and body every time it attacks me.

Never be frightened by any condition no matter how forbidding, how impossible the case may be.

Never give up. A born-again believer will always win in the game of life.

I cannot be defeated because of Jesus.

You know and confess; you and GOD are masters of the situation.

I know I'll never for a moment lose my confession of
my supremacy over the works of the adversary.

These diseases and calamity are not of GOD.

It has but one source, satan. I cast it out in the name of Jesus.
Come out of me and don't return in the name of Jesus.

Keep commanding your rights continually and take authority
over the disease and symptoms with the name of Jesus and
cast them out. Faith says in Jesus' Name, I am master.

I have taken Jesus' place; I am acting in His stead.

The name Jesus ; JESUS is above every name in the universe.

All mountains and problems have names but the name of
Jesus trumps their names, and you can move them out of your
life with that name that is above every name, Jesus.

I will always remember that Jesus met, and defeated and
conquered it all. I am facing defeat everywhere as a master
because of Jesus. I cannot be defeated in the name of Jesus.
Faith says that in all things I am more than a conqueror.

I can't be conquered because Jesus lives in me. Every disease
is of the adversary and I refuse to accept it in my soul or
body in the name of Jesus. GOD my Father and I are victors.
Greater is He that is in me than this opposition.

There is no lack that Jesus has not already met for me.
I am united with GOD, Abba Father, Lord Jesus, Holy
Spirit, and the Word of GOD. I am one with GOD.

"I [Jesus] am the light of the world: he that followed me shall not
walk in darkness, but shall have the light of life." I have the life

and light of Jesus living in me. Light means wisdom, and Jesus has become my wisdom. Jesus is my light for life's problems.

I don't walk in the darkness of sensory knowledge any longer. Jesus is all that the heart could ever want to know.

The Bible doesn't say you will have what you think, it says you will have what you say what are you confessing? GOD's confessions never repeat scandal. Never repeat talk of calamity. Let others do the talking about that.

You keep your lips for beautiful things, helpful things, comforting things. That is your job.

To maintain our faith the Word has to be more of a reality to us then the symptoms. What comes out of your mouth is healing if you are speaking the Word.

Faith will enforce the Word on the devil and your soul and body. "And hath raised [me] up together, and made [me] sit together [with Jesus] in heavenly places in Christ Jesus."

This is a spiritual thing. This is not a mental or physical thing. Our spirits are seated with Christ Jesus in heavenly places at the right hand of the throne of GOD our FATHER.

The benefits we have because of being seated with Christ Jesus in heavenly places are listed in the Word of GOD.

We have to know and activate the promises that we need in our souls and bodies by believing in our hearts and confessing with our mouths. GOD is omnipresent so He can be seated in heavenly places and live in our spirits at the same time.

I see that I am identified with Jesus, that I am actually seated with Jesus in that place of authority far above all principality, and power, and might, and dominion, and every name that is named in heaven, earth and hell.

In those three worlds, every being is subject to the name of Jesus, and now He gives me the power of attorney to use that name. Every disease, sickness, weakness, bondage, demon spirit, principality, power, and anything that steals, kills, or destroys is under my feet because I am the body of Christ and I have control over them.

The devil can only take advantage of me if I permit him. I am a master of demons; I am a master of sickness and disease in the name of Jesus.

I am seated in heavenly places in Christ Jesus and I will not be defeated by the devil, sickness, the world, or mankind in the name of Jesus. Fear knocked on the door and faith answered, fear fled.

I refuse to fear in the name of Jesus! flows in every subatomic particle of every atom of my soul and body, removing all sickness, disease and bondage, and causing everything to conform to the Word of GOD. Soul and body, I'm speaking to you! I command you to conform to the Word of GOD and be healed, work perfect and be made whole in Jesus' name.

That which GOD has not created is dissolved and is rooted out of my soul and body in Jesus' name. I bind every sickness, disease, bondage, weakness, malfunction, deterioration, and confusion in my soul and body and command them to come out of me and never return in the name of Jesus.

I call in and receive new soul and body in the name of Jesus. I call in and receive a new central nervous system, new nerve cells, new nerves, and new myelin around my nerves from the top of my head to the tip of my toes and from the top of my head to the tip of my fingers in the name of Jesus.

Nerves, be strong, healed and function properly in Jesus' name.

My soul and body are chemically balanced and my metabolism is normal in the name of Jesus. Jesus my healer, the Word of GOD my healer, and the Holy Spirit my healer lives inside of my spirit. I call them into my nervous system, and I am completely healed by faith in the name of Jesus. They go with me wherever I go.

The Kingdom of GOD lives in me! "Every plant which my heavenly Father hath not planted, shall be rooted up."

Every sickness disease weakness malfunction bondage lack and deterioration that my Father has not planted is rooted up and removed from my soul and body in the name of Jesus.

I call it done until I have what I need in my soul and body in Jesus' name. Get your mind fixed on the Word of GOD—your answer. Do not let sickness and symptoms remain in your thinking. Get a mindset that's programmed with the Word of GOD.

By Jesus' stripes I am healed. Call in and receive your answer night and day from the Word of GOD until you are completely healed. Get busy! Jesus, I receive Your mind, the mind of Christ. I will no longer think negative thoughts, because I have the mind of Jesus operating in my brain continually.

My mind is clear, healed, sharp, and chemically balanced with an outstanding memory in Jesus' name. Jesus, I thank you. Thank you, Jesus. instructs us to speak to the mountain [cancer, etc. name them] and command them to come out and not return in the name of Jesus.

Keep speaking! Hold on to this confession! Call in and receive new soul and body parts in the name of Jesus. says faith, "calleth those things which be not as though they were," and faith "calls those things which do not exist as though they did."

I call in and receive healing, health, deliverance, and new soul and body parts until I am completely restored in Jesus' name. I resist and rebuke the devil and his symptoms, sickness, bondage, fear, and anything that causes my soul and body to malfunction with the name of Jesus.

My faith takes hold of the answer and pulls it into my soul and body in the name of Jesus.

I call in and receive healing, wholeness, and health in my colon, stomach and intestine.

My colon and stomach are chemically balanced and working perfect from the top to the bottom in the name of Jesus.

My digestive system is operating properly, and all the nutrition is being removed from my food and sent to every subatomic particle of every atom and cell in my soul and body in the name of Jesus.

I confess that I am a son of GOD I am redeemed by the blood of Jesus Christ and his blood cleanses me from all my sins in the name of Jesus

I am redeemed from sicknesses I am redeemed from death
I am redeemed from poverty in the name of Jesus.

Psalms 1:1-3

1 Blessed is the man that walketh not in the counsel of the ungodly, nor standeth in the way of sinners, nor sitteth in the seat of the scornful.

2 But his delight is in the law of the Lord; and in
his law doth he meditate day and night.

3 And he shall be like a tree planted by the rivers of water,
that bringeth forth his fruit in his season; his leaf also shall
not wither; and whatsoever he doeth shall prosper.

4 The ungodly are not so: but are like the chaff
which the wind driveth away.

5 Therefore the ungodly shall not stand in the judgment,
nor sinners in the congregation of the righteous.

6 For the Lord knoweth the way of the righteous:
but the way of the ungodly shall perish.

RENOUNCE & RENOUNCING

MOST NEARLY MEANS DISOWN, REJECT, unacceptable, ABANDON, STAYAWAY FROM, RESIGN FROM, NO LONGER BE A PART OF, QUIT, STOP, DENY, RECANT your statement of what was said, abort, get out, Release, get rid of, let go. More to do with what's going on evil plans

St Luke 10:19 Behold, I give unto you power to tread
on serpents and scorpions, and over all the power of the
enemy: and nothing shall by any means hurt you.

I receive your power Lord Jesus I receive your instructions; I
receive your spirit to lead me and guide me into all truth in the
name Jesus that you have given me I continually put it to work
in my life daily in the name of Jesus Christ of Nazareth

I have power over all my enemies that includes all demonic
occultic practices dark arts, of all or / any kinds that rises up
against me be defeated in the name of Jesus. IT WONT BE
PRACTICED BY ME AND IF I DID, I NOW DENOUNCE and
RENOUNCE IT GET RID OF IT AND BURN UP THROW IT
AWAY AND STOP DOING IT SEPARATE MYSELF FROM ALL
ITS CONTENT DISMANTLE THE PROJECTS ON MY PART
IN THE ONLY MATCHLESS NAME OF JESUS CHRIST.

I shut down all communications of the enemies that comes
against me distracting and attempting to hinder my progress
be destroyed with the fire of GOD in Jesus name.

By the confession of my faith and belief in the word of GOD in Jesus name
I now have power that was given to me to use the name of JESUS to
tread or walk on subdue and bind the works of the enemy in Jesus' name.

I have the power in the name of Jesus to walk on serpents or snake's
cobra's python's restrictor demons that try to squeeze the living life
out of me to be bound up and thrown in the fire in Jesus name.

I take Authority & Dominion and control over every demonic or occultic
attack against me. All of those include scorpions and snakes of all kinds.
Reptilian demons oceanic queens of the sea demons, dragons, vipers, dogs,
spiders, owls, foxes birds of all kinds. Those that are in demonic form
or demons. Marine demons of the waters monitoring demons. Witches,
both male or female. Warlocks both male and female in organizations
or in a coven of some type. Wizards, Occult workers for the devil. All of
those that are practicing unrighteousness evilness, and all that's working
witchcraft. All of those that like to control me, those that are evil in
character working for the devil with evil intentions. Those that like to

trap and put snares. Those that are planting evil devices in my way. Those who working wickedness in scheming against me, be exposed and bound be tied up stop your activities your assignments are all canceled out destroyed, and burned in the fire of GOD. Never to come back into my life ever again and I will never open that door again in the name of Jesus.

The enemy can't hurt me as long as I stay within the
borders of GOD's boundaries in Jesus' name.

All that are working evilness against, me I send it back to the senders, in Jesus name. No weapon shall destroy me nor formed against me shall neither bring any type of hurt harm or danger in the mighty name of Jesus. Nothing shall by any means hurt me. I have the power of GOD in the name of Jesus to rout out, throw out, drive out, pitch out, burn out, cast out, remove from me, each and every demonic force that comes up against me and be destroyed in Jesus name. it is so and so it is true now.

CHAPTER 9

DECREES & DECLARATIONS, RESULTS BY SPEAKING, OUT LOUD

WHAT DOES IT MEAN TO DECREE AND DECLARE?

What exactly does it mean to decree and declare GOD's Word over our lives? Is this Biblical? What does it really accomplish? Many of us have been taught to do this or have avoided it because of the possibility that it is not sound doctrine. I have heard some state that this is a mentality that comes from the "prosperity movement of distorted doctrine". When it comes to this word distorted, Our Heavenly FATHER, JEHOVAH, has nothing that he has done or created to be distorted, tainted, or corrupt, twisted, or perverted. These words in meaning simply mean that they are not a lie, they are not fakes, or imitations, not mixed with anything. This is simply the word and thoughts of GOD, downloaded to his children. We are the children of GOD, and we are in covenant, or in agreement, with what GOD, has said, written, spoken, and declare and decree in the way of promises, proclamations and the inheritance, he has promised us that keep, his commandments. His words are sure and true down to the very letter and they, will harm anyone, but the words of GOD, gives and brings life blessings, health and strength to those that follow his divine plan. The things that GOD, has made are first pure, clean and Holy. Our Heavenly FATHER GOD, has all the power to back up, anything, that he has spoken or said in promises, that he would do for us this children. Let's examine this together today and see what the Word of GOD really has to say.

DECREE & DECLARE IN MEANING;

- <u>Thou shalt also decree a thing, and it shall be established unto thee: and the light shall shine upon thy ways.</u>

The Word Decree & Declare, are used together in the fellowship, the body of Christ. Prayers and mean distinctively two separate things. Let's take a look at the definition of Decree & Declare.

THE WORD DECREE;

❖ According to Dictionary.com, the decree is defined as "a formal and authoritative order having the force of law, a judicial decision or order. Google's definition includes "a mandate; proclamation; edict; command; an official order issued by a legal authority." Other definitions include "to state emphatically; to show; reveal; manifest; and to declare one's position in a controversy." Job 22:28 states "Thou shalt also decree a thing and it shall be established unto thee and the light shall shine upon thy ways". Many of us have read this passage without understanding the power of what this Word from GOD truly means. Let's go further. Numbers 23:19 GOD is not a man, that he should lie; neither the son of man, that he should repent: hath he said, and shall he not do it? or hath he spoken, and shall he not make it good? Psalms 2:7 I will declare the decree: the LORD hath said unto me, Thou art my Son; this day have I begotten thee.

❖ The word established is defined as:" to set up on a firm or permanent basis; to achieve permanent acceptance or recognition for, to sow, reveal to be true based on the facts." Any person who makes a decree must be in a position of power and authority. As Saints of GOD, Luke 10:19 reminds us that Jesus gave us all authority to trample on snakes and scorpions and over all the power of the evil, which is our enemy, we must always remember that one, so that nothing can harm us, and we must be able to memorize, meditate, and hide these words in our heart, which is the mind, or the thoughts, that are downloaded from the spirit of man, or GOD, or maybe even the enemy.

❖ The enemy can speak to us sometimes,if were not on guard and catch all of his tactics.

❖ We as Saints of GOD, must be sharpe and on our post, at all times guarding and watchingf or the schemes of the devil. This is one thing I want to make clear and precise. That what GOD, has said is true, that nothing by any means shall hurt us, but if we dabble in it open the door, and start playing with it, intentionally, knowing what we are doing, it has the potential to harm us.

❖ 2 Corinthians 2:11, lest satan should get an advantage over us.

❖ For we are not ignorant of his devices. 2 Tim 2:26 And that they may recover themselves out of the snares of the devil, who are taken captive by him at his will. We have trespassed into the devil's mess or stuff, tread on his territory.

❖ This will bring to us, or ourselves some consequences. We must not forget these principles of THE LAW OF PREVENTION, WHAT IT HAS TO SAY TO US; AND THAT IS. IF WE PREVENT IT FROM HAPPENING, WE DO NOT HAVE TO DEAL OR FACE THE CONSEQUENCES. Messing with the devils' mess will bring indeed some type of consequences, which may be very harmful to our lives or the lives of others if they're involved.

❖ The Scripture also reminds us in Matthew 16:18-19 that Jesus has given us the keys to the kingdom of heaven and whatever we bind on earth will be bound in heaven and whatever we loose on earth will be loosed in heaven when we pray in His Name.

❖ There are many other verses on spiritual authority. Proverbs 18:21 further reminds us that the tongues have the power of life and death.

Just as GOD spoke everything into existence, we as His children have a powerful weapon in our Words. We can declare blessings or curses upon our lives and others. We can cancel out our prayers in moments of doubt, stress, anxiety by complaining and thinking/speaking about what "we" can or cannot handle.

Let's take a look now at what decree means. The English definition of decree is "a statement of truth that carries the authority of a court order". A great example of this is when you go to court and a sentence or judgment is made. It cannot be ignored because of the authority of the court issued the decree or declaration. A more familiar expression would be "the court made a judgement".

Decrees are used to fulfill Matthew 6:10 "Thy Kingdom come, Thy Will be done on earth, as it is in heaven". Decrees cause truths from the Word and the heavenly realm to be manifested in our earthly realm. In Hebrew, decree, means "to divide, separate and destroy." When we decree for example "I am blessed" (based on Psalm 112:1) we establish blessing while separating from anything purposed against it by the enemy. We simultaneously are destroying the enemies plans against us.

I believe we can reason then with a sound mind that we have the power and authority to make decrees and expect them to be carried out. When we decree, we use the Word of GOD to state our case concerning our home, family, ministry and any other concerns we have. We have the authority to expect to see our words manifested in our life. As Ambassadores of Christ we must understand our legal right to have those decrees upheld. We must be careful to decree GOD's will (His Word) and not our own.

The German "diktat" is the equivalent of decree in the English language and means "a harsh judgment imposed on a defeated enemy that cannot be opposed".

"The spiritual Strategies are stunning. We see when we decree, we:

• Speak GOD's blessings upon your (our) as well as other lives,

• Institute the very will and purposes of GOD.

• Separate, uproot, and destroy the plans of the enemy.

• Impose a judgment; the enemy cannot oppose"
And shut down his Operations in Jesus.

As we can see, GOD has truly given us authority to equip us in our walk. Sadly, most of us are not using this authority, thus not walking in as much victory as Our Heavenly FATHER has provided for us.

➢ THE <u>WORD DECLARE;</u>

➢ comes from the Hebrew word "achvah" which means to "make known" or "to set forth. "declare". In general, an order, Edict; so this brings us to this word call or pronounced as (Edic) an edic is according to the bible hub topical bible, as A public ordinance by the sovereign power. This Sovereign power is none other, than the ALMIGHTY of GOD. THERE IS NO OTHER POWER BUT THE POWER OF GOD. Romans 13:1 Let every soul be subject unto the higher powers. For there is no power but of GOD: The Powers that be are ordained of GOD, GOD ALMIGHTY THAT IS, Because there is no other god. This god is with a little g signifying that GOD ALMIGHTY, our Heavenly FATHER, is the only REAL AND TRUE GOD. So GOD made the laws or law made by a superior as a rule to govern inferiors. In theology, predetermined purpose of GOD's plan ; the purpose or determination of an immutable Being, whose plan of operations is, like himself, unchangeable

➢ The act of declaring, or publicly announcing; explicit asserting; undisguised token of a ground or side taken on any subject; proclamation; exposition; as, the declaration of an opinion; a declaration of war, Acts 20:27 Psalms 50:6 Isaiah 21:6 Romans 3:26 on declares the word of GOD.

➢ That which is declared or proclaimed; announcement; distinct statement; formal expression;

Psalms 2:7

<u>I will declare the decree: the LORD hath said unto me,</u>
<u>Thou art my Son; this day have I begotten thee.</u>

Psalms 73:28

<u>But it is good for me to draw near to GOD: I have put my</u>
<u>trust in the Lord GOD, that I may declare all thy works.</u>

DECREEING AND DECLARING OUR HEALING IN
JESUS NAME, OF WHATEVER SORT IT IS.

ALL TYPES OF SICKNESSES.

PRAISES TO MY GOD, FOR HIS WISDOM & ENCOURAGEMENT:

1 Blessed is the man that walketh not in the counsel of the ungodly, nor
standeth in the way of sinners, nor sitteth in the seat of the scornful.

2 But his delight is in the law of the Lord; and in
his law doth he meditate day and night.

Ps93 - The Lord reigneth, he is clothed with majesty; the Lord
is clothed with strength, wherewith he hath girded himself:
the world also is stablished, that it cannot be moved.

2 Thy throne is established of old: thou art from everlasting.

3 The floods have lifted up, O Lord, the floods have lifted
up their voice; the floods lift up their waves.

4 The Lord on high is mightier than the noise of many
waters, yea, than the mighty waves of the sea.

5 Thy testimonies are very sure: holiness
becometh thine house, O Lord, forever.

Ps- 97 The Lord reigneth; let the earth rejoice; let
the multitude of isles be glad thereof.

2 Clouds and darkness are round about him: righteousness
and judgment are the habitation of his throne.

3 A fire goeth before him, and burneth up his enemies round about.

⁴ His lightnings enlightened the world: the earth saw, and trembled.

⁵ The hills melted like wax at the presence of the Lord,
at the presence of the Lord of the whole earth.

⁶ The heavens declare his righteousness, and all the people see his glory.

⁷ Confounded be all they that serve graven images, that
boast themselves of idols: worship him, all ye gods.

⁸ Zion heard, and was glad; and the daughters of Judah
rejoiced because of thy judgments, O Lord.

⁹ For thou, Lord, art high above all the earth:
thou art exalted far above all gods.

¹⁰ Ye that love the Lord, hate evil: he preserveth the souls of his
saints; he delivereth them out of the hand of the wicked.

¹¹ Light is sown for the righteous, and gladness for the upright in heart.

¹² Rejoice in the Lord, ye righteous; and give thanks
at the remembrance of his holiness.

CHAPTER 10

ACTIVATE YOUR FAITH IN GOD

So, let's talk about what faith is, and what faith isn't, in Hebrews 11:1,6,

says now faith is,

the substance of things hoped for, the evidence of things not seen.
So, then faith cometh by hearing and hearing by the word of GOD.
Romans 10:17. Faith is Simply following what GOD has said in his
word, and that takes us following his instructions, and applying what
he has said into action. for EXAMPLE LETS suppose GOD said to
you; your called to be a Pastor then first of all your already praying;

which is the first line of defense, and studying GODs Word, already.
But you're not having a heart to be very watchful, what's that,
so Shepherds are called watchmen for the sheep so you're going
to study about how to be a great watchman on the wall, so you
begin to read the word about watchmen, in the word of GOD.

Finding out all the details.

Ok enough said for now just telling of example of. what faith is not
it's not fearful, scared and worrying about this or that. Wishing
that everything would come together without putting any action
to the works with your hands. By the way, we as Saints of GOD,
do not practice, talk about, think about, ponder on, wishing.

We don't wish for nothing because we don't have to.

We do not talk about luck, these things belongs to the
devil, and that is where we want to leave them their.

If you have any of these types of words in your vocabulary you need to get rid of them and do not pick them up ever again. Some things we pick up give ourselves a curse and that is not our lot in life. Thinking, experiences knowledge and asking seeking and knocking on the LORDS DOOR IN PRAYER in the name of Jesus, some of these words we need to leave off so we can get what we are praying for.

When we follow the instructions with the proper applications given, then,you will see the manifestations of the spirit moving on our behalf, because we have met the proper requirement.

GODS WORD OF FAITH

WHAT IS FAITH?

Faith is defined as belief with strong conviction; firm belief in something for which there may be no tangible proof; complete trust, confidence, reliance, or devotion. Faith is the opposite of doubt, & fear. Faith is really and actually believing the word of GOD, without doubt, without wavering, without looking at other ways, or not being persuaded by others, in words, actions, feelings, thoughts, or speech of our tongue's things coming out of our mouths.

The book of Hebrews plunges the depths of Saints by addressing many false beliefs, choices and hardships that believers face.

In this get-back-to-basics book, that is the word of GOD, with the purpose of clarifying that only Christ, not sacred traditions or new ideas, was to be the center of a life of Faith in Hebrews.

It's natural to read this book in view of our daily life. But it's better to read it in light of who it was written to: men and women who were wrestling with faith in a life and death way that we may never experience.

Hebrews wasn't written merely for the purpose of correction or encouragement but also to fortify their souls because they were in desperate need. It is mentioned several times throughout this book that the audience was a specific group of believers who were facing persecution for their faith. With this solemn purpose in mind, we can look to Hebrews when life feels complicated, we feel our faith wavering and we need our souls realigned to truth.

Among the many topics the book covers, one topic it speaks to most extensively is faith. The author wanted the readers to hold fast to their commitment to GOD no matter what came their way. Faith in Christ was the foundation for this level of commitment.

faith is believing that GOD exists, that he rewards those who seek him and that we can hope in him because his promises will always be true. After the author defines faith, they put flesh on it in ways that both the intended readers, Saints of the most high GOD. Today can look to understand how to live an authentic life of faith.

WHAT IS FAITH?

Faith is defined as a constant outlook of trust toward GOD, abandoning all reliance on their own efforts and put their full confidence in him, GOD word, and his promises. As Sons of GOD, we know that faith is foundational to our relationship with GOD, and found in right standing with GOD and we can LOOK BACK throughout Scriptures.

Faith is the only means of Salvation or deliverance but also Healing of all types through faith and trust in his abilities.

Jesus is the object of saving faith, which is our examples of showing walking demonstrating, moving speaking to them by faith.

Faith shows itself through works, actions and instructions applied that shows a manifestation that will be seen with the natural eyes.

Faith produces peace in our lives when we continue to trust rely and lean on what he has promised us through his wonderful word.

Lack of faith leads to falling away from what GOD has said. What GOD has promised, written about us and for us. Lack of faith comes when we don't read, the words of GOD.

Do not study, research, or trust in his everlasting promises. Do not Stand on what he has said that he will do for us if we do this or that. Whatever this or that is, and he has promised to do for us.

Lack of faith starts with one being impatience. No longsuffering, is ever present to assist. Less of a tolerance for waiting on GOD, Wanting to do it ourselves.

Lack of faith wants it like right now. Not willing to work, but sometimes wants instant results.

Lack of faith also could be moving too fast. Wanting to be in a hurry to get something and not realizing that it will take more than what they anticipated. In their thinking, mindset, thoughts, ideas, and sometimes feelings. GODS word is SPIRIT and Life and so if we truly want to receive what he has promised us, we must begin to trust and rely on his Everlasting power.

His Directions and believe in him with all of our hearts not leaning on our own understanding and in all of our ways acknowledge him. Proverbs 3:5-6. Meaning to believe in what he has said, ask him for his wisdom to guide us without making our own mind up what we want to do. Then when it don't work, we decide to come back to him. One of the most important things we forget is to have a second to none RELATIONSHIP with our Heavenly Father, Jesus, and The Holy Spirit. Constantly from the time we surrender our lives to him, giving up our own wills, choices, plans and all the things we want to do and take up his plans for our lives. Taking up our crosses and following him all the way until we reach his ETERNAL KINGDOM from above.

Until then we should stay in constant prayer and communication. Loving the Lord of our lives, loving, and living out in his wonderful words of life through our lives. Enjoying all that he has for us through his inheritance. Through his promises, through his blessings, his gifts, his favors, his talents, anointings, mantles, signs wonders & miracles, with revelations of the word of GOD flowing in and out of our lives constantly. I intentionally put emphasis, in the word HIS, because all of these things belongs to him.

We don't have to remind ourselves that we are believers that trust, believe, stand, meditate confess and decree and declare his word of life. It is his word that gives life to those things that we speak in the mighty name of Jesus. If we want to strengthen our faith in GOD then the word tells us that faith cometh by hearing and hearing by the word of GOD; Roman 4:17 and that Faith is also, the substance of things hoped for and the evidence of things not seen, Heb 11:1. If we continue to have or maintain strong faith, we must exercise it on a daily basis just like a muscle. Speaking the word of GOD Over our own lives. Decreeing and declaring his word, memorizing hiding it in our hearts and allowing the Holy Spirit to bring it back to our remembrance. Faith has to be used each and every time, each and every day of our lives. We must keep it active, believing and not living by what we feel.

We literally live, depend on faith. It's a lifeline to all of those that trust in the Lord . To bring them out of all of their troubles, situations, dilemmas'. That's another part of what faith is all about. Faith is living not by our feelings. Reasons why they change each moment of the day and from time to time on a constant basis. Just like the clock on the wall referring the middle hand it never stops moving unless the battery is dead and that's not what we want when it comes to our faith. We want living faith, we do not want to produce dead faith and think, that we will be receiving a blessing out of faith that is dead or not active, or faith as the size of a mustard seed,

GOD is looking for faith that is lively. We want faith that moves mountains of all types of shapes, and sizes. At any given moment of each day of our lives in the mighty name of Jesus. That's how we accumulate strong faith by using it constantly never-ending,and it will begin to grow and become huge, big, large, and every word that describes when it begins to grow.

Faith activates GOD's power; In our lives, through our lives, to others that are connected with our lives in the mighty name of Jesus.

Let's read what the word of GOD said about faith. From his wonderful words of inspiration and life. Its faith that gives life to all that will be speaking it with faith, in faith, by faith, and living in that faith that is spoken in the mighty name of Jesus, and it's so.

FAITH IN ACTION.

Faith is substance, something we want that can be seen or it maybe intangible that; that can not be seen but never the less its their. Faith has evidence following it otherwise its not faith, and to add to this faith is an action word it requires us to do something not just to say something and let it do whatever it suppose to do on its on.

These men and women of GOD who lived by faith has a wonderful report of action that comes along with them. What they have accomplished through faith, listen what they have done through faith.

They have obtained and good report.

Stop lions mouth was shut through them believing, that they did not get any hurt, harm or danger come to them through their believing the Lord through faith.

Faith helped them to making through the rough times they where faced with. The word of GOD declares that without faith we can not even please GOD, we must come to him believing that whatever it is that we are asking him that we will receive it by faith trusting in his word that can not lie.

Faith caused them deny themselves, rather than live and accept the ways of the world systems of operations.

Their faith caused many to be healed, set free and delivered, faith caused some to be translated that they did not see death. Faith caused them to hold on to their testimony.

Faith caused Noah to get the dimensions of an ARK to build without any drops of rain, preparing to the saving of souls, as many as would come into the ark, but few souls were saved that is eight souls out of the world that they were living in at that time, pending a world flood to cover the whole earth for 40 days and 40 nights of rain, to destroy the earth of all of its evilness.

Now we want to mention others that did and had tremendous faith and works that did not give in the ways of the devil or evil men and women, while they were here on earth,

Abraham, Isaac, Jacob, Joseph, and the twelve tribes of Israel,

Moses the great work being a vessel to hep delver the children of Israel out of the land of Egypt which was a land of bondage and slavery.

Gideon, barak, David the slewing of the giant in the land.

Sarah and Ester, Ruth, Paul, Peter, James John from the Isles of Patmos, St Luke, Matthew, Mark, and many others, not to forget the mighty works of Jesus our Savior of the world, from the new and Old Testament did, the saints in those times many mighty works in whom they were fully persuaded they loved GOD, JESUS, AND THE HOLY SPIRIT. They loved not their lives unto to the death. They have committed all that they have went and been through all the cause of GOD ALMIGHTY, JESUS OUR REDEEMER.

While the whole Bible resonates, vibrates brings spiritual insight, illumination, strength and confidence in your faith. Sometimes is referred to as the "faith hall of fame." But unlike modern day halls of fame, entrance into this distinguished group wasn't reliant on outward achievements but an inner resolution to believe GOD's promises in the face of trial and adversity. Faith give us the simplest definitions we can find anywhere in GOD's word, that is simply believe what the word of GOD says, trust in, rely and lean on, depend on and in his promises.

These definitions are backed up by examples of faith throughout centuries of Bible history. Each person in the list acted with true faith, and as a result GOD approved them. He accepted them as his own and saved a place for them in eternity with him. The faith-filled actions of these people range from simple words they spoke to the giving of their very life. This shows us that faith permeates every area of our life and every act of faith holds weight with GOD.

WHAT DOES IT LOOK LIKE TO LIVE BY FAITH?

Living by faith is a simple concept that requires massive commitment, trust, in our lives. A life of faith is constantly, However, constantly isn't the same as perfectly. The faithful in GOD, called the Children of GOD, Sons of GOD had plenty of mess ups in their stories & LIVES but their faith remained constant still.

Faith requires living life he has promised in the word of GOD; that is true, whether we see the evidence of that or not. Faith doesn't need to see, to believe.

A life of faith starts in the heart, that is believing what GOD has written, promised us, and that we do not doubt, or allow anyone else to deter us, but always shows itself through works and actions. In the same way, a lack of faith shows in our actions as well, that would be doubt, or fears. Faith will not doubt but trust.

Faith sees life through the lens of eternity. It always looks towards the day when physical life ends. Only spiritual life remains, Therefore, faith can tolerate pain, shame and disgrace if they are done for the Glory of GOD.

Living a life of faith is a tall order. It requires the power and presence of GOD in your life. No matter how faith filled or faithless you're currently feeling. Be assured that faith comes not from those who try hard but those who lean into GOD hard and trust whatever his word declares for them shall be complete, satisfied, enjoying the benefits of the Lord.

St Mark 11:22

THE WORDS OF GOD WE SPEAK ARE CONTINUALLY HAPPENING IN MY LIFE AND THE LIFE OF THOSE THAT ARE SPEAKING THESE GOD, GIVEN WORDS INTO, AND FOR THEIR lives in JESUS name.

Decree & declare these for your life, in the mighty name of Jesus.

I NOW HAVE; In meaning that as soon as it leaves my mouth that I have spoken it; it begins to form, take

place and be activated into manifestations that will be
seen, that came out of the spirit into the natural.

And Jesus answering saith unto them, Have faith in GOD

I now have faith in GOD, and I believe whatsoever his word
says I will find myself doing it because I trust what his
powerful creative word says for me to do in Jesus' name.

I have the measure of faith that GOD has given me and
I now receive it in the mighty name of Jesus.

I now have faith to start something finish & complete
and see it to the end in the name of Jesus.

I now live by the faith GOD has given me in Jesus' name.

I now walk in faith, not by sight in Jesus' name.

I now have faith to be obedient in Jesus' name.

I now have faith to be confidence and not walk in any
type of fears what soever in Jesus' name.

My faith decrees in Jesus' name.

My faith declares the spoken word of GOD in Jesus name.

I now have faith to produce bountiful blessing in Jesus name.

I now have faith to heal the sick, raise the dead
and cast out devils in Jesus' name.

I believe in faith in Jesus' name.

I now have faith to overcome any situation
that comes my way in Jesus' name.

I now have explosive faith in Jesus' name.

I now have atomic faith that will cause an
explosion in the spirit in Jesus' name.

I now have imperial faith that, that Abraham had and it pleased GOD. And I will believe even when I do not see any type of results why because this type of faith is a knowing faith that beings result in due time.

I now have nuclear, biological, faith to explode in with Dunamis power in Jesus name when I put it to work in Jesus name.

I now have determined faith in Jesus' name.

I now have world overcoming faith in Jesus' name.

I now have power with my faith in Jesus' name.

I now have security in my faith in Jesus' name.

I now have global faith that can reach anywhere and everywhere in Jesus' name.

I now have faith all the time in Jesus' name.

my faith works by love in Jesus' name.

I now have faith and NO doubt NO unbelief and disbelief in Jesus' name.

I now have faith to speak life and not death in Jesus' name.

I now have faith to cast out devils' unclean spirits, foul evil spirits in the name of Jesus.

I now have faith in the word of GOD in Jesus name.

I now have faith in GODs instructions each and every day in Jesus' name

I now have faith that will bring my dreams alive in Jesus' name.

I now have faith that will get results at all times, I'm putting it to work in my life in Jesus' name.

I now have faith that will launch the ministry and ministries that GOD has given, spoken, showed me in visions and it is so in the name of Jesus.

I now have enduring steadfast, unwavering, unfaltering faith that will not be moved by present circumstances or situations in the mighty name of Jesus.

I now have faith that will go around the Globe
many times over in Jesus' name.

I now apply my faith in every situation I encounter in Jesus' name.

My faith never gets tired of being in use, because the
more I use the stronger it gets in Jesus' name.

I will activate my faith in all that I do for the
cause of Christ Jesus, in Jesus' name.

I now have faith that moves swiftly with precision in Jesus name.

I now have strong faith in Jesus name.

I will now follow in his footsteps in Jesus' name.

I now have faith that will bring miracles, signs, wonders and marvels
with exploits of demonstrations, in the mighty name of Jesus.

I now progress forward at all times with my faith in GOD in Jesus name.

I will not waver in faith any more from this point on in the name
of Jesus because I know in whom I believe in Jesus' name.

I will not be moved by others in what they do
with their faith. In Jesus name.

I now have faith that is whole in Jesus' name.

My faith is solid in Jesus' name.

My faith is complete in the name of Jesus.

I am steadfast in my faith and unmovable,
unshakeable in the name of Jesus.

I now have faith to move mountains in Jesus' name.

I now have faith to think beyond the sky's stars moon and the sun
and beyond all the spheres out there in the name of Jesus.

I now have faith with no limits or restrictions, or boundaries
that my faith cannot go perform in the name of Jesus.

I now have triumphant; faith that's victory in every
area in my life in the mighty name of Jesus.

MY FAITH.

My faith will bring production in the way of fruits around
the world in all that I do for Christ, in Jesus' name.

My faith calls down fire from Heaven.

My faith calleth those things which be not as though
they already are in the mighty name of Jesus.

My faith releases Angelic forces from Heaven in the name of Jesus.

My faith produces same day results in the name of Jesus.

My faith drives out demons in Jesus' name.

My faith scatters the plans of the enemy through the
strategies of wisdom and tactics skill in Jesus' name.

My faith shatters the strategies of my enemies In Jesus name.

My faith loose the band of wickedness in Jesus' name.

My faith breaks and destroys negative words of the enemy.

My faith undo heavy burdens and lets the oppressed
go and be free in the mighty name of Jesus.

My faith uproots his evil seeds called the devil that
were planted in my fields In Jesus name.

My faith cancels out all the attacks against me in Jesus' name.

My faith shoots out spear's javelins and throws out nets
to capture and subdue my enemies in Jesus' name.

My faith stops the witches, warlocks, wizards, and witchdoctors,
in their tracks from, saying, or speaking, casting, spells or

incantations, words of darkness, that I count null & void and stop them from moving forward in the mighty name of Jesus.

My faith can move north, south, east, and west in any direction in Jesus name.

My faith trust in the name of JESUS.

My faith goes along with the plans of GOD in Jesus name.

My faith breaks me and anyone out of prison in Jesus' name.

My faith melts and destroys, chains, and fetters, releases me from the captivity, and bondages of all types of demons & demonic forces over, my life and the lives of others in Jesus' name.

My faith uses the word of GOD skillfully in Jesus' name.

My faith knows how to use the sword of the Spirit in spiritual warfare to fight and combat the enemy and put him on a chase in Jesus' name.

My faith doesn't receive the evil suggestions of the enemy or anyone else that's speaking for the enemy in Jesus' name.

I SAY THROUGH THE WORD OF GOD.

I say to this mountain of debt be removed in Jesus name.

I say to this body of infirmities be healed in Jesus name.

I say to this mind be renewed with new parts and new thoughts, I renounce old, & evil, negative energy, stealing, draining thoughts of the enemy in Jesus' name.

I say to these bones be made whole in Jesus' name.

I say to these hands legs and feet be made whole in Jesus' name.

I say to the demon spirit, of cancer be removed and never return again in Jesus' name.

I say to all these sicknesses & diseases be healed in the name of Jesus, and bow to the ONLY POWERFUL name of JESUS.

I say to my spirit, soul and body & my mind, will & emotions and I rebuke any and all distractions, interferences from the enemy in Jesus' name and command you to leave now in Jesus' name.

I say to this mountain of fears and all types of phobias, be thou tilled up and removed, to be destroyed in the name of Jesus and never return again in Jesus' name.

I say to all these mountains of strongholds, religious, and all man-made, demonic, religions and doctrines of devils. Traditions, entities of evilness rudiments, old wives' fables, lies deceptions, and all the works of the devil, with all the occults, witches, warlocks, wizards, and witch doctors that studying and calling out our names into this atmosphere, I bind you and stop you, block all of your activities, be uprooted, tilled up from the roots, be handcuffed, shackled, and destroyed, thrown in the fire, and be burned up in Jesus' name.

I say in the mighty name of Jesus I take authority & dominion over all, spirits, of satan, the spirit of pride rebellion, and idolatry, Beelzebub, the lord of the flies, lord of the dung, Baal, spirits of Ashdod, Moab, Edomite demons, Sodom & Gomorrah, nimrod spirits, all evil kings in the old testament, the seven wicked nations, Canaanites, Amorites, Girgashites, Hittites, Hivites, the Jebusites, and the perrizzites. All the evil caesars of Egypt, jezebel, Ahab, Kora, Absalom, alexander the Coppersmith, Herodias, Herod, Nero, Cain, the spirit of murder and Judas spirits, of Betral, and I will add the devilish Roman empire, the laws, ordinances, statutes, that caused a lot of chaos throughout the whole entire world. The 200 fallen angels, not to forget about Lucifer, who rebelled against the plans of Heaven and con one-third of angels out of their first estate, as well as in the days of Enoch, and all that they have opened up to the Greek mythology, the Babylonian kingdom Medes & Persians, other evil entities, occult workers in our day, that has worked for the devil, that have caused trouble and chaos in our world. The Egyptian rules, and rulers of evil laws, evil plans, I bind all your activities words covenants, blood pacts, word curses spoken over myself and my wife and all my family members that are in the earth, period in the mighty name of Jesus it is so, NO harm or hurt shall come to us in the mighty name of Jesus.

I take authority over all anti-christ spirits, false prophets, the beast, the son of perdition, and I renounce, and denounce null and void all of their evil activities, I stop and block them from ever working in my life in the mighty name of Jesus.

23For verily I say unto you, That whosoever shall say unto this mountain, Be thou removed, and be thou cast into the sea; and shall not doubt in his heart, but shall believe that those things which he saith shall come to pass; he shall have whatsoever he saith.

BE REMOVED

The enemy desires to remove us but HE CAN'T, why? because he did not plant us. He do not own us, he did not create us. We do not belong to the devil. SO, SAINTS OF GOD. AMBASSADORS OF CHRIST JESUS, PEOPLE IN THE WORLD STOP LETTING THE ENEMY CONTROL YOUR LIVES. Stop opening doors for the enemy, letting him come in through us having his properties of things he has attached himself to through other of his workers of evil occult, religious, traditions, dogmas dark blood covenants with the enemies whether its ancestral or whatever.

The devils' plans are removed from my life in Jesus' name.

The darts and daggers are removed from my body in Jesus' name. The darts are removed from my back, my mind my arms legs and all parts of my head and no part of my body belongs to the enemy and I'm not going to open any more doors, windows, portals or any types of entrance ways for the enemy to come, in Jesus' name. To give the enemy for any reason. I command him to take all his things and leave and I shut the doors and seal it tight in Jesus' name.

I revoke all his licenses that I may have given him, access, legal rights, through my ignorance, unlearned actions and choices. It also goes for our family members, as well, that may have collected, such things as any kind of clothing, jewelry and personal items. These items that any one may have given me, us, or any food or drink that I have consumed or things that have been contacted. In the mighty name of Jesus I throw it out, get rid of it and not to give it to anyone else. I bind and stop these evil spirits, that have been spoken over or may have been attached, a curse may have been written or said over my life, I destroy it in the mighty name of Jesus. So that the LORD WOULD reveal to me anything that is evil. I get rid of it and throw It out of my house, car, mind, books and even if things inside of me may be apart, I command it to come out in the name of Jesus Christ of Nazareth never to return anymore in Jesus name.

1 The enemies' attacks are no longer effective against me because they are removed in the name of Jesus.

2. Mind controlling demons be removed in Jesus name.

Every obstacle that has invaded interfered and brought roadblocks obstruction that standing in my way be removed in Jesus name.

3. Every demonic spirit that's causing confusion strife contentions and angers of rage in my life be removed in, all discomforts distractions, upsets, setbacks losses divisions, and shames of condemnation in Jesus name.

4. All the evilness that came up from the sea; this is the spirit of leviathan, marine demons, siren & monitoring and recording demons, queens and mermaids, evil princess and princes and every evil unclean nasty perverted, hybrid demons, that are part human, and demon, corrupt, twisted, slimy, deceptive manipulating cunning worker of darkness you are defeated in JESUS NAME NOW LEAVE AND BE REMOVED IN JESUS NAME, I command them to NEVER return, ever to come back ever again, you are bound restrained forbidden from returning to my life in the name of Jesus.

5. All sicknesses and diseases be removed of whatever sort you are, you are subject to the name of Jesus, now bow and submit to the name of JESUS CHRIST.

6. Be removed all things that are hindering my natural, emotional, and my spiritual, financial, social, and physical body, be gone uprooted, any bacteria or microorganism's virus germs, all toxins that are hindering my body flow be uprooted and excreted out in the name of Jesus.

CHAPTER 11

I GIVE THE COMMAND, AUTHORITY FOLLOWS, THE BIG EXPLOSIONS !!! HERE IT COMES GET READY! WOW

I COMMAND AND TAKE AUTHORITY IN THESE AREAS OF MY (LIFE) or our lives IN THE NAME OF JESUS. THAT

Authority: means to assume authority in a controlling manner, and it is our GOD-given rights to use this power and authority by permission from our ALMIGHTY GOD AND SAVIOR, JESUS THE CHRIST. To bind down not up, and I step on the head of the devil and all of his nasty demonic cohorts in Yeshuas name, or tie up, stop the enemy, and his moving, and movement from going forward, in any of my situations in the mighty name of Jesus. Any evil forces from moving forward on, or others behalf in the mighty name of Jesus,

I command it and it is so. In Jesus name, we do stop the devil and all cohorts from moving into our space, areas, and territories that's off limits. no deception, manipulations, or any types of evil schemes, tricks or arrangements, plans, diagrams, or traps, in the mighty name of Jesus.

I command them all to go and never to return again, you are forever banished from appearing here, ever in Jesus name.

Any and all Ailments found in my body or (our)

Bodies, Soul, or maybe secretly hiding in our lives, I command it, to go, in the name of Jesus, NOW!

I AM NOT ASKING THEM, I AM TELLING THEM THAT THEY HAVE TO GO AND I AM DRIVING, PUSHING THROWING THEM OUT AND FOR THEM TO NEVER RETURN EVER AGAIN. That's not ordained to be there, be removed in the name of Jesus. I take authority over Every negative spirit, thought, and thought that attempts to invade my mind, actions, Ideas evil suggestion that the enemy has interjected or comes to deceive making attempts, to implement his diabolical plans into our lives through manipulation of any kind.

I take authority and command all attacks at this moment in my life and the lives of others to cease and desist, meaning to stop, discontinue their actions or plans, and don't go any further in the mighty name of Jesus NOW!

I take authority over all evil mind sets, evil forces that comes to invade my thinking capacities. That tries to come against my actions motives and intentions that have been given to me to complete. I will not let anything stop me from completing GOD'S divine plan. This plan that's been handed down and predestinated from the foundation of the world in the mighty name of Jesus. I will finish it in Jesus name, and it is so, and so it is spoken and so it is being carried out now!

I take authority over all traps, hinderances roadblocks, obstacles, obstructions, boulders, and barriers, of all types. It could be offenses, unforeseen situations, that I might not see, that has the potential to be a hindrance, be removed, driven out of my way right now in the mighty name of Jesus. That is seemingly to stop me; be moved out of my way right now, you cannot stand in my way or you can not stop me from going forward either, any more in the name of Jesus.

I take authority over all witchcraft, workers, making attempts, or inroads, to control my life, with various plots, tricks, and all types of evil ways. That can not hinder and will not progress forward. All wizards, and warlocks that's scheming, against me, wherever they are, doing, maneuvers, that is exercising your evil plans against me, to trap to set up an ambush against me; be removed in the mighty name of Jesus. No maneuvers, or none of your tactics will ever work into my life ever again.

I command them to be destroyed, crushed in many pieces, and broken and uprooted in the name of Jesus.

I take authority over every lying spirit, familiar spirit, deception dark plan, evil demons making attempts, strategies to overcome to overtake me in any area of my life.

I command it to stop and return back and destroy those that sent you in the mighty name of Jesus it is so. Every barricade, mountain that seems to be too large for me to move in my life I speak to it to be removed and cast in the sea and never to come up, or attack me ever again in the mighty name of Jesus. I stop it and uproot, cut, till up, get rid of all of his devices that's been preplanned into my life. I am rendering him and them harmless, ineffective, null and void, and they are all stripped of any access, any power over me, any actions that they had intended to do, I restrict its authority, actions, words, sounds, and all attacks in the mighty name of Jesus. They are none affective against me or anyone else in my family in the mighty name of Jesus and it is so.

All the devils, demonic spirits, evil workers, and unclean spirits, that are planning to make plans against me are destroyed. When it comes to my destiny and nothing by any means can hurt me in the mighty name of Jesus.

I take authority and command over all psychic workers, attacks, demonic ditches that's been Dugged for me, that they will fall into their own traps, instead of me and snares in Jesus name.

I take authority and destroy all spiritual, emotional, financial, and social assignments that seeks to put me into bondages of any type be removed now in the mighty name of Jesus.

I take authority over every evil encounter that's been set out and set up, and let out to cause me a setback be destroyed, in the mighty name of Jesus, that was against me.

I command All of his plans to be revoked, stripped away and removed permanently for good and never to come together ever again and his plan is eternally terminated in Jesus name.

I command all of these 11 operating systems or more are as follows: -- _Nervous system_ and all of it make up by authority decree and declared to be healed, set free made whole fixed and made complete in the mighty name of Jesus.

I take authority and command all threats, that's been strategically planned be silenced in the name of Jesus.

Integumentary system

and all of its make up by authority decree and declared to be healed, set free made whole fixed and made complete in the might name of Jesus.

Respiratory system

and all of its make up by authority decree and declared to be healed, set free made whole fixed and made complete in the might name of Jesus.

Digestive system

and all of its make up by authority decree and declared to be healed, set free made whole fixed and made complete in the might name of Jesus.

Excretory system

and all of its make up by authority decree and declared to be healed, set free made whole fixed and made complete in the might name of Jesus.

Skeletal system

and all of its make up by authority decree and declared to be healed, set free made whole fixed and made complete in the might name of Jesus.

-- Muscular system

and all of its make up by authority decree and declared to be healed, set free made whole fixed and made complete in the might name of Jesus.

-- Circulatory system

and all of its make up by authority decree and declared to be healed, set free made whole fixed and made complete in the might name of Jesus.

-- *Endocrine system*

and all of its make up by authority decree and declared to be healed, set free made whole fixed and made complete in the might name of Jesus.

- *Reproductive system*

and all of its make up by authority decree and declared to be healed, set free made whole fixed and made complete in the might name of Jesus.

- *Lymphatic (Immune) system* TO Operate properly in the name of Jesus. I decree & declare that these systems will operate in their proper functions as ALMIGHTY has designed them in the name of Jesus, and I further command take all authority over any demon, unclean foul any spirit of infirmities that is a spirit that's weak and sickly to lose itself off of me and to get out; I'm not asking you to get out I'm COMMANDING YOU TO LEAVE IN THE NAME OF JESUS AND I REBUKE YOU spirit of sickness to leave in the mighty name of Jesus now and never to return every again.

I Command and take authority

Over all types of sicknesses and diseases,to be HEALED SET FREE AND DELIVERED IN THE NAME OF JESUS,SUCH AS ALL OF MY BONES, JOINTS,,MUSCLES, LIGAMENT'S, BLOOD, CELLS, red & white,TISSUES,FIBERS, nerves, tendons, eyes,ears, nose and mouth,tongues,hands, feet, arms,legs,toes,fingers, knees, elbows,neck, shoulders,, chest OF MY BODY TO BE REGULATED, AND GET IN MOTION THE WAY GOD HAS MADE,it to operate IN JESUS NAME, I COMMAND IT NOW.

I SILENCE.

I silence, and Quiet the mouth of the enemy and, I command all my enemies to shut their mouths, from a wagging tongue, in Jesus' name.

I silence the mouths of the devils, that working, schemes, traps, and snares of the enemy, to be none effective, against me and they are being burned with the fire of GOD from this point on forever in Jesus' name.

I walk in faith and not any type of doubt But I believe every word spoken by GOD almighty in Jesus mighty name.

I speak the word of GOD and I see results, And My tongue,will speak only the word of GOD.

I SHALL NOT DOUBT IN MY HEART

ST MARK 11:24-26

I shall not doubt but I'm a believer of GODS word

24 Therefore I say unto you, What things soever ye desire, when ye pray, believe that ye receive *them*, and ye shall have *them*.

25 And when ye stand praying, forgive, if ye have fought against any: that your Father also which is in heaven may forgive you your trespasses.

26 But if ye do not forgive, neither will your Father which is in heaven forgive your trespasses.

I want to say that sometimes we that are living and breathing on the face of this earth. We get ourselves in troubles through our unforgiveness. I said this once before if I have repeated a matter in my book, its because its necessary to drive the thoughts, ideas and situations home. So many times: we are sick with some type of ailment its most times if we would check our situations out. We have caused our sicknesses and diseases through holding unforgiveness against someone else or even sometime it starts with not forgiven ourselves. This is a start of a major sickness or a terminal disease such as cancer, strokes, heart diseases, heart attacks. These situations happens due to stress from our thinking, worrying about something that we have done. What we should have done at the time is get on our knees and begin to pray. I have said many times that prayer is one of the first lines of defense along with the words of GOD. To pray ourselves out of all of the messes that we have gotten ourselves in and the LORD GOD, & JESUS had nothing to do with it. We did not sought them for what we should do in the case of these troubles, and things we have caused.

I decree and declare, that I have forgiven all of those who have offended me, and I release them all and will not hold any type of ill feelings, of hate revenge, anger, bitterness, rage, retaliation, or guilt over their heads as well as myself and I release them and let them go free in Jesus name. I hold nothing against them whatsoever in the mighty name of JESUS.

I decree and declare that I am forgiven, because I have been forgiven, so therefore I forgive, those all that have ever hurt me, slandered, talked about me, cut me down with their tongues. Murdered me on verbally on a platter that slices & diced me up, like mincemeat. I forgive them for all their actions, words, deeds, of plots, that have taken advantage of me, for putting me down. Underestimating or assumed that I knew this, information,

or that about whatever, that may have been at the time.

Those that may have given up on me, was'nt patient or did not have enough patients with me, even myself.

I forgive myself of all the faults, mistakes, things I did, the many ways I felt about myself in the past.

I hold no blame against myself or anyone, else, with no ought's or anything holding against any in the way of: words, actions, deeds, choices, feelings that came across my mind. Thoughts and feelings, I have entertained them causing them to be planted in the soil of my ground called my mind and thoughts.

I forgive myself and I do not hold myself or others in debt for whatever they have done or said transgressed, sinned, blocked, became a stumbling block in my way and I did nothing at the time.

Because I was either ignorant, scared, blind, vulnerable, fearful, frightened, terrified, or horrified in a paralyzing way. I forgive my parents, dad, mom, sisters' brothers, all in-laws, and all relatives that have touched me, or said things to me that was hurting in some kind of way that was not appropriate or right. I forgive all those that, for whatever reason did not trust or trusting me, helping or help me, protecting or protected me. Holding me and telling me that they love me, and that they really care, for me. That they are here for me and will let nothing happen to me as long as they are around in the mighty name of Jesus and it is so.

I believe when I pray that GOD hears my prayers and petitions.

GOD hears my heart cries, and knows all about whatsoever I go through.

So I give him all my situations to him now and never worry about how they are going to get or be fixed in the mighty name of Jesus. That is my release to him, all my problems, not to worry, panic or be under stress with all the things that are going on in my life in the mighty name of Jesus.

GO in Jesus name;

TELLING THE ENEMY TO GO AND NEVER TO RETURN

TAKING YOUR RIGHTFUL PLACE IN THE KINGDOM OF GOD AS A CHILD OF THE HIGHEST GOD AND SOVEREIGN SAVIOR IN JESUS NAME.

In the name of jesus all demonic activities that came up against me attacked me through sicknesses or any types of diseases I command you to leave and I cast you out in the name of Jesus. You are not welcome on me, or any part of me on the inside of my thoughts or actions in the name of Jesus now!

St Matthews 8:32

And he (Jesus)said unto them, Go. And when they were come out.

I command hate anger,revenge, rejection, abandonment,unacceptance, every evil thought, rage,vengeance, evil speaking, malicious way, every occult practice, to GO in the mighty name of Jesus.

Witches, being female, warlocks, being males all practicing any type of evilness, & wizards, attempting to do any type of magic spells, incantations, making evil potions, dirty food, calling up evil spirits from the underworld, I bind and stop your activities in the name of Jesus right this moment in the mighty name of Jesus.

Those that are practicing witchcraft, doing evil things, mentioning our names in the atmospheres, I block it, and shred, your plans, crush the head of the serpent, viper, dog, wolf, or whatever type of spirit, that is at work against me, I command in the name of Jesus, you to GO NOW!

I command barriers and blocks of boundaries to be put up against these attacks, and I send it back to the sender 100-fold in Jesus' name. These tactics of the enemy will not come back to do me any harm, or danger of any other type of pain in the mighty name of Jesus.

I command all demons to go and never to return ever again you are not wanted in this place in fact you are banned from ever coming here.

I close every door that is opened to the enemy to be closed in the name of Jesus and I get rid of any materials such as books, pictures, statues and anything that might have been given to me that is evil or that might have or carry a curse, or a spirit may have been attached on it, or in it in the name of Jesus .

Our prayers send out ENERGY, power, & Authority against our enemies. So, he encourages and fight the good fight of faith in the MIGHTY name of JESUS CHRIST.

When we talk about atomic powers, what are we referring to and about?

We're talking about energy being sent out or released or supplied to fulfill to activate combustions and outbursts of power.

WARFARE SCRIPTURES

When we speak about warfare, what are we really talking, about and referring to? Are we talking about war, attacks without defense and no power just getting ran over by the enemy and nothing to do about it? BY no means ARE we defeated not letting the enemy trample all over us. We have power & authority, that is what we called dumamis power, and esousia, that's our authority we use against our enemies. We use weapons, tools, armor, this is the whole armor of GOD, in Ephesians 6:10-18 to with stand the blows, the hits, and all that he may throws or launch at us in a way of an attack. These things we should already know through reading and studying this book up to this point. You should be on fire, armored up, suited up, and dangerous against the devil and all of his cohort. You should by now, all that have been said, have gotten rid of any type of demons, and know how to attack the devil.

Knows his tactics, knows what a lot of these terms are and how to put them to use. By now you should be to a point where you can spot and identify the voice of the devil any evil spirit, anything that is not from GOD. BY NOW, you should be able to understand the word of GOD, know the benefits of fasting and most of the components, the blessings and the strengths of doing whatever it may be; be it studying the word of GOD, MANY other things you should already know about this time, and at this point.

Our job is to drive out any type of devil and all evil spirits all unclean demons, and foul spirits, including marine demons in the oceans, seas, and all those demons that pass through; the waters. Queens, princesses, and princes that are evil occultic; witches, warlocks, witchcraft, wizards, demonic, and all dark evil contrary to the plans of GOD. Whether in the air, land, water, or under the earth or wherever they may appear. We're going to attack and STOP THEM, from all their activities, make no difference how big or small how dark or large, evil they may appear to be we have superior power.

This happens, ONLY IN AND THROUGH the MIGHTY name of JESUS. THE devil is defeated at the name of JESUS, and in the mighty name of Jesus as well. He is terrified of the precious powerful name of Jesus.

WARFARE includes every way the enemy comes in at us. Any time and any place.

Our job is to recognize, what is going on and put a stop to it in the name of Jesus. Something that GOD has ordained and sanction for his children to partake in. We should enjoy lifting up his HOLY name in the MIGHTY name of JESUS. WE fight with his WORD, HIS SPIRIT, HIS ANGELS OF LIGHT AND POWER FROM ON HIGH INCLUDING MICHAEL THE ARCH and chief warrior angel. In Heaven to fight for us and with us in the mighty name of Jesus. We fight with his blood, armour, spears and praise worship, waving banners, javelins, fires of GOD.

GOD INDIGNATION and his fierce wrath, his anger that can be kindled against the devil and all his armies. We defeat and conquer, means to defeat overcome by fighting against him and putting him under our feet, taking back what he has stolen. Letting our Lord have his way in our lives and submitting to the Lord of our life in the name of Jesus. In all that we do we do it all for the glory of GOD our Heavenly Father.

A name that's above each and every other name in Heaven and on the Earth as well. Has the power to subdue and bring down satan, Beelzebub, the devil, Lucifer, these and many other names he has and have been called from time to time.

All that he stands for, and all his cohorts, his agents of evil, his fallen army, and many more, many that have been mentioned many times. All that he tries to do against us, because he's defeated.

Warfare Is fighting and stopping the devil, and all our enemies from moving forward to distort distract, or even try to disrupt or corrupt, what GOD has made pure and clean. Our job, to come against him and not to be afraid, but attack him many times as he comes up against us, in any type of way. We should never be fearful and terrified but be bold with the fire of GOD.

Enjoy these scriptures and most of all repeat them, say them out loud. Say them so you can hear what you are saying. Begin to see and feel results; decree and declare them before the Lord, your families each and every day of your lives.

The word of GOD is here to protect you and give you, whatever you may need. It might be, that you need to be protected my his awesome shields, a place of safety. All that are around may be blessed and strengthen. It will encouraged, you the words of GOD. It will add years to your life and life, to the years that you are living for the Lord. GOD which is energy power strength and all that the word of GOD HAS to offer. Anyone that will put in the time and receive the bountiful blessings, in the words of GOD, it will build you up and make you a strong warrior, a soldier in the army of the LORD.

Ephesians 6:12 - For we wrestle not against flesh and blood, but against principalities, against powers, against the rulers of the darkness of this world, against spiritual wickedness in high places (***and may I add low places as well.***)

We are not fighting with natural weapons such as guns, knives, tanks, cannons, poisons, chemicals, nuclear bombs, missiles, mines, and Bobi-traps of any kind. No gas warfare of biological, atomic plutonium rockets, and all that make up natural things that can destroy the earth. These are natural weapons and things that destroy the earth, land, and humans as well.

We do not fight as SAINTS OF GOD WITH THESE TYPES of natural physical weapons. OUR weapons are in prayer, SPIRITUAL power that cannot be seen with the natural eyes. But the power we have been given can be demonstrated. This power will be seen and felt in the spirit and the demons know that when they are hit with these weapons they feel this type of power with the fire of GOD. THE WORD THAT HITS THEM AS WE SPEAK IT. fasting to humble our souls to the Lord. Praise is a weapons as I described in some the of previous chapters, so don't fail to go back and review and learn and ask the Lord to help you grasp what he is saying to you through his word. All that he has to offer you in the name of Jesus.

Let us talk about some more types of weapons such as FAITH IN THE WORD OF GOD, living a holy and clean life; is a weapon against our enemies, because we live free from SIN.

Ephesians 6:11 - Put on the whole armour of GOD, that ye may be able to stand against the wiles of the devil. The wiles may represent tricks, schemes, deceptive tactics, evil plots to trap someone, dangerous harmful things to cause one to have little to no movement, and can even cause death to the one involved. We put on the ARMOUR OF GOD and never take it off. So if anyone has taken off their armour because they may get tired of fighting. That is not a smart idea to do in the heat of the battle. Put on all that GOD has given us and put it to use each day while we are living in this side of the world, earth, or even this side of heaven.

2 Corinthians 10:3-5 - For though we walk in the flesh, we do not war after the flesh: for the weapons of our warfare are not Carnal but mighty through GOD to the pulling down of STRONGHOLDS. These strongholds; what are they? how did they get here? How did I grab this type of stronghold into my life. How did I not realize that this was ruling in my life without me knowing it?

Could I somehow be operating in some form of ignorance? Yes perhaps, without knowing. Maybe my heart at the time or my spirit was not aware of. Maybe I did not take interest, did not notice, was unable to detect what was going on in my life. When these things were taking place or even taking shape in my life without me, realizing, it at all whatsoever. Did not care? or pick up,on the warning signs, or did I ever know what the signs we're at all?

Did I have a sense of what was going on at the time in my life.? Could it be that so much was happening in my life that my attention was diverted to other things? Seemingly to be more important at the time?

Needing more of my time than other things went unattended with no attention paid to them whatsoever?. By what means and avenue did these strongholds enter my life without me ever paying attention to them? Did I even know what a stronghold is? The answer is no ? I did not know. I was not taught this before in my entire life. Have I ever heard of such a word? YES in GOD's word only.

It was because of our IGNORANCE NOT having a sense of awareness, alertness, focus, lacking in knowledge as Hosea 4:6 WE NEED TO START; studying GOD'S word for ourselves and not always depend on everyone else to give us what they want to give us. We must be seasoned as a veterans, Elders, that is learned students of GOD, in his word. As the word of GOD had said, These were noble than those in Thessalonica, in that they received the word with the all readiness of mind, and searched the scriptures daily, whether those things were so.

Acts 17:11 . this takes away all types of excuses away from all leaders, Saints and all who are in the body of Christ, how by studying GOD'S word, his messages, his thoughts, his plans and all that he has for us. GOD'S WORD IS HIS WILL, THE WILL OF GOD IS THE THOUGHTS OF GOD, WRITTEN FOR HIS PEOPLE TO FOLLOW. WHAT IS THE WILL OF GOD? IT IS HIS WORD THOUGHTS AND PLANS AS STATED BEFORE, SO HOW TO BE LED BY HIS SPIRIT, THAT IS READ THE WORD OF GOD AND TO FOLLOW ALL THE CONTENT THAT HE HAS SAID FOR US. THIS IS HIS WILL, PLANS, INSTRUCTIONS, INFORMATION ON PAPER PLAIN AND SIMPLE TO FOLLOW.

THE PROPHET OF GOD SPEAKING TO THE PEOPLE AND THE LORD IS TELLING THEM, US AND ALL WHO IS READING; MY PEOPLE ARE DESTROYED FOR LACK OF KNOWLEDGE: WHY? BECAUSE (WE, THEM, THOSE YOU, ME US) THOU HAST REJECTED KNOWLEDGE, AND THE LORD IS SAYING STILL SAYING HAS SAID) I WILL ALSO REJECT THEE THAT THOU SHALT BE NO PRIEST TO ME: SEEING THOU HAST FORGOTTEN THE LAW OF THY GOD, I WILL ALSO FORGET THY CHILDREN. LET'S stop coming up to these types of experiences.

These experiences that pronounces types of indictments from the Lord of Glory on us as a people. This is not a great and comfortable good place to be with the Lord so let's learn from our ignorance's, or choices. Because they really do not belong to us so we need to stop claiming things that's not ours in the name of Jesus. Not having enough of knowledge as much as knowledge in this season time, period, & dispensation.

We have experienced the age of information in the 20th Century. The 21st Century presented to us as the age of Technology. Where we can do extensive research, with great devices, equipment, electronics, the digital age movement. Computers, has also been a big part of our lives as they have help us in many areas of our lives at this time. I pads, and the A.I. artificial intelligence, like watches on our wrist that convert to a phone, and camera all together, we have the ability to search and research on subjects not given or even hidden, anymore. But are now being revealed to us, The mystery or secrets have come out of the ages for us to enjoy and take full advantage, that has never been discovered until now. Lets start taking advantage of these great studies and researches across the globe like never before heard of or seen, We are truly blessed.

Psalms 91:1-16 - He that dwelleth in the secret place of the most High shall abide under the shadow of the Almighty. Dwelling in the secret's places with the Lord, is a sure foundation of confidence security, protection, silence, a safe place to hide in and have a place called shield buckler, a wall of defense and so much more.

BRINGING SOME EXPLANATION FOR UNDERSTANDING,

1 Peter 5:8 - Be sober, be vigilant; because your adversary the devil, as a roaring lion, walketh about, seeking whom he may devour:

What does the word _**SOBER**_ mean really, a sober person who is alert to all types of dangers, of the world, at home, on the job and in an anointed ministry under leadership of careful watchmen and women? The flesh, and the devil, will not be easily distracted by side issues, that may cause one to lose their lives or get hurt or wounded because they are steadfastly on their post, watching, and will not suffer any situations to happen while on duty in the mighty name of Jesus.

Being vigilant, always watching for all types of dangers, and will not let anything take place if they have the power on their watch to do something about it. At this moment no one will be taken away due to negligent behavior, being caught off guard, or not paying attention to what is happening in the spirit,

James 4:7 - Submit yourselves therefore to GOD.
Resist the devil, and he will flee from you.

SUBMIT simply in meaning yielding to spiritual guidelines according to GOD'S WORD. Coming under to follow rules and regulations, information, instructions that has been given, will be rendered to one or receive what is handed down to one by those that are in charge watching for their souls. Not given in to the enemies traps or being overtaken by temptations of the flesh, far as lust of the flesh, lust of the eyes, or the pride of life will not over take them, but they will be triumphant. The ability to overcome in the hour of temptation, and pass the test with flying colors, in Jesus name. 1 John 2:15-17 please read it at your leisure.

Ephesians 6:13 - Wherefore take unto you the whole armour of GOD, that ye, *(you)* may be able to withstand in the evil day, and having done all, to stand.

TAKING ALL THE EQUIPMENT THAT HAS BEEN ISSUED TO YOU AND USE TO YOUR FULLEST EXTENT.

Deuteronomy 28:7 - The LORD shall cause thine enemies that rise up against thee to be smitten before thy face: they shall come out against thee one way, and flee before thee seven ways.

Luke 10:19 - Behold, I give unto you power to tread on serpents and scorpions, and over all the power of the enemy: and nothing shall by any means hurt you.

THE ABILITY WALK ON THE HEADS OF THE ENEMY, AND OBTAIN THE VICTORY.

2 Corinthians 10:4 - (For the weapons of our warfare are not carnal but mighty through GOD .

THESE WEAPONS ARE SPIRITUAL ONES THAT WE FIGHT NOT FLESH AND BLOOD BUT demon spirits. Evil spirits without bodies looking for someone to enter into them, and start acting out there desires and evil plans.

1 John 5:4 For whatsoever is born or GOD overcometh the world: and this is the victory that overcometh the world, even our faith.

Because we are born from GOD ALMIGHTY, we have, the victory, the ability to overcome anything that stands in our way. We hurdle over that thing in our lives and keep moving forward by and through FAITH, trusting in what GOD has said about me. What I can have, and who I am and my reliance is in him and on him, and not myself, this is the ANTIDOTE FOR VICTORY, THE ABILITY TO OVERCOME ANY OBSTACLES I MAY FACE AT ANY GIVEN TIME IN MY LIFE.

Matthew 18:18-20 - Verily I say unto you, Whatsoever ye shall bind on earth shall be bound in HEAVEN and whatsoever ye shall loose on earth shall be loosed in HEAVEN.

Ephesians 6:11-12 - Put on the whole armour of GOD, that ye may be able to stand against the wiles of the devil.

Psalms 84:11 - For the LORD GOD is a sun and shield: the LORD will give grace and glory: no good thing will he withhold from them that walk uprightly.

There hath no temptation taken you but such as is common to man: but GOD is faithful, who will not suffer you to be tempted above that ye are able; but will with the temptation also make a way to escape, that ye may be able to bear it.

1 Corinthians 10:13

Then he answered and spake unto me, saying, this is the word of the Lord unto Zerubbabel, saying, Not by might, nor by power, but by my Spirit, saith the Lord of hosts.

Zechariah 4:6

These things I have spoken unto you, that in me ye might have peace. In the world ye shall have tribulation: but be of good cheer; I have overcome the world.

John 16:33

Put on the whole armour of GOD, that ye may be able to stand against the wiles of the devil.

Ephesians 6:11

Have not I commanded thee? Be strong and of a good courage; be not afraid, neither be thou dismayed: for the Lord thy GOD is with thee whithersoever thou goest.

Joshua 1:9

Ye are of GOD, little children, and have overcome them: because greater is he that is in you, than he that is in the world.

1 John 4:4

And no marvel; for Satan himself is transformed into an angel of light.

2 Corinthians 11:14 the ability to transform into other look alikes, for example certain angels in heaven, of sometype, that, but are fallen spirits or demon & devils

Make a joyful noise unto the Lord, all ye lands.

2 Serve the Lord with gladness: come before his presence with singing.

3 Know ye that the Lord he is GOD: it is he that hath made us, and not we ourselves; we are his people, and the sheep of his pasture.

4 Enter into his gates with thanksgiving, and into his courts with praise: be thankful unto him, and bless his name.

5 For the Lord is good; his mercy is everlasting; and his truth endureth to all generations.

Psalm 100:1-5

13 Enter ye in at the strait gate: for wide is the gate, and broad is the way, that leadeth to destruction, and many there be which go in thereat:

14 Because strait is the gate, and narrow is the way, which leadeth unto life, and few there be that find it.

Matthew 7:13-14

And we know that we are of GOD, and the whole world lieth in wickedness.

1 John 5:19

13 Who hath delivered us from the power of darkness, and hath translated us into the kingdom of his dear Son:

14 In whom we have redemption through his blood, even the forgiveness of sins:

Colossians 1:13-14

But thanks be to GOD, which giveth us the victory through our Lord Jesus Christ.

1 Corinthians 15:57

4 (For the weapons of our warfare are not carnal, but mighty through GOD to the pulling down of strong holds;)

5 Casting down imaginations, and every high thing that exalteth itself against the knowledge of GOD, and bringing into captivity every thought to the obedience of Christ.

2 Corinthians 10:4-5

37 Nay, in all these things we are more than conquerors through him that loved us.

38 For I am persuaded, that neither death, nor life, nor angels, nor principalities, nor powers, nor things present, nor things to come,

39 Nor height, nor depth, nor any other creature, shall be able to separate us from the love of GOD, which is in Christ Jesus our Lord.

Romans 8:37-39

3 For though we walk in the flesh, we do not war after the flesh:

4 (For the weapons of our warfare are not carnal, but mighty through GOD to the pulling down of strong holds;)

5 Casting down imaginations, and every high thing that exalteth itself against the knowledge of GOD, and bringing into captivity every thought to the obedience of Christ.

2 Corinthians 10:3-5

The Lord shall cause thine enemies that rise up against thee to be smitten before thy face: they shall come out against thee one way, and flee before thee seven ways.

Deuteronomy 28:7

Behold, I give unto you power to tread on serpents and scorpions, and over all the power of the enemy: and nothing shall by any means hurt you.

Luke 10:19

9 Whom resist stedfast in the faith, knowing that the same afflictions are accomplished in your brethren that are in the world.

1 Peter 5:8-9

But the Lord is faithful, who shall stablish you, and keep you from evil.

2 Thessalonians 3:3

Nay, *(or no)* in all these things we are more than conquerors through him that loved us.

Romans 8:37

In whom the god of this world(the god of this world in which we are living is satan,) the devil in case someone did not know(hath blinded the minds of them which believe not, lest the light of the glorious gospel of Christ, who is the image of GOD, should shine unto them.

satan is the god of this world with a little g not the GOD of creation, not the GOD that is everywhere all at the same time. Satan is not the GOD that has all power and knows all things and can do anything and there is not limits or restrictions to what he can do. Because GOD, JEHOVAH IS EVERLASTING, OUR HEAVENLY FATHER. So people do not get this statement mixed up with the god of this world who's name is satan or was lucifer, the fallen angel that has lost his first estate in Heaven.

2 Corinthians 4:4

What shall we then say to these things? If GOD be for us, who can be against us?

Romans 8:31

Fight the good fight of faith, lay hold on eternal life, whereunto thou art also called, and hast professed a good profession before many witnesses.

1 Timothy 6:12

No weapon that is formed against thee(US) shall prosper; and every tongue that shall rise against thee in judgment thou shalt condemn.

Isaiah 54:17.

The thief cometh not, but for to steal, and to kill, and to destroy: I am come that they might have life, and that they might have it more abundantly.

John 10:10

This charge I commit unto thee, that thou by them mightest war a good warfare.

1 Timothy 1:18

7 And there was war in heaven: Michael and his angels fought against the dragon; and the dragon fought and his angels,

8 And prevailed not; neither was their place found any more in heaven.

9 And the great dragon was cast out, that old serpent, called the Devil, and Satan, which deceiveth the whole world: he was cast out into the earth, and his angels were cast out with him.

Revelation 12:7-9

Are you aware of the attacks of the enemy?

Descriptive Words to attack our enemies; we take authority over & dominion to drive back every evil spirit.

Dismantle, destroy, disrupt, Hinder, uproot, crush & demolish, till up, break, strip away, revoke the license of our enemies. Close all open doors, windows, portals entry points to the enemy. To shut the mouth of all the Lions wannabes, gainsayers, scoffers, mockers. Terrorize all our adversaries. Burn to ashes the devils all unclean spirits, and handcuff all evil demons. Throw all those evil spirits, that are in the water which is marine, leviathan octopus, mind-controlling demons, and all that passed through the sea psalms 8:6-9 into the abyss to be burned forever. For we fight against and wrestle, attack, chase, pursue run down, drive back, hunt down, cast out, beat down, strip down, tear down, devour, through consumption, all with the word of GOD, JESUS BLOOD AND ALL THE TOOLS AND WEAPONS THAT WE HAVE IN OUR ARSENAL TO TAKE OUT THE ENEMIES OUT OF OUR LIVES. We put to shame and confusion the works of our enemies. We overcome we are triumphant, which is victory in every area of our lives over every strategy of the devil or evil spirits. We smite against, slaughter, prevail, over, and against every demonic force that tries to hinder, us or cause some type of delay.

SPIRITUAL STRENGTH

Ephesians 6:10 Finally, be strong in the Lord and in the *POWER (or strength and his ETERNAL LIMITLESS ABILITIES, ENERGIES DOMINIONS and all that He GOD can do by himself)* of His might.

Finally, be strong in the Lord and in the strength of His might.

DISARM

We need to learn how to disarm our enemies not just speaking or uttering with our own mouths, things of no avail. We are just uttering things out of our mouths we are wasting time and precious energy. So, to disarm our enemies we need to with GODS words NOT OURS that is why we do not walk in the flesh but walk in the spirit. Walking in the spirit each and every day requires prayer, consecration of the flesh mortifying or killing out the deeds of this old man, our old nature this carnal nature and carnal man get this picture and frame of mind. Colossians 2:15 And having spoiled principalities and power, he made a shew of them openly, Triumphing over them in it.

SYNONYMS FOR THE WORD DISARM.

❖ Deactivate; means to make something inactive by disconnecting and destroying it.

❖ Demilitarize means to get rid of all military forces from an area.

❖ Demobilize means to make something incapable of movement or unable to go or move.

❖ Disband means to cause something to breakup or stop functioning!

❖ Neutralize means to limit something in their movement.

❖ Subdue means to overcome or bring under Control, defeat by force.

❖ Cripple

❖ Debilitate means to make something weak!

❖ Disqualify meaning someone are ineligible, can not any more, at this point, be a part of activities.

❖ Incapacitate means to prevent from functioning in any way, shape, form, or fashion.

❖ Invalidate means to void someone or something out.

❖ Paralyze means to stop their movement from going forward.

❖ Strip means to take things away from them where they are torn down completely to one naked to uncover expose, undress, to clean out.

❖ Weaken means to take away their strength, energy, power to function!

❖ DeEscalate

This means to reduce the intensity of a conflict or potentially violent situation.

Deuteronomy 28:7

The Lord shall cause thine enemies that rise up against thee to be smitten before thy face: they shall come out against thee one way, and flee before thee seven ways.

Exodus 23:22

But if thou shalt indeed obey his voice, and do all that I speak; then I will be an enemy unto thine enemies, and an adversary unto thine adversaries.

Genesis 22:17

That in blessing I will bless thee, and in multiplying I will multiply thy seed as the stars of the heaven, and as the sand which is upon the sea shore; and thy seed shall possess the gate of his enemies;

Genesis 14:20

And blessed be the most high GOD, which hath delivered thine enemies into thy hand. And he gave him tithes of all.

Luke 10:19

Behold, I give unto you power to tread on serpents and scorpions, and over all the power of the enemy: and nothing shall by any means hurt you.

Leviticus 26:6

And I will give peace in the land, and ye shall lie down, and none shall make you afraid: and I will rid evil beasts out of the land, neither shall the sword go through your land.

Psalm 81:14

I should soon have subdued their enemies, and turned my hand against their adversaries.

1 John 4:4

Ye are of GOD, little children, and have overcome them: because greater is he that is in you, than he that is in the world.

Genesis 12:3

And I will bless them that bless thee, and curse him that curseth thee: and in thee shall all families of the earth be blessed.

Luke 6:27-30

But I say unto you which hear, Love your enemies, do good to them which hate you, Bless them that curse you, and pray for them which despitefully use you. And unto him that smiteth thee on the one cheek offer also the other; and him that taketh away thy cloak forbid not to take thy coat also. Give to every man that asketh of thee; and of him that taketh away thy goods ask them not again.

Psalm 143:12

And of thy mercy cut off mine enemies, and destroy all them that afflict my soul: for I am thy servant.

2 Corinthians 10:3-5

For though we walk in the flesh, we do not war after the flesh: (For the weapons of our warfare are not carnal, but mighty through GOD to the pulling down of strong holds;) Casting down imaginations, and every high thing that exalteth itself against the knowledge of GOD, and bringing into captivity every thought to the obedience of Christ;

Deuteronomy 30:7

And the Lord thy GOD will put all these curses upon thine enemies, and on them that hate thee, which persecuted thee.

Genesis 49:8

Judah, thou art he whom thy brethren shall praise: thy hand shall be in the neck of thine enemies; thy father's children shall bow down before thee.

Isaiah 54:17

No weapon that is formed against thee shall prosper; and every tongue that shall rise against thee in judgment thou shalt condemn. This is the heritage of the servants of the Lord, and their righteousness is of me, saith the Lord.

Proverbs 24:17

Rejoice not when thine enemy falleth, and let not thine heart be glad when he stumbleth:

Mark 12:36

For David himself said by the Holy Spirit, The Lord said to my Lord, Sit thou on my right hand, till I make thine enemies thy footstool.

1 Peter 5:8-9

Be sober, be vigilant; because your adversary the devil, as a roaring lion, walketh about, seeking whom he may devour: Whom resist stedfast in the faith, knowing that the same afflictions are accomplished in your brethren that are in the world.

Jeremiah 30:20

Their children also shall be as aforetime, and their congregation shall be established before me, and I will punish all that oppress them.

Psalm 138:7

Though I walk in the midst of trouble, thou wilt revive me:
thou shalt stretch forth thine hand against the wrath of
mine enemies, and thy right hand shall save me.

Romans 12:20

Therefore if thine enemy hunger, feed him; if he thirst, give him
drink: for in so doing thou shalt heap coals of fire on his head.

Luke 1:74

That he would grant unto us, that we being delivered out of
the hand of our enemies might serve him without fear,

Numbers 24:9

He couched, he lay down as a lion, and as a great lion: who shall stir him
up? Blessed is he that blesseth thee, and cursed is he that curseth thee.

Romans 12:19

Dearly beloved, avenge not yourselves, but rather give place unto wrath:
for it is written, Vengeance is mine; I will repay, saith the Lord.

Deuteronomy 20:1

When thou goest out to battle against thine enemies, and seest horses, and
chariots, and a people more than thou, be not afraid of them: for the Lord
thy GOD is with thee, which brought thee up out of the land of Egypt.

Luke 19:27

But those mine enemies, which would not that I should reign
over them, bring hither, and slay them before me.

Ephesians 6:11-17

Put on the whole armour of GOD, that ye may be able to stand against the wiles of the devil. For we wrestle not against flesh and blood, but against principalities, against powers, against the rulers of the darkness of this world, against spiritual wickedness in high places. Wherefore take unto you the whole armour of God, that ye may be able to withstand in the evil day, and having done all, to stand. Stand therefore, having your loins girt about with truth, and having on the breastplate of righteousness; And your feet shod with the preparation of the gospel of peace; Above all, taking the shield of faith, wherewith ye shall be able to quench all the fiery darts of the wicked. And take the helmet of salvation, and the sword of the Spirit, which is the word of GOD:

Luke 6:28-30

Bless them that curse you and pray for them which despitefully use you. And unto him that smiteth thee on the one cheek offer also the other; and him that taketh away thy cloak forbid not to take thy coat also. Give to every man that asketh of thee; and of him that taketh away thy goods ask them not again.

1 Peter 5:8

Be sober, be vigilant; because your adversary the devil, as a roaring lion, walketh about, seeking whom he may devour:

Luke 21:15

For I will give you a mouth and wisdom, which all your adversaries shall not be able to gainsay nor resist.

Romans 8:37

Nay, in all these things we are more than conquerors through him that loved us.

1 Thessalonians 5:15

See that none render evil for evil unto any man; but ever follow
that which is good, both among yourselves, and to all men.

Ephesians 6:12

For we wrestle not against flesh and blood, but against
principalities, against powers, against the rulers of the darkness
of this world, against spiritual wickedness in high places.

Proverbs 16:7

When a man's ways please the Lord, he maketh
even his enemies to be at peace with him.

1 Corinthians 15:57

But thanks be to GOD, which giveth us the
victory through our Lord Jesus Christ.

Luke 6:35

But love ye your enemies, and do good, and lend, hoping for nothing
again; and your reward shall be great, and ye shall be the children
of the Highest: for he is kind unto the unthankful and to the evil.

Leviticus 26:7

And ye shall chase your enemies, and they
shall fall before you by the sword.

Romans 12:14

Bless them which persecute you: bless, and curse not.

Matthew 5:43

Ye have heard that it hath been said, Thou shalt
love thy neighbour, and hate thine enemy.

Matthew 5:43-45

Ye have heard that it hath been said, Thou shalt love thy neighbour, and
hate thine enemy. But I say unto you, Love your enemies, bless them
that curse you, do good to them that hate you, and pray for them which
despitefully use you, and persecute you; That ye may be the children
of your Father which is in heaven: for he maketh his sun to rise on the
evil and on the good, and sendeth rain on the just and on the unjust.

Leviticus 26:8

And five of you shall chase an hundred, and an hundred of you shall put
ten thousand to flight: and your enemies shall fall before you by the sword.

1 Peter 3:9

Not rendering evil for evil, or railing for railing: but contrariwise blessing;
knowing that ye are thereunto called, that ye should inherit a blessing.

Micah 5:9

Thine hand shall be lifted up were cast out with him.

Psalm 37:1-6

Fret not thyself because of evildoers, neither be thou envious
against the workers of iniquity. For they shall soon be cut down
like the grass, and wither as the green herb. Trust in the Lord,
and do good; so shalt thou dwell in the land, and verily thou shalt
be fed. Delight thyself also in the Lord: and he shall give thee the
desires of thine heart. Commit thy way unto the Lord; trust also

in him; and he shall bring it to pass. And he shall bring forth thy righteousness as the light, and thy judgment as the noonday.

Micah 7:10

Then she that is mine enemy shall see it, and shame shall cover her which said unto me, Where is the Lord thy God? mine eyes shall behold her: now shall she be trodden down as the mire of the streets.

3 John 11

Beloved, follow not that which is evil, but that which is good. He that doeth good is of GOD: but he that doeth evil hath not seen GOD.

Leviticus 26:17

And I will set my face against you, and ye shall be slain before your enemies: they that hate you shall reign over you; and ye shall flee when none pursueth you.

Ephesians 6:11

Put on the whole armour of GOD, that ye may be able to stand against the wiles of the devil.

Romans 13:4-6

For he is the minister of GOD to thee for good. But if thou do that which is evil, be afraid; for he beareth not the sword in vain: for he is the minister of GOD, a revenger to execute wrath upon him that doeth evil. Wherefore ye must needs be subject, not only for wrath, but also for conscience sake. For this cause pay ye tribute also: for they are GOD's ministers, attending continually upon this very thing.

Matthew 18:18-19

Verily I say unto you, Whatsoever ye shall bind on earth shall be bound in heaven: and whatsoever ye shall loose on earth shall be loosed in heaven. Again I say unto you, That if two of you shall agree on earth as touching any thing that they shall ask, it shall be done for them of my Father which is in heaven.

Psalm 54:5

He shall reward evil unto mine enemies: cut them off in thy truth.

Leviticus 26:36

And upon them that are left alive of you I will send a faintness into their hearts in the lands of their enemies; and the sound of a shaken leaf shall chase them; and they shall flee, as fleeing from a sword; and they shall fall when none pursueth.

Colossians 2:1

And having spoiled principalities and powers, he made a shew of them openly, triumphing over them in it.

Psalm 6:10

Let all mine enemies be ashamed and sore vexed: let them return and be ashamed suddenly.

Psalm 18:48

He delivereth me from mine enemies: yea, thou liftest me up above those that rise up against me: thou hast delivered me from the violent man.

Psalm 23:5

Thou preparest a table before me in the presence of mine enemies:
thou anointest my head with oil; my cup runneth over.

John 16:33

These things I have spoken unto you, that in me ye
might have peace. In the world ye shall have tribulation:
but be of good cheer; I have overcome the world.

1 Corinthians 10:13

There hath no temptation taken you but such as is common
to man: but GOD is faithful, who will not suffer you to be
tempted above that ye are able; but will with the temptation
also make a way to escape, that ye may be able to bear it.

Psalm 109:2-5

For the mouth of the wicked and the mouth of the deceitful are
opened against me: they have spoken against me with a lying
tongue. They compassed me about also with words of hatred;
and fought against me without a cause. For my love they are
my adversaries: but I give myself unto prayer. And they have
rewarded me evil for good, and hatred for my love.

PULLING DOWN STRONGHOLDS

WHAT ARE STRONGHOLDS?

So, a stronghold is, or can be considered a fortress. A place that's
surrounded by gates, walls or even iron bars, no one comes in or typically
no one comes out. They can not go out due to the gates being locked,
secured, closed, and shutdown. Unless they have keys, codes, cards to

swipe, or buttons to push to get some type of access of entrance in or out. Strongholds, A fortified place of being in lockdown, these can take place In our minds, patterns of thinking. Mental cycles of thinking, patterns. Ways in which, we put together our thoughts, wrongfully, erroneous, evil, wrong, ways of thinking about something that is not right, but is not the right way or the truth about something that stop us from moving forward.

It has become a strong barrier, iron bars to keep everyone out. It is called a left field of wrong, iron bar thinking patterns. Ways that we think, someone has told us about, or someone has been teaching us about practically all or most of our lives. This kind of thinking that one person, or family members, be it groups, church's, organizations, clubs and other forms has gotten, information from deceptive sources, because they either were feed some type of information and believed it, or was forced to take in believe a certain way.

Someone may have put them in a state of being trap in their thinking, this happens when others are left to themselves, or the people that's giving out the knowledge do not know what they are saying so they are giving out false information.

This kind of message sends others into a mindset of deception, believing something others have no proof or truth to stand on just giving out info so people begin accept what others are teaching, and no one is doing a research to find out if its truth or a deceptive lie.

Believing something is one way and it may well not be that way. They do not think that this thing is

wrong, that's not really sound as far as results. It's a metaphoric thinking, thoughts, ways, and even ideas that has been embedded in us through our life experiences. Information that has not been verified caused us to think these ways and Behavioral attitudes, cycles of thinking. Personal experiences that was taught to some ways as most times they become a lifestyle of things we have thought about most probably all or some of our lives.

That puts us in these mindsets or a rut thinking something over and over until it becomes a pattern cycle of thinking this is what we call

RUT OR ruts, that is doing something over and over again digging a ditch or a deep hole for their lives and they excepted this kind of life and style a way of life for themselves and others that join their groups or inner circles. Carefully read and meditate on the story of the digger and see if you can Identify with his kind of mindset and what happened to him and why has he allowed himself to get into this kind of thinking pattern. 2 Timothy 2:15 tell us to :

<u>Study to shew thyself approved unto God, a workman that needeth not to be ashamed, rightly dividing the word of truth.</u>

SCRIPTURES AND THE THOUGHTS, & THE WORD OF GOD ON DECEPTION, DECEIVING, AND DECEIT ;

Galatians 6:7-8 · Be not deceived; God is not mocked: for whatsoever a man soweth, that shall he also reap.

Proverbs 12:22 · Lying lips are abomination to the LORD: but they that deal truly are his delight.

Proverbs 10:9 · He that walketh uprightly walketh surely: but he that perverteth his ways shall be known.

Psalms 52:2 · Thy tongue deviseth mischiefs; like a sharp razor, working deceitfully.

Romans 12:2 · And be not conformed to this world: but be ye transformed by the renewing of your mind, that ye may prove what is that good, and acceptable, and perfect, will of God.

Galatians 5:16-26 · This I say then, Walk in the Spirit, and ye shall not fulfil the lust of the flesh.

James 1:22 - But be ye doers of the word, and not
hearers only, deceiving your own selves.

Proverbs 11:3 - The integrity of the upright shall guide them:
but the perverseness of transgressors shall destroy them.

Luke 6:31 - And as ye would that men should
do to you, do ye also to them likewise.

Ephesians 4:31-32 - Let all bitterness, and wrath, and anger, and
clamour, and evil speaking, be put away from you, with all malice:

Mark 7:20-22 - And he said, That which cometh
out of the man, that defileth the man.

Colossians 3:9 - Lie not one to another, seeing that
ye have put off the old man with his deeds;

John 8:44 - Ye are of your father the devil, and the lusts of your
father ye will do. He was a murderer from the beginning, and abode
not in the truth, because there is no truth in him. When he speaketh
a lie, he speaketh of his own: for he is a liar, and the father of it.

THE STORY OF THE DIGGER.

So, this is a story of a man that was thinking in his mind one day, I'm
looking for something, I want to have and I think it will make me a
very rich man one day. It could be gold, silver, precious stones, or jewels
of some kind. How can I find it? So, he thought, in his thoughts, and
ways that his mind process information, since he had purchased a large
piece of land some time ago. and was told by some of the neighbors in
the town that your land has gold on it. but no one has never found any

in hundreds of years. If this was true why then they have not bought the land if gold and jewels of treasure was suppose to be in the ground, somewhere on the land. He should have been thinking this kind of way and it would have eliminated some of his doubts and waste of time and money trying to find something that is not their. This is his thoughts as he walked around and thinking, so he decided to go to the shed and pick up a shovel, thinking that he need to find something or dig up something that was lost. This man started digging and digging for a long while.

He was digging down through the night and up till the day. Light has sprung up looking for something that he thought he has entitlements. So, in his community they were looking for this man because he was a man that has taken care of certain needs in that city as an Administrator of the city. So, when they could not find him at home, they decided to look in his backyard where he started to dig. This man has Dugged and Dugged a hole so deep that he did not realize how deep the hole was and paid no attention to his surroundings that it the hole grew and it brought attention to the city of that town, where it began to draw crowds of people and commotion in that particular area and city and the nearby cities.

This situation begins to be rather big and out of control because this man has dug a hole so large that he could not get out so he begins to ask questions? HOW DO I GET OUT OF THIS HOLE I HAVE DUG? Can anyone help me the poor man asked.? Because the hole was so deep everyone had to look down at him in the very large deep hole that he has dug for himself. Looking for exactly what they were asking him. No one was willing to go down there, and he certainly could not get out. The man said I am searching for my treasure.

The man was thinking that he would find it down there, so he kept, digging and asking for help to get out. So he asked again as the crowd grew and others heard his statement how do I get out of this hole that I have dug for myself. The man's reply". Do anyone know he asked? No one really had an answer for him, no one really said to much about the situation, but to think about him and all that he has done to get himself into this deep trap, a stronghold and patterns of thinking. Leaning on what he heard others say about the land a while back.

No one could or would, be willing to help him out. So, there was young man heard all the commotion and decided to come and see what was going on over there, with all the people standing around in a large crowd looking down into this very deep and larger hole; thinking that something was being built here. This young man came over and said to this man what are you doing down their? digging a deep hole, the man replied, how can I get out of this hole that I have dug for myself, the young man looked at all the situations that was going on down there and around where they were standing and he finally said PUT THE SHOVEL DOWN AND STOP DIGGING BECAUSE YOU HAVE DUG yourself a deep hole that you can't get out. Finally, they hoisted a long rope and apparatus to put him in to help him to get out.

Sometimes we dig ourselves into a very deep and large troubles. One that we cannot even see until its too late or too deep to get out on our own. This mess that we have decided to take upon ourselves to start. Our thoughts and things we have done and is doing, acting and applying what we think is right for ourselves. In these situations, it is not so, when we look at the situation what has taken place.

In this story were reading about a man that cannot get out and no one is willing to go in after him. This is the case with our hearts, or our spirit or our soul which is our minds, parts of us that thinks with thoughts, ideas, and sometimes pictures come with the thoughts if were thinking about it and want to see it. Our wills or our emotions feelings are behind the things we do. But sometimes we ignore some of our feelings. We sometimes think we know what we are doing, because we do not or cannot identify what we are feelings are telling us. So many times we bi - pass or put off not realizing these feelings, what is going on, these are warning signs. The signs that gives us indications when things are about to go wrong or Off course.

The signs are here to help us so when we can not detect what is right from wrong then we are in real big trouble. The things that are wanting, and making effort to help us. We do not even know the events that will take place after the tragedy. Can this situation have been even prevented, from problems, injuries, dangers to others as well as ourselves from happening.? When we have had strongholds built or allowed to enter without us fully knowing into our space and or lives. Analyzing counting the cost of what will take place thinking patterns, thoughts of ours through whatever means deemed to be necessary.

It can be overwhelming because the hole is too deep to climb out. We have nothing to get him, or them out, not even ourselves or even others out with if we decided to help. We dig ourselves into a stronghold of situations that is deep. E.g... examples this is what (e.g., means) (as a side note;) We as men & women get into relationships with other men and women and that could potentially involve children, diseases, money for this, and money for that will send us into a life of struggling to pay for what cannot have at the time but we find ways to get it despite.

We put ourselves in harm's way of dangerous relationships, crimes, financial crises, community rivals, clubs, gangs of trafficking and so many more to discuss the list could be endless if we are not educated. As well as being stamped into the prison systems some get set into these strongholds no way seems to get out. So they get into or fall into a mind-blowing trap that seems to be no way out.

We must be very careful not to dig ourselves into a trap that we need a lot of help. Sometimes our neighbors,' friends, and associates cannot even get us out of. The thing is that sometimes we are not listening to ourselves, and others as well that's one of the first mistakes. We are not listening and paying attention because too many things have gotten our attention, and we become distracted, loss of focus. I want to say this we must become good listeners it causes us to avoid pitfalls and webs that trap us into a stronghold that no one else will be able to get us out of it.

If the Lord GOD, & Jesus do not get us out, where in trouble. You and I cannot be thinking that we know best uhm, I got this it now... thank you for your help they say. But when all the waters settled down at the bottom of the lake we were in a lot of trouble. This is what we do to ourselves not everyone and not all situations have this type of chaos take place but we have put ourselves in a stronghold that's holding us so strong we can barely move.

2 CORINTHIANS 10:4

(For the weapons of our warfare are not carnal, but mighty through God to the pulling down of strong holds;) Holds one in thoughts very strong and don't want to let go. Can be in chains of and or bondages in their ways of thinking if they do not get some type of breakthrough from the Lord. They will remain in this state of mind for a very long time even die with this situation in their life.

STRONGHOLDS COME FROM:

> What could be considered strongholds in our lives?

> Some of our beliefs can cause a stronghold.

> the ways we were raised with our parents and neighborhood's city states town at that time things took place.

> Religious beliefs and traditions these were ways teachings from our parents and great grandparents that is handed down through generational bloodlines and ancestors that were before them we handed down all the way in time.

> The things that we were taught by certain teachers in the school systems coming up as small children young teens, seeing certain things happened that should or did not happen the way it should have, and so forth.

> or ministers doing and saying things, teaching things or not teaching things that should have been taught but was not.

> in our upbringings can stay with us for a lifetime and somethings we will never forget happened as little children and still with us till this day.

> in various doctrines

> foundations

> ➤ seminars,

> ➤ conferences

> ➤ universities & colleges

> ➤ organization's & clubs

> ➤ not to forget our own actions ideals thoughts, feelings & applications the parts we played in these matters.

> ➤ and systems of Operations with all its rules and regulations laws being established commandments, Ordinances and so forth.

BE STRONG IN THE LORD

What does it mean to be strong in the Lord? And exactly how do (we) (do) that? It's not a strength of our own.

Deuteronomy 31:6

[6] Be strong and of a good courage, fear not, nor be afraid of them: for the Lord thy GOD, he it is that doth go with thee; he will not fail thee, nor forsake thee.

I will not TREMBLE AS long as the Lord is with me nor will I allow my feet to be moved out of the way that I'm charted navigated to and sanctions with the call of God with a mandate in the ONLY powerful name of Jesus.

I am strong and I will continue to be strong only in the Lord and in the power of HIS MIGHT.

I am not afraid nor will I be dismayed. I will not be Shocked or under any kind of stressful demanding, taxing situations, or be shaken moved, or thrown off course. I will not be persuaded or hindered by what I see or feel. I will RE-SUME my path. I will stay focused and I will stay in line with what the Lord has for me. I will see my destiny come to pass as long as I continue to do what I'm supposed to do in the name of Jesus

I AM very courageous with the help of my Lord and SAVIOR JESUS CHRIST, I can do all things through Christ that strength me I am strengthened in Christ Jesus by his words instructions plans Obedience, his Spirit and His Blood cleanses me from all my sins in the name of Jesus me Phil 4: 13

Deuteronomy 31:7

Then Moses called to Joshua and said to him in the sight of all Israel, "Be strong and courageous, for you shall go with this people into the land which the Lord has sworn to their fathers to give them, and you shall give it to them as an inheritance.

I now receive all the INHERITANCES THAT THE LORD JESUS HAS FOR ME

Deuteronomy 31:23

Then He commissioned Joshua the son of Nun, and said, "Be strong and courageous, for you shall bring the sons of Israel into the land which I swore to them, and I will be with you."

Joshua 1:6

Be strong and courageous, for you shall give this people possession of the land which I swore to their fathers to give them.

Joshua 1:7

Only be strong and very courageous; be careful to do according to all the law which Moses My servant commanded you; do not turn from it to the right or to the left, so that you may have success wherever you go.

I am careful to do all of your will Lord Jesus and to follow your plans

Joshua 1:9

Have I not commanded you? Be strong and courageous! Do not tremble or be dismayed, for the Lord your GOD is with you wherever you go."

Joshua 1:1

Anyone who rebels against your command and does not obey your words in all that you command him, shall be put to death; only be strong and courageous."

Joshua 10:2

Joshua then said to them, "Do not fear or be dismayed!
Be strong and courageous, for thus the Lord will do
to all your enemies with whom you fight."

2 Samuel 10:12

Be strong, and let us show ourselves courageous for the
sake of our people and for the cities of our GOD; and
may the Lord do what is good in His sight."

1 Kings 2:2

"I am going the way of all the earth. Be strong,
therefore, and show yourself a man.

Isaiah 35:4

Say to those with anxious heart,

"Take courage, fear not.

Behold, your GOD will come with vengeance.

The recompense of God will come,

But He will save you."

Daniel 10:19

He said, "O man of high esteem, do not be afraid. Peace be with you; take
courage and be courageous!" Now as soon as he spoke to me, I received
strength and said, "May my lord speak, for you have strengthened me."

Haggai 2:4

But now take courage, Zerubbabel,' declares the Lord, 'take
courage also, Joshua son of Jehozadak, the high priest, and
all you people of the land take courage,' declares the Lord,
'and work; for I am with you,' declares the Lord of hosts.

Zechariah 8:9

"Thus says the Lord of hosts, 'Let your hands be strong, you who are listening in these days to these words from the mouth of the prophets, those who spoke in the day that the foundation of the house of the Lord of hosts was laid, to the end that the temple might be built.

Zechariah 8:13

It will come about that just as you were a curse among the nations, O house of Judah and house of Israel, so I will save you that you may become a blessing. Do not fear; let your hands be strong.'

1 Corinthians 16:13

Be on the alert, stand firm in the faith, act like men, be strong.

1 Kings 20:22

Then the prophet came near to the king of Israel and said to him, "Go, strengthen yourself and observe and see what you have to do; for at the turn of the year the king of Aram will come up against you."

James 5:8

You too be patient; strengthen your hearts,
for the coming of the Lord is near.

Psalm 31:24

Be strong and let your heart take courage,

All you who hope in the Lord.

Ephesians 6:10

Finally, be strong in the Lord and in the strength of His might.

2 Timothy 2:1

You therefore, my son, be strong in the grace that is in Christ Jesus.

Luke 10:27

And he answered, "You shall love the Lord your God with all your heart, and with all your soul, and with all your strength, and with all your mind; and your neighbor as yourself."

Revelation 3:2

Wake up, and strengthen the things that remain, which were about to die; for I have not found your deeds completed in the sight of My GOD.

❖ RECOGNIZING THE ATTACKS OF THE ENEMY

with his signs.

❖ When things happen that do not normally happen. In our lives, through relationships. They will work in some experiences, things not going to our schedule plans, with money. These things will cause our time. These things will cause thoughts that we think about from time to time, to go all wrong.

These experiences with people, it could be husband, wives, kids, family members and the likes or even places. All of the things that can go wrong in our lives, it seems at this time, that everything all at once, is going out of control. It could be our homes, cars, office, and our things, that we can lose or misplace, for example it could be lost keys.

❖ Lost or misplaced wallets, our paper work for school reports, Ministry notes or even a good teaching book, that, you have either set down some where. Your machine might be acting up, at work or just not working, properly. Your at a restaurant with some friends or family members ordering Food & drinks, not right as we have ordered it. in your everyday life, it will bring you all types of thoughts like what in the world is going on. This could be a sign that you're under an attack. The thing we need to realize, think about understand, ponder in our great minds.

❖ The questions are that do we know the signs and know how to come back or bounce back out of one of these types of situations, without causing us a setback. These things can cause upset, or a setup for a worser situation like a snowball effect taken place. We cannot forget about our bodies becoming sick, sore in some kind of pain, soreness, rashes, hurts internally. There is a long list of things that can go wrong. It goes on and on, you may say to yourself or others when do all of this stops?

What are some of the signs that you are under an attack? have you ever asked yourself this? This is for born again believers, that has a mission, mandate on their lives. People in the world have problems as well but they have problems on a different set of situations because they are living in sin and living for the devil. Many are living under a curse if they are not saved.

❖ Not being saved from their sins and have been previously given their lives to Christ Jesus. These situations cause them to be living under a curse from Adam to Christ Jesus. Until they give their lives and surrender to Christ their lives are going to constantly be in some type of trouble, turmoil, discuss utterly, problems on every side and then some.

❖ When your unorganized when you use to be organized and can get much done, and things seems to be out of order at this time you did not really get much done as before, your thoughts may come upon your mind, and you ask yourself where have all my time gone? You may certainly be under some kind of an attack.

When you are all confused and discombobulated and may be all over the page.

❖ When you start losing things and start becoming forgetful, of where you laid something down. For example like your phone, keys in your hand, but you are looking for them and going all over the house and bedroom, and just realize you have them in your hand this could be a sign you're under an attack. Your wallet, your Lunch, your bookbag, or even your money, your morning coffee cup full of hot delicious tasty coffee, but don't know where you laid it down., you might be under an attack, do to so much distractions or just running behind on this particular day.

❖ You might be under an attack, if you go to start up your car and its very quiet outside, and no traffic is coming from either direction, so you go to pull out the drive way or turn around seemingly, No cars are coming as you see it, It seems then all of a sudden, cars begin to storm down the road. Be it sunlight or at night, cars flood the road and you almost have an accident. This is potential for an attack, this could very well be known as a set up by the enemy, because you were caught off guard.

❖   You might be under an attack, if you are all of sudden, feel sick on the stomach, or you begin to get a cough,or a headache, or head cold or some kind, or some pains hit your body, heart, chest or feeling, not well or up to full strength, you could be up under an attack these attacks come on you all in a few moments in time at the lest time, like right when other things are out of place or going in the opposite direction. This is a set up for an attack.

❖   You could be under an attack when you began to pray but don't remember, the things that you were ask to pray for others. You could be under an attack when you forget, what to pray for or about and you just don't know where to start or your words just don't come out quite, the right way, feelings of fears nervousness or uptightness can set in on you and throw you off course.

❖   You could be under an attack; when a lot of thoughts of evil things like bad profanity, nasty sexual perverted thoughts about others, body parts. All of a sudden begin to flood the mind with these thoughts, Ideals, images, pictures logos, symbols or other things come into the mind. Maybe even begins to fill your mind and you're hearing all of these thoughts coming from within.

❖   You could be under an attack, when you have made up your mind not to fall into any type of temptations. Relationships or going out to dinners with others that are saved or not saved. Someone approach you and ask you out for a dinner or trying to flirt with you. You previously have had bad ties, experiences with others and made up your mind to stay single, not sexually active but dedicated to Christ Jesus you could be under an attack.

Just REMEMBER You could be under an attack spiritually, emotionally, financially, mentally, verbally, or maybe even physically, that is spirit, soul & body. These attacks can come from demonic forces, demon spirits, the dark side, occults, or evil organizations. Witches is both male & female Warlocks, wizards Astro projectors. They are people coming out of their bodies to do some type of evil, harm to someone or for someone.

When you want to do right and everything around you talking, seeing on tv, media, or groups. Your peers trying making attempts to get you to do or say something that is not right or that could be sin or transgressions.

Lets take a look at the attacks with the list of some.

THE DIFFERENT TYPES OF ATTACKS THAT COMES INTO OUR LIVES ;

This is a list of some of the attacks that I have to share with my audience of Saints, Warriors, Intercessors, Soldiers, newcomers to Christ as babes, Ambassadors, Sons of GOD, AND LEADERS WORLDWIDE GLOBALLY.

❖   Spiritual attacks: can include but are not limited to our thoughts and confusion

❖   Mental blocks the inability to not remember the things that I should be able to recall back into my life due to me having and using, memorizing and saying and doing it a number of times in my life. Spiritual attacks are related to the spirit. Anything that is spiritual that was either said, given, talked about, or quoted to me written down, I should be able to resight it back without any problems.

❖   SOULISH ATTACKS: Dealing with the choices, which is the will, the will is very strong and determined, the will deals with the power to make wise choices, but when someone is under an attack, they find it hard to make good sound decisions, this person very well could be under some type of an attack, and we need to remember this right, away and stop the plans and traps of the enemy, from hindering us, from doing what is right.

❖   PHYSICAL ATTACKS: things that happen to the flesh, the body, things we eat, things we put on, such as clothes, and the vehicles, such as cars, we get in and drive, Your going down the highway and all of a sudden the police pulls you over, and gives you a ticket of a hundren and ten dollars, you are under an attack. These things that are temporal, in life and we must be on guard and alert, and watchful at all times,these things that will vanish away because they are for a short period of time, but we must be aware of what is going on. Various attacks deal with the body and any part of the body that the enemy can get a hold of if the person can be lured in.

❖ FINANCIAL ATTACKS; Dealing with the MONEY ATTACKS, when a person loves or enjoy, or knowing that money is needed. But the enemy will cause an attack on a person's money or financial business. Sometimes when the Lord wants to bless you and you are blessed but the enemy will cause someone to look at your blessing and begin to be jealous. When the enemy can attack your finances.

❖ VERBAL ATTACKS; When attacks come when a person begins to run the mouth and get themselves in trouble due to the tongue. Smart mouthing, Sarcasm. Some of them begin to tell lies, deceive, and manipulate others.

❖ SOCIAL ATTACKS; People get around their peers and begin to talk

❖ COMMUNITY ATTACKS: When a person is attacked in the neighborhood due to being selfish, territorial, or private, and when that privacy is violated, then the trouble starts. The tongue, and the mouth get a lot of people in deep trouble; too much mouth will cause the lips to be loose and will sink some good ships.

❖ FAMILY ATTACKS: When the family has things happening behind the scenes, dipping deep in the dark arts, working witchcraft, or trying to control a person or individual or a group of people. Something in the family the devil will start some type of trouble. What did the dad do when he was drunk, having sex with other children or other women? You get the picture some if the enemy can start something within the family He will. We must remember if the seeds of SIN are planted deep within the recesses of the soul, which is the mind, will, or emotions, the enemy, the devil, our adversary, will bring it out at a time that will bring some embarrassment to others so the turmoil in the family will start. When the troubles start and begin to take OFF, then the enemy is gone to the next project in life to stir up some troubles or turmoil in other places.

❖   BUSINESS ATTACKS on the business when shady and shyster deals or made for selfish reason. Stealing money. The business partners are holding out or back some of the money, or the books are not balancing out due to mismanagement, mishandling funds or some kinds of bribes or blackmail.

❖   MENTAL ATTACKS; This can take place when it starts in the family ancestral line of the genetics of the bloodlines of individuals. These things just do not happen over night but have been going for sometime, and its just now being exposed, brought to the light and made aware of by someone that has been paying attention and catch all of the signs and put 2 and 2 together and figured out.

❖   MEDIA ATTACKS;

❖   When others are posting things about others that can bring some type of embarrassment. People post things about family members, husband or wife. Things about there friends or work associates. Some of these things that were posted online should not have been posted. These types of things cause fights, and attacks civil rivalry. They may even cause someone to get shot and eventually die due to things inappropriately posted online. Listen young and old people. We should avoid posting things online about others it may come back to bite or hunt us so we need to be very careful posting things about our lives that we want to deem personal, even about other lives.

❖   MINISTRY ATTACKS; When loose ends are not tight, everyone is not on one accord and there is not a lot of love being spread across the fellowship. This could be a setup for an attack loopholes are left open, gaps in relationships. It does not matter if it's in the leadership or through the members of the body of KINGDOM believers. THE devil has no respect for a person when it comes to breaking up a spirit-filled place once where GOD was moving in a GLORIOUS TIME AND HAVING HIS WAY.

❖   GROUP & ORGANIZATIONAL ATTACKS: GANGS are territorial with colors, street hand signs, clothes, drugs, and so forth. The list can be a bit much. Just want to give you some type of idea as to how these things get started with the people and the devil,

❖   ALL TYPES OF SCHOOLS PRE, JR & SR, COLLEGE ATTACKS;

❖ POLITICAL, GOVERNMENTAL, AND POSITIONAL ATTACKS CAN ALL HAPPEN WHEN THE DOORS TO THE ENEMY ARE LEFT WIDE OPEN. THE ENEMY HAS ALL TYPE OF ACCESS TO COME IN AND START CHAOS. SITUATIONS, LIES, DECEPTIONS OF ALL KINDS AND TYPES ON EVERY LEVEL. THESE ARE JUST SOME OF THE MANY WAYS THE DEVIL CAN COME IN AND TAKE OVER AND BEGIN TO ATTACK. BUT HE CAN NOT COME IN IF THE DOORS, PORTALS, ENTRANCEWAYS, WINDOWS, BACK DOORS, AND FRONT DOORS ARE CLOSED AND LOCKED, AND HE IS NOT TO TRESPASS ON THIS PROPERTY. THIS IS A RESTRICTED AREA ALL VIOLATORS WILL BE PROSECUTED AND BROUGHT TO JUSTICE IN THE NAME OF YESHUA, JESUS THE CHRIST.

ALL ATTACKS COME FROM THE ENEMY IN SOME KIND OF WAY:

These attacks that comes, some may say why is this happening to me??? The enemy uses others to do his dirty work. Such as people working in the OCCULT, the dark arts of all kinds this is another topic and subject for another day and time.

When you want to sit down and meditate on the word of the Lord. There are all kinds of distractions just begin to flood your world. Thoughts like the doorbell is ringing and you are cooking and the phone is going off at the same time. You can get or feel frustrated, aggravated or even irritated this maybe a sign that your under an attack. Maybe even that day you did not get to pray and reach the level that you normally reach in the spirit. Doors could be open and unrepented sins of angers upsets, tries to come into your mind.

Your day is just not going well this could be
that you are in an awkward position.

You might be under an attack, if things around you all of a sudden began to bombard your mailbox with bills. Creditors calling you about money that was owed to them more than five years ago or less or more. We do know everyone wants to get paid. But have not heard from them in several years and then you get a bill that you owe this that and so on.

You may be under an attack, that all of a sudden people in the family begin to either die, get hospitalized. Maybe get sick, and the doctor don't really know what is going on in their lives after running as many tests as they can to figure out what in the world is going on in this body or life of this person.

You might be under an attack, if when you go to the market to shop, and all the food is going up, without warning, and you don't have enough money, to pay for your groceries, and maybe short of funds already, from the start.

You might be under an attack, when you used to drink, or smoke, and all of these thoughts are trying to infiltrate your thoughts to enter in and take over. Especially when a person has been delivered from these desires, or urges, that came from the enemy, and it is a spirit of the enemy or a demon of lust and sex, and all of a sudden, you get an urge for a stronger drink, or smoke a cigarette, or maybe even want to, smoke crack, crystal meth, marijuana and have sex with someone.

I am going into some deeper details, for example only: a man wants to have sex with another man, that's a homosexual, and this or that person has a girl female spirit trying to take over. This is a demon trying to take over, and the same with women, or females wanting to go to bed with another female, that is a lesbian demon or a male spirit wanting to take over a woman. Men and women want to masturbate or have sex with themselves, for themselves, and by themselves. Especially when you are attracted to the opposite sex, not the same sex as you are. It is not a sin to be tempted but, even if these thoughts cross our minds, but we do know these are the thoughts of the enemy. We need to at this time rebuke these nasty thoughts and start pulling down these thoughts out of the air by binding them in Jesus or Yeshua name.

This is a possible means that you are under attack, and you need to be on guard and continue to bind those evil thoughts and feelings and sometimes, they double-team you. You want to drink, smoke, and do drugs, which in terms you have desires to have sex. By the way doing and dealing with drugs opens one up to want to have sex, and all kinds of dirty, and sinful ways, just be aware. When we are saved from our sins we are free to serve the Lord from all types of mess. So we need to really get some deliverance if we have some type of involvement in this type of living after coming to Christ. Just be on guard of the tactics of the enemy. While you are free from these types of sins and addictions you need to stay free and clean in the name of Jesus.

You are already in deep trouble if you do not get rid of these thoughts in the name of Jesus, by binding these attitudes, mindsets, actions and deeds and thoughts, that seem to flood your mind.

Pray and read the word of GOD, AND PRAISE THE LORD UNTIL YOU GET A BREAKTHROUGH.

When all of these things began to flood your mind all at once, it's time to pray, put on some soft music inspirational, anointed worship music or praise music, dance, shout or sit, stand or kneel down to pray ; but do something to get in the presence of GOD ALMIGHTY AND DECLARE AND DECREE HIS WORD BACK TO HIM OR EVEN READ, LISTEN, QUOTE, CONFESS, THE WORD OF THE LORD, UNTIL YOU GET SOME TYPE OF RELEASE, RELIEF, AND BREAKTHROUGHS IN THE MIGHTY NAME OF JESUS. WHILE ALL OF THIS MESS IS GOING ON ALSO ADD SOME REAL HUMBLE REPENTENCE TO YOUR TIME WITH THE LORD, FOR CLEANSING AND BEING PURIFIED.

CHAPTER 12

DO NOT BE AFRAID!

Isaiah 41:10

'Do not fear, for I am with you;

Do not anxiously look about you, for I am your GOD.

I will strengthen you, surely, I will help you,

Surely, I will uphold you with My righteous right hand.'

2 Timothy 1:7

For God has not given us a spirit of timidity, *(fear, is false evidence appearing to be real but it's not REAL)* but of power and love and (a sound mind) discipline.

Deuteronomy 31:6

Be strong and courageous, do not be afraid or tremble at them, for the Lord your GOD is the one who goes with you. He will not fail you or forsake you."

John 14:27

Peace, I leave with you; My peace I give to you; not as the world gives do I give to you. Do not let your heart be troubled, nor let it be fearful.

Romans 8:28

And we know that GOD causes all things to work together for good to those who love GOD, to those who are called according to His purpose.

Psalm 27:1

The Lord is my light and my salvation;

Whom shall, I fear?

The Lord is the defense of my life;

Whom shall I dread?

Joshua 1:9

Have I not commanded you? Be strong and courageous! Do not tremble or be dismayed, for the Lord your GOD is with you wherever you go."

Matthew 10:28

Do not fear those who kill the body but are unable to kill the soul; but rather fear Him who is able to destroy both soul and body in hell.

1 John 4:18

There is no fear in love; but perfect love casts out fear, because fear involves punishment, and the one who fears is not perfected in love.

1 Peter 5:7

casting all your anxiety on Him, because He cares for you.

Proverbs 3:5-6

Trust in the Lord with all your heart

And do not lean on your own understanding.

In all your ways acknowledge Him,

And He will make your paths straight.

1 Corinthians 10:13

No temptation has overtaken you but such as is common to man; and GOD is faithful, who will not allow you to be tempted beyond what you are able, but with the temptation will provide the way of escape also, so that you will be able to endure it.

Isaiah 41:13

"For I am the Lord your GOD, who upholds your right hand,

Who says to you, 'Do not fear, I will help you.'

Be anxious for nothing, but in everything by prayer and supplication
with thanksgiving let your requests be made known to GOD.
And the peace of GOD, which surpasses all comprehension,
will guard your hearts and your minds in Christ Jesus.

Psalm 34:4

I sought the Lord, and He answered me,

And delivered me from all my fears.

Psalm 55:22

Cast your burden upon the Lord and He will sustain you;

He will never allow the righteous to be shaken.

2 Corinthians 12:9

And He has said to me, "My grace is sufficient for you, for power is
perfected in weakness." Most gladly, therefore, I will rather boast
about my weaknesses, so that the power of Christ may dwell in me.

Jeremiah 29:11

For I know the plans that I have for you,' declares the Lord, 'plans
for welfare and not for calamity to give you a future and a hope.

Isaiah 40:31

Yet those who wait for the Lord

Will gain new strength.

They will mount up with wings like eagles,

They will run and not get tired,

They will walk and not become weary.

Romans 8:15

For you have not received a spirit of slavery leading to
fear again, but you have received a spirit of adoption
as sons by which we cry out, "Abba! Father!"

Hebrews 13:5-6

Make sure that your character is free from the love of money, being
content with what you have; for He Himself has said, "I will never
desert you, nor will I ever forsake you," so that we confidently say,

"The Lord is my helper; I will not be afraid.

What will man do to me?"

Psalm 23:4

Even though I walk through the valley of the shadow of death,

I fear no evil, for You are with me;

Your rod and Your staff, they comfort me.

Matthew 6:33

But seek first His kingdom and His righteousness,
and all these things will be added to you.

Philippians 4:6

Be anxious for nothing, but in everything by prayer and supplication
with thanksgiving let your requests be made known to GOD.

Hebrews 11:1

Now faith is the assurance of things hoped for,
the conviction of things not seen.

Hebrews 13:6

so that we confidently say,

"The Lord is my helper; I will not be afraid.

What will man do to me?"

Luke 12:32

Do not be afraid, little flock, for your Father has
chosen gladly to give you the kingdom.

Philippians 4:13

I can do all things through Him who strengthens me.

John 16:33

These things I have spoken to you, so that in Me you
may have peace. In the world you have tribulation,
but take courage; I have overcome the world."

1 Chronicles 28:20

Then David said to his son Solomon, "Be strong and courageous,
and act; do not fear nor be dismayed, for the Lord GOD, my
GOD, is with you. He will not fail you nor forsake you until all
the work for the service of the house of the Lord is finished.

Psalm 56:3-4

When I am afraid,

I will put my trust in You.

In GOD, whose word I praise,

In GOD I have put my trust;

I shall not be afraid.

What can mere man do to me?

1 Corinthians 16:13

Be on the alert, stand firm in the faith, act like men, be strong.

Psalm 118:6

The Lord is for me; I will not fear;

What can man do to me?

Luke 12:25

And which of you by worrying can add a single hour to his life's span?

Psalm 27:14

Wait for the Lord;

Be strong and let your heart take courage;

Yes, wait for the Lord.

Deuteronomy 31:8

The Lord is the one who goes ahead of you; He will be with you. He will not fail you or forsake you. Do not fear or be dismayed."

Psalm 56:11

In GOD I have put my trust, I shall not be afraid.

What can man do to me?

Psalm 46:1-3

GOD is our refuge and strength,

A very present help in trouble.

Therefore we will not fear, though the earth should change

And though the mountains slip into the heart of the sea;

Though its waters roar and foam,

Though the mountains quake at its swelling pride. Selah.

Proverbs 29:25

The fear of man brings a snare,

But he who trusts in the Lord will be exalted.

Jeremiah 31:3

The Lord appeared to him from afar, saying,

"I have loved you with an everlasting love;

Therefore I have drawn you with lovingkindness.

James 1:5-6

But if any of you lacks wisdom, let him ask of GOD, who gives to all generously and without reproach, and it will be given to him. But he must ask in faith without any doubting, for the one who doubts is like the surf of the sea, driven and tossed by the wind.

Exodus 14:13

But Moses said to the people, "Do not fear! Stand by and see the salvation of the Lord which He will accomplish for you today; for the Egyptians whom you have seen today, you will never see them again forever.

Psalm 23:1

The Lord is my shepherd,

I shall not want.

Matthew 5:10

"Blessed are those who have been persecuted for the sake of righteousness, for theirs is the kingdom of heaven.

James 1:2-4

Consider it all joy, my brethren, when you encounter various trials, knowing that the testing of your faith produces endurance. And let endurance have its perfect result, so that you may be perfect and complete, lacking in nothing.

Matthew 6:34

"So do not worry about tomorrow; for tomorrow will care for itself. Each day has enough trouble of its own.

Psalm 31:24

Be strong and let your heart take courage,

All you who hope in the Lord.

2 Timothy 1:7

For God has not given us a spirit of timidity,
but of power and love and discipline.

Psalm 27:14

Wait for the Lord;

Be strong and let your heart take courage;

Yes, wait for the Lord.

Joshua 1:9

Have I not commanded you? Be strong and courageous! Do not tremble or be dismayed, for the Lord your GOD is with you wherever you go."

I must remember always that the Lord is always with me and never, let the enemy cause me to be afraid, lacking in confidence, or speak anything on myself as a way of a curse. I will not walk or entertain doubts, unbelief's, or speaking negative words out of my mouth.

Psalm 138:3

On the day I called, You answered me;

You made me bold with strength in my soul

Daniel 10:19

He said, "O man of high esteem, do not be afraid. Peace be with you; take courage and be courageous!" Now as soon as he spoke to me, I received strength and said, "May my lord speak, for you have strengthened me."

Joshua 1:7

Only be strong and very courageous; be careful to do according to all the law which Moses My servant commanded you; do not turn from it to the right or to the left, so that you may have success wherever you go.

271

Hebrews 13:6

so that we confidently say,

"The Lord is my helper, I will not be afraid.

I will not be afraid of what men and man can do unto me.

The Lord is my helper I will not be afraid, but I
will walk in the confidence of the Lord.

I will not let man cause me to walk, talk, or possess any
type of fears or speak these things out of my mouth.

What will man do to me?"

Joshua 1:6

Be strong and courageous, for you shall give this people possession
of the land which I swore to their fathers to give them.

Isaiah 41:6

Each one helps his neighbor

And says to his brother, "Be strong!"

1 Corinthians 16:13

Be on the alert, stand firm in the faith, act like men, be strong.

Deuteronomy 31:6

Be strong and courageous, do not be afraid or tremble
at them, for the Lord your God is the one who goes
with you. He will not fail you or forsake you."

Ephesians 6:10

Finally, be strong in the Lord and in the strength of His might.

Micah 3:8

On the other hand I am filled with power—

With the Spirit of the Lord—

And with justice and courage

1 Chronicles 28:20

Then David said to his son Solomon, "Be strong and courageous, and act; do not fear nor be dismayed, for the Lord GOD, my GOD, is with you. He will not fail you nor forsake you until all the work for the service of the house of the Lord is finished.

When we begin to walk in the strength of the Lord, it gives us confidence.

The Lord will never forsake or fail me, because there is no failure in his abilities, power, his words, and all that he can do for me.

There is no failure nor forsaken me when I begin to call on his Great name of strength almighty power, shields of faith righteousness, becoming my armour of protection in the times of battles, times of heated intense tribulations, when I cannot see my way, he is the way and will be the way that I should go.

When I begin to walk in the Lord's power, might, courage, and not faint lose heart, give up or let these things cause me to become weak and forsake the plans that has been set before me.

I will be strong in the Lord when I begin to get into his presence, sing songs of praise and worship, speak out loud his words of strength.

I will be strong when I remember who the Lord told me that I am.

I will remember the Lord when I am going through my trials and test, I will become strong and stay focused.

2 Chronicles 15:7

But you, be strong and do not lose courage, for there is reward for your work."

Isaiah 35:4

Say to those with anxious heart,

"Take courage, fear not.

Behold, your GOD will come with vengeance.

The recompense of GOD will come,

But He will save you."

Isaiah 41:10

'Do not fear, for I am with you;

Do not anxiously look about you, for I am your GOD.

I will strengthen you, surely, I will help you,

Surely, I will uphold you with My righteous right hand.'

Thank you, Lord GOD ALMIGHTY, for upholding me with your strong righteous right hand of power might and your strength in Jesus name.

2 Timothy 2:1

You therefore, my son, be strong in the grace that is in Christ Jesus.

Proverbs 24:10

If you are slack in the day of distress,

Your strength is limited.

Joshua 2:11

When we heard it, our hearts melted and no courage remained in any man any longer because of you; for the Lord your GOD, He is GOD in heaven above and on earth beneath.

Proverbs 24:5

A wise man is strong,

And a man of knowledge increases power.

I decree & declare that I am a man of wisdom, strength that is increasing on a daily basis, power, and the Lord has given me authority and dominion to use it against my enemies, and reign on this earth, while I am here, in Jesus name it is so and so it is.

Ezra 10:4

Arise! For this matter is your responsibility, but we
will be with you; be courageous and act."

Isaiah 12:2

"Behold, GOD is my salvation,

GOD is my deliverance, my deliverer, and the one that will deliver
me, out of all of my troubles, situations, and circumstances when
I depend on him, rely, trust and make him my defense.

I will trust and not be afraid.

We should trust the Lord and never let any types of
fears grip our life to paralyze us to a standstill, halt, a
point of being in a none movement, or stoppage.

I will not let any type of fears cause me to stand still and just
do absolutely nothing with no type of movement at all.

For the Lord GOD is my strength and song,

And He has become my salvation."

Deuteronomy 31:7

Then Moses called to Joshua and said to him in the sight of all
Israel, "Be strong and courageous, for you shall go with this
people into the land which the Lord has sworn to their fathers to
give them, and you shall give it to them as an inheritance.

When we have the Lord on our side it should make us feel
strong in his abilities, depending on him for all our needs.

We are strong when we can look to him for all of our
needs, feel confidence, know that he is our defense,
protection, and help in times of great need.

1 Chronicles 19:13

Be strong, and let us show ourselves courageous for the
sake of our people and for the cities of our GOD; and
may the Lord do what is good in His sight."

Philippians 1:20

according to my earnest expectation and hope, that I will not be put
to shame in anything, but that with all boldness, Christ will even
now, as always, be exalted in my body, whether by life or by death.

2 Samuel 10:12

Be strong, and let us show ourselves courageous for
the sake of our people and for the cities of our GOD;
and may the Lord do what is good in His sight.

Fear is not a terror to us, because we do not walk in fear,
live or Operate in any type of fear whatsoever.

Fear And Worry

Fear is false evident Obvious Plain and apparent appearing real

He that dwelleth in the secret place of the most High
shall abide under the shadow of the Almighty.

Psalms 91:1-16 READ IT AT YOUR OWN LEISURE!

HE THAT DWELLETH IN THE SECRET PLACE OF THE MOST HIGH SHALL ABIDE UNDER THE SHADOW OF THE ALMIGHTY.

Fear and worry come when we try to do things on our own. But not
include the Lord in our plans. When we run into a situation and we
run out of answers then we are in a bit of an what do I do situation
and we seek other ways and means to get our problems resolved.

WE DO NOT WALK IN ANY TYPE OF FEARS FOR GOD HAS NOT GIVEN US A SPIRIT OF FEAR BUT OF POWER LOVE AND A SOUND MIND.

Matthew 6:27

And who of you by being worried can add a single hour to his life?

Jeremiah 1:8

"Do not be afraid of them,

For I am with you to deliver you," declares the Lord.

Luke 12:11

When they bring you before the synagogues and the rulers
and the authorities, do not worry about how or what you
are to speak in your defense, or what you are to say;

Luke 12:29

And do not seek what you will eat and what you
will drink, and do not keep worrying.

Luke 12:4

"I say to you, My friends, do not be afraid of those who kill
the body and after that have no more that they can do.

Psalm 91:5

You will not be afraid of the terror by night,

Or of the arrow that flies by day;

Matthew 14:27

But immediately Jesus spoke to them, saying,
"Take courage, it is I; do not be afraid."

Mark 5:36

But Jesus, overhearing what was being spoken, *said to the
synagogue official, "Do not be afraid any longer, only believe."

Psalm 94:19

When my anxious thoughts multiply within me,

Your consolations delight my soul.

Philippians 4:6

Be anxious for nothing, but in everything by prayer and supplication with thanksgiving let your requests be made known to GOD.

Mark 6:50

for they all saw Him and were terrified. But immediately He spoke with them and *said to them, "Take courage; it is I, do not be afraid."

Matthew 10:28

Do not fear those who kill the body but are unable to kill the soul; but rather fear Him who is able to destroy both soul and body in hell.

Matthew 6:25

"For this reason I say to you, do not be worried about your life, as to what you will eat or what you will drink; nor for your body, as to what you will put on. Is not life more than food, and the body more than clothing?

Isaiah 57:11

"Of whom were you worried and fearful

When you lied, and did not remember Me

Nor give Me a thought?

Was I not silent even for a long time

So you do not fear Me?

Galatians 4:11

I fear for you, that perhaps I have labored over you in vain.

Psalm 56:3

When I am afraid,

I will put my trust in You.

Daniel 10:19

He said, "O man of high esteem, do not be afraid. Peace be with you; take courage and be courageous!" Now as soon as he spoke to me, I received strength and said, "May my lord speak, for you have strengthened me.

1 Peter 5:7

casting all your anxiety on Him, because He cares for you.

Proverbs 3:25

Do not be afraid of sudden fear

Nor of the onslaught of the wicked when it comes;

Matthew 6:34

"So do not worry about tomorrow; for tomorrow will care for itself. Each day has enough trouble of its own.

Matthew 6:31

Do not worry then, saying, 'What will we eat?' or 'What will we drink?' or 'What will we wear for clothing?'

Psalm 118:6

The Lord is for me; I will not fear;

What can man do to me?

Luke 12:32

Do not be afraid, little flock, for your Father has chosen gladly to give you the kingdom.

Luke 8:50

But when Jesus heard this, He answered him, "Do not be afraid any longer; only believe, and she will be made well."

John 14:1

"Do not let your heart be troubled; believe in GOD, believe also in Me.

Isaiah 41:10

'Do not fear, for I am with you;
Do not anxiously look about you, for I am your GOD.
I will strengthen you, surely I will help you,
Surely I will uphold you with My righteous right hand.'

Proverbs 3:24

When you lie down, you will not be afraid;
When you lie down, your sleep will be sweet.

Psalm 112:7

He will not fear evil tidings;
His heart is steadfast, trusting in the Lord.

Lamentations 3:57

You drew near when I called on You;

You said, "Do not fear!"

Ruth 3:11

Now, my daughter, do not fear. I will do for you whatever you ask, for
all my people in the city know that you are a woman of excellence.

1 Peter 3:14

But even if you should suffer for the sake of righteousness, you are
blessed. And do not fear their intimidation, and do not be troubled,

Proverbs 29:25

The fear of man brings a snare,
But he who trusts in the Lord will be exalted.

Matthew 10:31

So do not fear; you are more valuable than many sparrows.

2 Timothy 1:7

For God has not given us a spirit of timidity,
but of power and love and discipline.

Isaiah 54:14

"In righteousness you will be established;
You will be far from oppression, for you will not fear;
And from terror, for it will not come near you.

Proverbs 23:1

Do not let your heart envy sinners,

But live in the fear of the Lord always.

Deuteronomy 1:29

Then I said to you, 'Do not be shocked, nor fear them.

Isaiah 35:4

Say to those with anxious heart,

"Take courage, fear not.

Behold, your GOD will come with vengeance;

The recompense of GOD will come,

But He will save you."

Acts 18:9

And the Lord said to Paul in the night by a vision, "Do not be afraid any longer, but go on speaking and do not be silent;

Psalm 49:16

Do not be afraid when a man becomes rich,

When the glory of his house is increased;

Hebrews 13:6

so that we confidently say,

"The Lord is my helper, I will not be afraid.

What will man do to me?"

CHAPTER 13

THE GRACE OF GOD; HIS UNMERITED FAVOR.
WHAT IS GRACE?

Grace is GOD UNMERITED FAVOR; what we don't really deserved have or get, but GOD gives it to us anyway. Because we were so underserving of it. Our Lord sees fit to let us have it and that's love, being shown to his children and the grace he gives the people in the world.

Ephesians 2:8-9 - For by grace are ye saved through faith; and that not of yourselves: it is the gift of GOD.

I am saved by the grace of GOD and it is through faith, that is justified, meaning that I am in right standing with GOD, as if I have never sinned, causing me to be in a good position with my Heavenly Father.

2 Corinthians 12:9 - And he said unto me, My grace is sufficient for thee: for my strength is made perfect in weakness. Most gladly therefore will I rather glory in my infirmities, that the power of Christ may rest upon me.

Father GOD, your grace is sufficient, which means it is more than enough to do, and to carry me as far as I need to go and to do whatever it is that I need to do.

1 Peter 5:10 - But the GOD of all grace, who hath called us unto his eternal glory by Christ Jesus, after that ye have suffered a while, make you perfect, stablish, strengthen, settle you.

Titus 2:11 - For the grace of GOD that bringeth salvation hath appeared to all men,

Romans 3:24 - Being justified freely by his grace
through the redemption that is in Christ Jesus:

Ephesians 2:5 - Even when we were dead in sins, hath
quickened us together with Christ, (by grace ye are saved;)

John 1:17 - For the law was given by Moses, but
grace and truth came by Jesus Christ.

Romans 11:6 - And if by grace, then is it no more of works:
otherwise grace is no more grace. But if it be of works, then
is it no more grace: otherwise work is no more work.

Romans 5:2 - By whom also we have access by faith into this grace
wherein we stand, and rejoice in hope of the glory of GOD.

Titus 3:7 - That being justified by his grace, we should
be made heirs according to the hope of eternal life.

Ephesians 1:7 - In whom we have redemption through his blood,
the forgiveness of sins, according to the riches of his grace;

2 Timothy 1:9 - Who hath saved us, and called us with an holy calling,
not according to our works, but according to his own purpose and
grace, which was given us in Christ Jesus before the world began,

2 Corinthians 9:8 - And GOD is able to make all grace
abound toward you; that ye, always having all sufficiency
in all things, may abound to every good work:

Titus 3:5 - Not by works of righteousness which we have
done, but according to his mercy he saved us, by the washing
of regeneration, and renewing of the Holy Ghost;

1 Corinthians 15:10

**But by the grace of GOD I am what I am: and his
grace which was bestowed upon me was not in vain;
but I laboured more abundantly than they all: yet
not I, but the grace of GOD which was with me.**

James 4:6

But he giveth more grace. Wherefore he saith, GOD resisteth the proud, but giveth grace unto the humble.

Matthew 22:29

Jesus answered and said unto them, Ye do err, not knowing the scriptures, nor the power of GOD.

Mark 12:24

And Jesus answering said unto them, Do ye not therefore err, because ye know not the scriptures, neither the power of GOD?

Hebrews 4:16

Let us therefore come boldly unto the throne of grace, that we may obtain mercy, and find grace to help in time of need.

1 Corinthians 1:4

I thank my GOD always on your behalf, for the grace of GOD which is given you by Jesus Christ;

Romans 5:15

But not as the offence, so also is the free gift. For if through the offence of one many be dead, much more the grace of GOD, and the gift by grace, which is by one man, Jesus Christ, hath abounded unto many.

John 1:16

And of his fulness have all we received, and grace for grace.

Romans 16:26

But now is made manifest, and by the scriptures of the prophets, according to the commandment of the everlasting God, made known to all nations for the obedience of faith:

Romans 11:6

And if by grace, then is it no more of works: otherwise
grace is no more grace. But if it be of works, then is it
no more grace: otherwise work is no more work.

Romans 1:2

(Which he had promised afore by his
prophets in the holy scriptures,)

Zechariah 4:7

Who art thou, O great mountain? before Zerubbabel thou
shalt become a plain: and he shall bring forth the headstone
thereof with shoutings, crying, Grace, grace unto it.

Romans 1:7

To all that be in Rome, beloved of GOD, called
to be saints: Grace to you and peace from GOD
our Father, and the Lord Jesus Christ.

Matthew 26:54

But how then shall the scriptures be
fulfilled, that thus it must be?

Luke 24:45

Then opened he their understanding, that
they might understand the scriptures,

Titus 2:11

For the grace of GOD that bringeth salvation
hath appeared to all men,

Ephesians 2:8

For by grace are ye saved through faith; and that
not of yourselves: it is the gift of GOD:

Galatians 1:15

But when it pleased GOD, who separated me from
my mother's womb, and called me by his grace,

2 Corinthians 6:1

We then, as workers together with him, beseech you
also that ye receive not the grace of GOD in vain.

Romans 5:2

By whom also we have access by faith into this grace wherein
we stand, and rejoice in hope of the glory of GOD.

Ephesians 3:2

If ye have heard of the dispensation of the grace
of GOD which is given me to you-ward:

Mark 14:49

I was daily with you in the temple teaching, and ye
took me not: but the scriptures must be fulfilled.

John 5:39

Search the scriptures; for in them ye think ye have
eternal life: and they are they which testify of me.

Philemon 1:3

Galatians 2:21

I do not frustrate the grace of GOD: for if righteousness
come by the law, then Christ is dead in vain.

Romans 6:15

What then? shall we sin, because we are not under
the law, but under grace? GOD forbid.

CHAPTER 14

SPEAKING THE FIRES OF GOD INTO ACTION

As we begin to speak about fire and the effects that it can all do.

Fire is said to be a very destructive in whatever area it touches. Natural fire will destroy natural things in its pathway whatever it may be. When we begin to look at fire or think about fire and all the things that fire is used for. Fire in its very vast, in its many ways that can be used for all sorts of uses. The definition of what fire is; Fire is said to be an igniting substance mixed with Oxygen, resulting in a combustion with light, heat, and all the visible effects it gives off after it starts. Fire needs basically three key ingredients to get started, after it is lit, from a match or a lighter., #1 Heat, and the heat is hot, and carries high temperatures. These high tempertures can burn a lot man made materials. But the fires of GOD, burns out impurities, out of the soul, which again is explained in other writing chapters in this book, the mind, which is the seat of thought. The will, or our choices, we make from moment to moment and from day to day. The other part of the soul is our Emotions, which is our feelings, senses, or perception levels of understanding, with our emotions and feelings, #2 Fuel is needed to get things started, something, to get it to burn, like for examples paper, wood, clothing materials and so forth. #3 It needs Oxygen, what is oxygen? Is colorless, odorless gas, a chemical element, that, is used to keep our lives going for breathing purposes for sustaining life here while on this earth.

THE things we want to remember about fire, it is first spiritual fire, that is spirit. The SPIRIT of GOD is a fire, He is a SPIRIT.

THE SPIRIT OF GOD can be felt like a fire when we get into prayer, there is the holy Spirit fire, the angels of GOD is in the form of ministers of flames of fire. Fire can be used to burn our impurities, fire is use to hardened steel, cook with fire. Fire is used to bring healing to ourselves and others as well. Fire is used to as a weapon against our enemies. Fire is used for light. Fire is used for warming a house, homes, food and drinks, such as warming, a hot drink, making coffee, and tea, or taking a warm bath for cleansing the bodies of dirt and toxins. So, fire has many different uses and we have covered some of the many uses of what fire can do and what it can do in our lives. This is not an exhausting list of the many things of what fire can do both spiritually and naturally. There are many types and forms of fire in our world.

Fire can also burn up these demonic spirits, causing them to burn into ashes as things are cremated into ashes, that; that is left over after the fire has devoured what it has burned.

Sometimes we are in the fire of afflictions, or furnace of afflictions. The refiners fire. Sometimes we feel like we are in an oven of fire and everything around us is burning up. Sometimes we can smell the burning of smoke the rest of what the fire has done with what has been set to.

The fire of GOD is a hidden approach that has grasped the hunger, of those that are focused and spiritual seekers for long periods. Many marvels if it refers to the flames of divine judgment, those who might be standing in line for an indictment for their actions. While others ponder if it represents the burning passion and desires of GOD and for GOD's love.

The fires of GOD will burn away, all impurities, that which is not needed, can be a hinderance, roadblocks, and much interference, strengthening and sharpening, fine tuning the believers' commitment, their, dedications to follow Christ. James 1:2-9 and 1 Peter 1:6-7 describes distressing trials as the "fire" that tests and refines genuine faith, "more precious than gold" refined by fire.

² <u>My brethren, count it all joy when ye fall into divers temptations;</u>

³ Knowing *this*, that the trying of your faith worketh patience.

⁴ But let patience have *her* perfect work, that ye may
be perfect and entire, wanting nothing.

⁵ If any of you lack wisdom, let him ask of GOD, that giveth to all
men liberally, and upbraideth not; and it shall be given him.

⁶ But let him ask in faith, nothing wavering. For he that wavereth
is like a wave of the sea driven with the wind and tossed.

⁷ For let not that man think that he shall receive any thing of the Lord.

⁸ A double-minded man *is* unstable in all his ways.

⁹ Let the brother of low degree rejoice in that he is exalted:

⁶ Wherein ye greatly rejoice, though now for a season, if need
be, ye are in heaviness through manifold temptations:

⁷ That the trial of your faith, being much more precious than of gold
that perisheth, though it be tried with fire, might be found unto
praise and honour and glory at the appearing of Jesus Christ:

This fire of GOD cleanses and cleans out all the mess that
we have stored up for many years. This waste can become
a stench in the nostrils of OUR GOD. We want a good scent
going up before our GREAT GOD, ALMIGHTY.

Difficult circumstances train GOD's people to rely more fully on
him. Even so, GOD's loving discipline brings torment to our sinful
flesh. As Hebrews 12:29 states, "Our GOD is a consuming fire" not
only for the wicked but also for wayward saints he chastens.

I want to say this as the LORD IS SPEAKING TO ME AT THIS
MOMENT. IF YOU ARE NOT SERIOUS, ABOUT THE THINGS
OF GOD, DO NOT ASK FOR THE THIS TYPE OF FIRE IN YOUR
LIFE. IF YOUR NOT GOING TO ENDURE THE UNDERTAKING
OF THIS TYPE OF COMMITMENT. GOD WILL HOLD US

ACCOUNTABLE. Once we have ask for somethings in our lives, we cannot take it back, or say I have made a mistake. Please be very careful what we ask the Lord for. When it comes it will not look like what you or I thought it would be. Words to the wise, we can not say to the Lord I've made a mistake, making vows, or commitments that we do not want to keep. When the pressure gets hot in the kitchen.

Our prayers should be Lord GOD ALMIGHTY MAKE ME A MINISTER OF FIRE. Give me eyes burning with your fire, Lord GOD SET MY LIFE ON FIRE WITH YOUR SPIRIT IGNITING ME FROM THE INSIDE OUT.

Cause my life to be on fire for others to see me burn for you and be a help to them and for them. Bringing them out of the ETERNAL FIRES OF HELL. PULLING THEM OUT OF THE FIRES OF TROUBLES IN THIS WORLD.

Pulling them out of the fires of sin, darkness, and chaos.

Our prayers should be making your fire to burn in my mouth, my tongue, my eyes, my belly and burn me from the inside out in the mighty name of JESUS - GOD you are a consuming fire.

CONSUMING FIRE, FIRE THAT CAN DESTROY ALL THINGS. GOD CAN BE IN THE FORM OF SOME FIRE, AND CONSUME THINGS.

Not only will we be submerged in water but he shall overshadow us with the Holy SPIRIT and with fire:

BAPTIZED WITH THE HOLY SPIRIT AND FIRE; WHICH IS THE SPIRIT OF GOD AND HIS FIRE SPIRITUALLY. Who maketh his angel's spirits; his ministers a flaming fire:

GOD MINISTERS WHICH IS ANGELS; A FLAMING FIRE. GOD's word is like a fire and like a hammer that breaketh the rock in pieces? This is what GOD is saying to us about his word. When we start and end of praying, the fire, of GOD WILL come down from heaven, and consumed, whatever it is that needs to be destroyed or restored with the glory of the LORD.

FIRE TO FROM HEAVEN TO CONSUME what ever that is not of GOD and needs to be consumed out of the way. But his word was in mine heart as a burning fire shut up in my bones.

FIRE IN OUR HEARTS AS A BURNING FIRE

FIRE THAT IS KINDLED;

What is a kindling fire?

Fire that is stirred up for a period of time

The fires of GOD has many uses such as;

TRANSFORMATION;

Going from one form to another; taking something that was old turning it into something different, changing from one image to another, making one new all over again examples

Having a change of heart

Change of mind

Change of attitudes

Change of thoughts

Change of outlook or perception levels;

Changes in habits

Goals dreams, visions, and lifestyles can all be changed with the simple thought of wanting to be transformed

Romans 12: 1-2

[1] I beseech you therefore, brethren, by the mercies of GOD, that ye present your bodies a living sacrifice, holy, acceptable unto GOD, *which is* your reasonable service.

² And be not conformed to this world: but be ye transformed
by the renewing of your mind, that ye may prove what *is*
that good, and acceptable, and perfect, will of GOD.

TRANSFORMING; into the image of GOD
requires for to submit to the will of GOD.

IT requires for us to deny ourselves and take up our
crosses and follow him, GOD, & YESHUA, OR JESUS
THE CHRIST, AND LED BY THE HOLY SPIRIT.

The ways in which we look or view situations,
problems, and circumstances in our lives.˙

Purification; is the ability to be cleansed from pass waste, sin, and guilt,
shame, and condemnation, filthiness, and all types of unclean emotions,
attitudes, actions, and habits that were there before we were born. To be
cleaned and purified with water of the word of GOD. These things are
no doubt from the our past. The life we lived before coming to the Lord
just as we were, sinners practicing and living in SIN.!!! Psalms 51: 1-17

¹ Have mercy upon me, O GOD, according to thy lovingkindness: according
unto the multitude of thy tender mercies blot out my transgressions.

² Wash me throughly from mine iniquity, and cleanse me from my sin.

³ For I acknowledge my transgressions: and my sin *is* ever before me.

⁴ Against thee, thee only, have I sinned, and done *this*
evil in thy sight: that thou mightest be justified when
thou speakest, *and* be clear when thou judgest.

⁵ Behold, I was shapen in iniquity; and in sin did my mother conceive me.

⁶ Behold, thou desirest truth in the inward parts: and in
the hidden *part* thou shalt make me to know wisdom.

⁷ Purge me with hyssop, and I shall be clean: wash
me, and I shall be whiter than snow.

⁸ Make me to hear joy and gladness; *that* the bones
which thou hast broken may rejoice.

⁹ Hide thy face from my sins, and blot out all mine iniquities.

¹⁰ Create in me a clean heart, O GOD; and renew a right spirit within me.

¹¹ Cast me not away from thy presence; and
take not thy holy spirit from me.

¹² Restore unto me the joy of thy salvation;
and uphold me *with thy* free spirit.

¹³ *Then* will I teach transgressors thy ways; and
sinners shall be converted unto thee.

¹⁴ Deliver me from bloodguiltiness, O GOD, thou GOD of my
salvation: *and* my tongue shall sing aloud of thy righteousness.

¹⁵ O Lord, open thou my lips; and my mouth shall shew forth thy praise.

¹⁶ For thou desirest not sacrifice; else would I give
it: thou delightest not in burnt offering.

¹⁷ The sacrifices of GOD *are* a broken spirit: a broken and
a contrite heart, O GOD, thou wilt not despise.

Romans 3:23

"For all have sinned, and come short of the Glory of GOD;"

6: 23 "For the wages of sin *is* death; but the gift of GOD
is eternal life through Jesus Christ our Lord."

REBIRTH; It means to be spiritually transformed. Regenerated, made new all over again with all things being new and in right standings with GOD, in GOD, and through the plans; of GOD. This comes through the work of the HOLY SPIRIT, through, and by the word or thoughts plans, and actions of GOD ALMIGHTY. 2 Corinthians 5:17 "Therefore if any man be in Christ, he is a new creature: old things are passed away; behold, all things are become new."

RIGHTEOUSNESS; Living in a right standard, with GOD, as before. Justified, as if it has never happened, putting us back in place, the way it has been designed from the beginning, as has been established with his great covenant with his Patriarchs.

Galatians 3:6

Even as Abraham believed GOD, and it was accounted to him for righteousness.

Romans 6:18

Being then made free from sin, ye became the servants of righteousness.

Romans 3:26

To declare, I say, at this time his righteousness: that he might be just, and the justifier of him which believeth in Jesus.

[1] Therefore being justified by faith, we have peace with GOD through our Lord Jesus Christ:

[2] By whom also we have access by faith into this grace wherein we stand, and rejoice in hope of the Glory of GOD.

[3] And not only *so*, but we glory in tribulations also: knowing that tribulation worketh patience;

[4] And patience, experience; and experience, hope:

[5] And hope maketh not ashamed; because the love of GOD is shed abroad in our hearts by the Holy Spirit which is given unto us.

LOVE;

The unconditional agape or overwhelming compassion, love, charity, heartfelt, forgiving grace, and mercy of ALMIGHTY GOD extended to the likes of all creation on earth. St John 3:16 for GOD, so loved the world, that he gave his only begotten SON, that whosoever believeth in him, should not perish, but have Everlasting Life.

John 15:10

If ye keep my commandments, ye shall abide in my love; even as I have kept my Father's commandments, and abide in his love.

1 John 4:16

And we have known and believed the love that GOD hath to us. GOD is love; and he that dwelleth in love dwelleth in GOD, and GOD in him.

1 Peter 1:22

Seeing ye have purified your souls in obeying the truth through the Spirit unto unfeigned love of the brethren, see that ye love one another with a pure heart fervently:

Truth; That which is backed up with true facts, really actually happened, and can be substantiated. That which is not only scientifically proven. It has the ability to stand alone due to its realities, proven track records, and information. That which can be verified and the truth, when all others have proven to not stand alone by itself.

John 17:17

Sanctify them through thy truth: thy word is truth.

1 Thessalonians 2:13

For this cause also thank we GOD without ceasing, because, when ye received the word of GOD which ye heard of us, ye received it not as the word of men, but as it is in truth, the word of God, which effectually worketh also in you that believe.

1 John 3:18

My little children, let us not love in word, neither in tongue; but in deed and in truth.

Psalms 119:43

<u>And take not the word of truth utterly out of my mouth; for I have hoped in thy judgments.</u>

2 Timothy 2:15

<u>Study to shew thyself approved unto GOD, a workman that needeth not to be ashamed, rightly dividing the word of truth.</u>

Holiness;

His absolute pureness, cleanness, righteousness in all of who he is. Completeness, His perfect ways, and all of his attributes, within his plans for men. It describes his standards, values, and none changing ways. An awesome consecrated, setting apart and setting aside for a particular work, with pureness, clean standards, and outlooks of things concerning mankind, and his divine plans.

2 Corinthians 7:1

<u>Having therefore these promises, dearly beloved, let us cleanse ourselves from all filthiness of the flesh and spirit, perfecting holiness in the fear of GOD.</u>

Psalms 93:5

Thy testimonies are very sure: holiness becometh thine house, O LORD, for ever.

Hebrews 12:14

Follow peace with all men, and holiness, without which no man shall see the Lord:

1 Thessalonians 4:7

For GOD hath not called us unto uncleanness, but unto holiness.

Psalms 97:12

Rejoice in the LORD, ye righteous; and give thanks
at the remembrance of his holiness.

1 Timothy 2:15

Notwithstanding she shall be saved in childbearing, if they
continue in faith and charity and holiness with sobriety.

Ephesians 4:24

And that ye put on the new man, which after GOD is
created in righteousness and true holiness.

Psalms 96:9

O worship the LORD in the beauty of holiness:
fear before him, all the earth.

Titus 23 The aged women likewise, that they be in
behaviour as becometh holiness, not false accusers, not
given to much wine, teachers of good things;

Psalms 30:4

Sing unto the LORD, O ye saints of his, and give
thanks at the remembrance of his holiness.

Psalms 47:8

GOD reigneth over the heathen: GOD sitteth
upon the throne of his holiness.

Romans 1:4

And declared to be the Son of GOD with power, according to the spirit of holiness, by the resurrection from the dead:

Compassion of GOD's Grace & Mercy; read the information on the chapter, on grace

HOLY SPIRIT FIRE IN THE FORM OF SPIRIT, WHICH IS THE TONGUES OF FIRE FOR UTTERANCE.

ANGELS OF FIRE

KJV) Bible, the "angels of fire" is found in Hebrews 1:7 "And of the angels he saith, Who maketh his angels spirits, and his ministers a flame of fire."

. This describes GOD's angels as being like flames of fire, signifying their power and intensity as his servants.

- **Reference:** Hebrews 1:7

❖ **Meaning:** "Flame of fire" is used to represent the angels' divine power and ability to execute GOD's will with great force.

1 Corinthians 3:15-17 -

Revelation 21:8 - But the fearful, and unbelieving, and the abominable, and murderers, and whoremongers, and sorcerers, and idolaters, and all liars, shall have their part in the lake which burneth with fire and brimstone: which is the second death.

2 Kings 1:9-12

Exodus 40:38 .

GOD CAN BECOME A FIRE IN A PILLAR, AND NOT BE CONSUMED.

Revelation 20:9 - **Jude 1:7** - Even as Sodom and Gomorrha, and the cities about them in like manner, giving themselves over to fornication, and going after strange flesh, are set forth for an example, suffering the vengeance of eternal fire.

WE NEED TO BE AWARE OF THE DIFFERENT TYPES OF FIRE IN THE WORD OF GOD AND IN THE WORLD, AND THERE IS A BIG DIFFERENCE. There are both natural fires and spiritual fires, but the ones talking spiritually are the fires of the spirit that never goes out and no one can put out the fires of GOD WHEN HE LIGHTS THEM, BUT WHEN MEN LIGHT A FIRE IT CAN BE PUT OUT, STOMPED OUT WATERED OUT DOUSE OUT AND SO ON.

LETS SPEAK AND SEEK THE FIRES OF GOD THAT CAN NEVER GO OUT.

CHAPTER 15

HOW I WILL BE OPERATING AS A 1000 X 'S MORE

THE WORD OF THE LORD GIVEN TO MOSES, TO SPEAK TO THE PEOPLE OF GOD.

You may see the word I, it has been a personal pronoun, which is taking ownership of what I am saying. If it's a group they can use other words to fill in to make all for them. As a group, organization, club, or couple.

Deuteronomy 1:8-11 8:18, 28:1-14

Behold, I have set the land before you: go in and possess the land which the LORD sware unto your fathers, Abraham, Isaac, and Jacob, to give unto them and to their seed after them.

And I spake unto you all at that time, saying, I am not able to bear you myself alone:

The LORD your GOD hath multiplied you, and behold, ye are this day as the stars of Heaven for multitude.

(The LORD GOD of your fathers makes you a thousand times so many more as ye are and bless you as he hath promised you!)

I Operate in the Wisdom, his abilities, to know how to successfully let the money work for me without doing a lot of hard, agonizing work, of myself; these blessings are of GOD.

I Operate in the Authority of GOD. The ability to use the power to command things to happen, speaking in the authority that has been given over to me through relationship. This relationship is with my Heavenly Father, this relationship is with my Savior Jesus Christ, and this relationship is with The Holy Spirit, all in the wonderful name of Jesus.

I Operate in the Dominion, which is rulership and reigning over, taking control, making sure things are under some type of submission to GOD.

I Operate properly with the finances, that I
have been entrusted with from GOD.

I Operate in the mindset of riches, having more than
enough to give out to others, on the behalf of GOD.

I Operate in the progress, and furtherance of GOD.

I Operate in the progressions and prosperity of GOD.

I Operate in the Mighty Power, which is Dunamis, TNT,
explosive, power that will move things and cause things to
happen when spoken with power and authority, of GOD.

I Operate in the advancement, enhancement, and advantage of GOD.

I Operate in the successfulness and bountiful blessings of GOD.

I Operate in the Wealth of GOD.

I operate as a Millionaire, billionaire, philanthropist, doing business with the talents, and desires, he has given me. I operate in all that he has downloaded in my life. I use all that he has designed, deposited, and passionately planted. So, I am not lazy to be looking for handouts. And get up and start putting all to work and become fruitful, with, addition and multiplication, that will cause, activation with duplication.

I do not Operate in the mindset of a procrastinator,
or a slothful, non-caring, that's not GOD.

Deuteronomy 28:1-14

I Operate and keep ALL of GODS commandments so
that I will be blessed and empowered in the city, state,
town, and countries wherever I may travel.

I Operate and am blessed, and empowered, in every land, that
my feet touch, every field, ground, seas, oceans, mountains that
I cross, it gives me the ability to be fruitful with increase.

I Operate and I am successful in my body, soul, which is
my mind, will and my emotions are blessed in GOD.

I am Operating in these blessings of coming and going, in my home, in
my businesses, in & on my jobs, careers, vocation, occupation, and I want
to add my Vacation, times of rest, times of fun, and laughter, site seeing,
games food, fun, and plenty of excitement. All my desires, passions,
dreams, goals, I am blessed and operating in them all through GOD.

I Am blessed when, I am Operating with my hands, to create. My
feet, I am able to walk, run, and move around as I want to. My
eyes, to see whatever I can see for learning, paying attention, with
notices, awareness. My nose, to smell the coffee, a breath of fresh
air, smell the beautiful flowers, fragrances of greatness and other
smells that will be impacting my life. My mouth will not be speaking
anything that is negative. But I will be speaking life in the mighty
name of Jesus not only for myself but on behalf of others as they
will be blessed to receive. They will also be blessed to speak life.

I am blessed when I am Operating in the Ministries, an
official Ambassador, sent from HEAVEN; to serve the creation
of my GOD & FATHER, that he has designed for me.

I am blessed when I am Operating to be a blessing to
my children, and all of my family members.

I Operate in all the gifts, talents, and treasures that has been,
given and designed, created, and written about me in GOD.

I Operate and blessed in the winter, spring, summer, and
autumn, through rain, sleet, shine, snow, thunder, flashes
of lightning, & bolts of powerful lightnings of GOD, hail,
and through the stormy seasons, I am blessed.

I am blessed when I can look up and see all the billions of
Stars, billions upon billions of Galaxies that are lightyears
away, milky ways, and the combustible gases out they're not
seen by man, but only our great FATHER has designed.

I Operate as a lender and never as a borrower, in GOD.

I ALWAYS Operate as the Head and never the tail or at the end of anything that was not designated for me to be a partaker of.

I Operate always as being above only and never beneath, below, or underneath, or in a place of being in a sub, up under something, not so.

I Operate in Repentance, as a person with humility, humbleness, in getting things that were wrong, making them right in GOD.

I NEVER Operate in doubt, unbelief, disbelief, any type of fear, never, lacking in faith, never wavering with doublemindedness, like an unstable sea that's tossed to and fro or frontwards and backward that is out of control, or like a great body of water, but trust in the Lord,

I only Operate in the Holy Spirit Anointing.

Ephesians 1:1-7

I Operate in the spiritual blessings In Heavenly places in Christ, far above, all principalities, might, and dominions.

I Operate in the quickening, Resurrection power of GOD.

I Operate in the Revelation knowledge of GODS word being revealed or uncovered to me, which is secrets, mysteries, that have been hidden as far as truths are concerned but have now been revealed to me by GOD, in the mighty name of Yeshua, Jesus my Christ.

I Operate in the Grace, things I did not deserve to get but have gotten in spite of, Mercies of GOD, things I deserved to get in the way of judgements, consequences, things that would and could have set me back, or cause a great delay. With Favor, things happening for me, that I did not either have the knowledge, experiences, degrees, or the money and network to cover for myself, but these things happened on my behalf from, the LORD GOD. Inheritance that has been passed down unto me, these are the blessings from the Lord.

I Operate in all the blessings of GOD; and never operate, or allow it, a curse in my life, that is which all things happening, wrong, having no favor, with GOD, things that I may have done, they are not working for me but against me, that is not good. Not able to fulfill itself in my life in the mighty name of Jesus.

I now Operate in the mighty forgiveness of GOD,
NEVER holding a debt over anyone's head, because
JESUS you have paid the debt for all mankind.

I operate in the Abundance of GOD.

I now Operate as an Ambassador, Saint, and Son of GOD.
Operating as the highest level and promotion, and position on
the earth, with the power, authority, and subduing all that's
out of order, will be back in order in the name of Jesus.

I NOW walk in the Eternal purpose, reason
with,GOD and for GOD. Eph 3:11

I NOW walk in all the Healings and deliverances of GOD.

I NOW walk in all the promises, covenants, vows, and agreements of GOD.

I NOW Operate in all the fruits of the SPIRIT of GOD, which is
love, joy, peace, long-suffering, gentleness, meekness, faith, goodness,
temperance, or walking in the balanced areas of, what GOD, has written
about me, has sown, into my life, given, songs that have been sung
for me, about me, and deposits that have to enter my life. Learning to
operate in the discipline in every area of my life that has been designed,
signed, planned, written, and prepared just for me with discipline. I am
building character with these 9 fruits, of the Spirit. Galatians 5:22-23

I Operate in diligence, with all his great commandments, statues,
ordinances, and laws that pertain to my everyday living.

I Operate in his Anointings that will overshadow, overtake me,
so that I will always have a cup running over to pour out.

I Operate in the ALL of GOD, that has been given
to me in the way of my gifts, and abilities.

I Operate in the Mega Vance of GOD, the mega vance is, the
mega being the bigness of what He has shown me, and the vance
is the forward, enhancing, ways to progress with execution.

I Operate in the Warp Speed of GOD., operating faster than the
speed of light, getting things done faster than normal, time.

I Operate in the Supersonic, operating, in that with GOD, much greater than sound, and Ultrasonic, operating in high sound frequency, above natural limits, Kinetic Energy, operating, in a faster energetic, concept of motion, through the Power of GOD.

I Operate in the Rapid Acceleration, Breakneck speed, of GOD.

I Operate in the Hypersonic Boom of GOD, the ability in which GOD, gives me to operate with a loud explosive sound of movement, to travel and carry out the business of GOD.

I Operate in the Massiveness of GOD, the ability to operate in the awesome, enormous, quantities of sizes, and qualities, that will be, immeasurable, with GOD.

I Operate in the Vastness, the Limitless, that which is with out any limits or restrictions, and the Super pursuit Mode in GOD, the stirring desire, with a strong passion after, the things of GOD.

I Operate in the Mega Force, the angels' armies of GOD, helping me to accomplish, all that GOD, has given me while here on earth, the Enthusiastically, the ability to be eager with intensity, and impact power of GOD.

I Operate in the Science, the Mathematical, Arithmetical, Exact & Precise physics of GOD.

I Operate in the Navigational course and Directional Path of GOD. The ability to get on course and get there on time and in time, with great focus, with the Spirit of GOD.

I Operate in the Divine Will and Predestination of GOD.

I Now Operate in the Strategies, Skillset, and Technologies of GOD, abilities to be trained, instructed, with hands-on, the job, knowing how to handle, various kinds of situations, that may occur, with the materials, devices, both digital and analogical, set up, in GOD.

I Operate through the Mind of GOD in the Mighty name of Jesus, that which is downloaded to my thoughts from GOD, himself, sharing his thoughts, with me, his Son,

I STRIVE TO SAVE

I strive to save, in my account, I strive to pay my tithes, and offerings, give and it shall be given unto me good measures pressed down, shaken together, and running over, shall men given unto my bosom declare St Luke 6:38.

I strive to use the time I have properly without wasting it on none productive items, ideas, and things not worthy of progress.

Ephesians 5:15-21

[5] See then that ye walk circumspectly, not as fools, but as wise,

[16] Redeeming the time, because the days are evil.

[17] Wherefore be ye not unwise, but understanding what the will of the Lord *is*.

[18] And be not drunk with wine, wherein is excess; but be filled with the Spirit;

[19] Speaking to yourselves in psalms and hymns and spiritual songs, singing and making melody in your heart to the Lord;

[20] Giving thanks always for all things unto GOD and the Father in the name of our Lord Jesus Christ;

[21] Submitting yourselves one to another in the fear of GOD.

I strive to pray without ceasing, or stopping, praying all through the day, while I am consciencely aware, relying on, him, the things I am in need of, that I need to pray to build Relationship with the Lord GOD, JESUS CHRIST and allow the Holy Spirit to use me.

I strive to fast and abstain from food but will drink plenty of water to cleanse and hydrate myself and be successful in GOD.

I strive to consecrate my life to GOD, which is a setting aside myself for him a work that he has blessed me and predestinated for me from GOD.

I strive to praise GOD, for all that he has done for me.

I strive to worship the lord, adoring him for all HE, is to me; with all my heart, that is with all that I know about HIM, how I feel about and know about who HE GOD IS, TOO ME. With all my soul which is my mind, ALL that I think about HIM, will, ALL of the choices that he has ordained just for me, & emotions, the way I feel toward him with a true LOVE, so affectionate, loving, heartfelt with passions, and real love flowing from me, my, feelings back to HIM.

CONCLUSIONS

Let me be the first to say to you thank you for purchasing and using all the content in this book. I hope you have gained much information and knowledge from this manual, teaching of a great set of instructions. The information in this book will continue to guide and direct you in many areas of your life and the life of all who comes in contact with this type of knowledge.

Hopefully by now with all these teachings, words of creativity, through your prayers, decreeing, and declaring what is rightfully yours, the thoughts of GOD. spoken words to enhance and bless your lives. You can use this information, over and over again to get more out of it. The more you use the better you will feel and more spiritual enlightening you will become. You will now be able to successfully Identify the works of our enemies, learn and discover new words with their meanings. These words and meanings will help you throughout the whole course of your entire life as a warrior, a soldier. This information has taught you to fight. Recognize what's going on in a battle with the devil and know how to counteract his attacks.

Thank you for supporting, THE GLOBAL LIFELINE/ HOUSE OF PRAYER IMPACT TRUTH/ ELITE WARRIORS TRAINING MINISTRIES.

IN THE MIGHTY NAME OF JEHOVAH GOD ALMIGHTY, JESUS YESHUA THE CHRIST & THE SPIRIT OF TRUTH; THE HOLY SPIRIT.

BOOK REFERENCES

Kingjamesbibleonline.org/
Kingjamesbibleonline.org/

AMP
The Lockman Foundation
PO Box 2279
La Habra, CA 90632-2279
(714) 879-3055
Privacy Policy

Decrees & declarations
Merriam-webster dictionary
www.Dictionary.com
www.Oxford Dictionary.com
www.wordpress.com
https://r.search.yahoo.com/_ylt=AwrC3TQq3HlhJSQAEA4PxQt.;
ylu=Y29sbwNiZjEEcG9zAzEEdnRpZAMEc2VjA3Ny/RV=2/
RE=1635404970/RO=10/RU=https%3a%2f%2fwsmin.org%2fwp-co
ntent%2fuploads%2f2018%2f10%2fHow-To-Activate-the-Promises-
of-God.pdf/RK=2/RS=h.i9TlbqFv98EJqLYcPTxoGHsL4-
https://youtube.com/https://www.kingjamesbibleonline.
org/search.php?hs=1&q=sins+of+iniquity
https://r.search.yahoo.com/_ylt=AwrCmmDL3Xlh8gcAtgUPxQt.;
ylu=Y29sbwNiZjEEcG9zAzEEdnRpZAMEc2VjA3Ny/RV=2/
RE=1635405388/RO=10/RU=https%3a%2f%2fwww.biblegateway.
com%2f/RK=2/RS=UKJN7cN9zyuH6t8hE6iXIUypOWY-KJV/AMP.
: https://bible.knowing-jesus.com/topics/Being-Afraid
Bible Dictionaries - Baker's Evangelical
Dictionary of Biblical Theology - Grace

https://christwin.
com/2021/09/9-fruits-of-the-spirit-meaning-and-purpose-kjv/
AMP BIBLE
www.compellingtruth.org/submit-to-God.html
www.bibletools.org
UCAR Center for Science Education https://scied.ucar>learning-zone
av1611.com › kjbp › kjv-dictionary
www.merriam-webster.com › di Kingjamesbibleonline.org/
ctionary › humble
Webster's Revised Unabridged Dictionary

Source: https://prayer.knowing-jesus.com/Prayers-for-Trust
https://r.search.yahoo.com/_ylt=AwrVk5fJV.dh6X0AyAIPxQt.;
ylu=Y29sbwNncTEEcG9zAzIEdnRpZAMEc2VjA3Ny/
RV=2/RE=1642580042/RO=10/RU=https%3a%2f%2fwww.
christianity.com%2fjesus%2fdeath-and-resurrection%2fthe-
crucifixion%2fwhat-is-the-power-in-the-blood-of-christ.
html/RK=2/RS=HTJr49hXhXg3pdgiuz70K9rLE40-
https://pixabay.com/images

THE END.

PLEASE GET READY AND BE ON THE LOOKOUT FOR SERIES #2

THANK YOU.

BY PROPHET CARL A BURDEN, GOD'S SCRIBE WRITER, IN YESHUAS NAME & IT IS SO.